To Obtain This Print (and others) Please see page 183

CARL HUNGNESS PRESENTS
THE INDIANAPOLIS 500 YEARBOOK

It was possible to leave The Indianapolis 500 Mile Sweepstakes in 1976 with mixed emotions: Who would have won if the race had gone the entire 500 miles? Or, we have just witnessed one of the best races ever run, no matter how long it lasted.

Annually, we try to represent the mood of the year as it took place and record it in not only a historical, but easily readable fashion. Again, our job was most pleasurable as it always is when there are no injuries to report.

Indianapolis 500 racing in the mid-seventies will be looked upon in the future as a time when some of the greatest drivers and builders the sport has ever known were competing against each other. Sit back, relax, and enjoy our journey into their world. We think the 60th running of this classic event, during our nation's Bicentennial will be recalled as one of the more memorable races.

As in the past, we sincerely appreciate your acceptance of our Yearbook and solicit your comments.

CARL HUNGNESS PRESENTS:

The Indianapolis 500 Yearbook

Volume IV   Number IV

Unequalled in Coverage of The World's Most Famous Automobile Race

EDITOR & PUBLISHER . . . . Carl Hungness
ASSISTANT EDITORS . . . . Dave Parker
                                                 Mark Wick
FEATURE EDITOR . . . . Jerry Miller
HISTORICAL EDITOR . . . . Jack C. Fox
STAFF PHOTOGRAPHERS . . . . David Stringer
                                                 Tom Dick
                                                 Steve (Link) Lingenfelter
CIRCULATION MANAGER . . . . Becky Featherston
TYPESETTING . . . . Shirley Cole
DISTRIBUTION MANAGER . . . . Dr. Harlen Hunter
MAILING . . . . Ray Briskey

A special thanks to Al Bloemker, Charlene Ellis and all Speedway personnel for their assistance in our annual compilation of this book.

Library of Congress Catalog Card Number: 76-84562
Library Binding . . . . $10.95   ISBN 0-915088-09-6
Paperbound . . . . 4.95   ISBN 0-915088-10-X

1976 Copyright Carl Hungness Publishing, Box 24308 Speedway, IN 46224 Telephone (317) 244-4792

Artist Ed Sullivan of Orphan Productions, Cincinnati, produced our '76 cover. Photo in frame by pro racing photographer, Dennis Torres.

COLOR CREDITS

Color pages produced by Indianapolis artist, Joe Stevens.

This publication subscribes to standards set by the American Auto Racing Writers and Broadcasters Association.

American Auto Racing Writers and Broadcasters Association

Contributing Photographers

Jim Chini	Mark Wick
Arnie deBrier	Dave Parker
Steve Ellis	Harlen Hunter
Steve Snoddy	John Mahoney
Jim Schweiker	Frank Fisse
Bruce Young	Gene Crucean
Tom Yzenbaard	Leroy Byers
Dennis Torres	D.R. Shuck
Phil Whitlow	Jack Fox
Rosie Rosenlof	Jerry Weeks
	Craig-Alvarez

Contributing Writers

Julie Klym
Ted West
Robin Miller
Bob Cutter
John Sawyer
Mark Wick

Johnny Rutherford.
No.1 at Indy. Again.

This year at Indy, Valvoline® Racing Oil went all the way with Johnny—from the first practice lap to the winner's circle. For some very good reasons.

Valvoline is one motor oil that stands up to the punishment. Of speeds of over 200 miles an hour—at close to 10,000 rpm's. Of mile after mile of intensive heat and piston-pounding pressure, at engine temperatures three times greater than in passenger cars.

This year, 31 out of the 33 drivers ran on Valvoline. For the eighth year in a row, Valvoline was the choice of more Indy drivers than all other motor oils combined.

Make it your choice, too. There's a Valvoline Motor Oil for every kind of car, every kind of driving.

Valvoline
No.1 at Indy. Again.

Valvoline Oil Company. Ashland, Ky. Division of Ashland Oil, Inc.

PRESENTING

The Content

Johnny Rutherford, 1976 Indianapolis 500 Winner

Hy-Gain travels in fast company.

From America's highways to her favorite race, you'll find Hy-Gain wherever there are active people.

Hy-Gain makes the reliable, high performance citizens two-way communications systems that are right for America's fast moving way of life. In addition to CB radios, antennas and accessories, we also manufacture equipment for amateur, government, commercial, professional, military and marine use. In fact, we are the world's largest manufacturer of marine antennas.

To millions of people around the world the more than 300 Hy-Gain products mean solid, dependable communications. Where time and speed count, people count on Hy-Gain. And Hy-Gain delivers.

Our congratulations to "Lone Star J.R." and the entire Hy-Gain McLaren racing team. They're our kind of people.

You've got a friend.

Hy-Gain Electronics Corporation   8601 Northeast Highway Six; Lincoln, NE 68505
Hy-Gain de Puerto Rico, Inc.   Box 68; Naguabo, PR 00718

© 1976 Hy-Gain

The month of May just wasn't the same. He wasn't riding around Gasoline Alley on his little bicycle and enjoying the people he loved to be with. And he did truly love his time that he spent in automobile racing.

When Jimmy Caruthers' little brother was killed a few years ago in a Midget accident, Jim and his dad, Doug, talked about the situation. Do you think you oughta quit, he was asked. No, Jim said, there wasn't anything else he enjoyed quite so much as being around the racing people. Nothing else matches it. And Doug Caruthers knew what Jim was talking about. Doug himself had been following auto racing for better than three decades.

Doug knew the challenges of the outside world, he'd proven that he was a successful businessman and knew how to make money. But he knew too that there's more to life than just money. He had been fielding Midget race cars since after the war and winning with tremendous consistency. His race cars have always been nice, but no better than others could buy. It was always the combination that counted: you've never seen a mediocre driver in a Caruthers Midget.

Even Jimmy Caruthers himself wasn't good enough to start his Midget racing career driving for the old man, as he always called him. By the time Jimmy was ready to begin racing, Doug Caruthers had already become one of the United States Auto Club's winningest car owners. Guys like Bobby Unser and Jimmy Bryan were names associated with his race cars.

"You want to drive my Midget?" he asked Jimmy once. "What, do you think I'm crazy? Better go out and get yourself a ride. A little experience."

That's father talking to number one son. To read it you might think of the old man as a stingy old coot not willing to give the kid a try. But that was Doug's method, and he'd been making his sons work for their salt for quite a few years and the combination worked. He gave them what they needed, but no more. The low-budget Midget racers might have always thought that the Caruthers kids were born with silver spoons in their mouths, but they didn't have it any easier than other kids on the block.

The record books show that Jimmy Caruthers won the 1970 USAC Midget title after a see-saw battle that lasted all season with Dave Strickland. They swapped the point lead back and forth some eight times. What the record books don't show is that Jimmy Caruthers almost single-handedly won that crown with little outside mechanical help. He drove the car, prepared it, crashed it, fixed it and towed it to the races.

This writer accompanied him throughout most of the season and at year's end we couldn't figure out whether I'd helped or hindered the campaign. Suffice it to say that I wouldn't win any mechanical achievement awards.

I'd met Jimmy and Doug in 1969 and they certainly weren't the Caruthers Racing Team I'd seen compete in Denver the years before that. Then, however, Doug had a fella named Vukovich driving and he must have been trying to imitate his famous father's style as they made shambles out of the competition. Doug and Jimmy in 1969 sure weren't Doug and Vuky though. They ran in the back.

But just getting a ride in Pop's car was an achievement for Jimmy. He had taken Doug's advice a couple years earlier and found an owner who had a Midget that was in the proverbial basket. Jimmy put it together, ran up front with it, spun out a few times, crashed a bit, and then got on with the task at hand of working his way toward a ride at the Indianapolis Motor Speedway. Had to get to the Speedway. . . .that was always the thought.

Long before he convinced his dad to put him in one

(Photos by Chini and Weeks)

of his Midgets, Jimmy (and later brother Danny) started their race driving careers in quarter-Midgets. Doug built the cars for them, then constructed a race track behind his trailer manufacturing plant so they could race. Soon others wanted to do the same and Doug was in the quarter-Midget building business. Jimmy and Danny both became quarter-Midget champions.

Soon as you become a teenager though, you can't race quarter-Midgets anymore. So Jimmy started taking flying lessons after he obtained his driver's license and then found that helicopters required even more coordination so he learned to fly those too. He wasn't old enough to start racing full size Midgets yet, so he built a Stock car and bumped around Los Angeles' Ascot Park.

After the Stock car he started going to race after race looking for a Midget ride. Got any experience kid? Sorry, come back after you've won a couple of features. The name didn't help much either. Why don't you go drive for your old man, they'd say. Finally, he found the willing ear and proved himself. Then he won his first USAC feature and was greeted the same night with army induction papers. Some guys would be bitter. You needed those years for experience if you wanted to get to the Speedway. Not Caruthers.

"You've just gotta learn how to have fun doin' anything Carlie," he would say to me.

So he went to the Army and raced too. They stationed him in Phoenix, Arizona and he convinced a Sprint car owner that he could drive a Sprinter at Manzanita, one of the fastest and most dangerous dirt half-mile race tracks in the country. He wheeled and dealed with the commanding officer enough to get time off for every race and staged a season-long battle for the title with Jerry McClung, a good-time Charlie who was legendary at Manzy. Caruthers and McClung would race holy hell out of

Continued on Page 222

Sugaripe

Mike Mosley retired last August, then decided that he missed racing more than he realized. We're glad to see him return for his eighth Indianapolis 500 and joined again with a greatly respected mechanic, Jud Phillips, above, and popular car owner, Jerry O'Connell, below. Mike surprised many with a fine qualifying effort and the Sugaripe people can be proud that he has returned to the racing world.

PATRICK RACING TEAM

George Bignotti, upper left, is the mechanical brain behind the Wildcat II machines for Gordon Johncock, upper right, Wally Dallenbach, center, and owner Pat Patrick, right. Bignotti's skill combined with his expert drivers beat the odds by bringing the new cars home third and fourth although we know that he had his sights on first and second.

NASCAR, SPORTSMAN, USAC, INDY, FORMULA 1. IN ALL OUR RACES, IN ALL OUR CRANKCASES, CAM2.™

For over seven years, the Penske Racing Team has been punishing a multigrade passenger-car oil in rugged race competition. CAM2.

In NASCAR, USAC, Indy, Can-Am and Trans-Am race cars, CAM2 took everything that was dished out.

In 1974, CAM2 20W50 became the first multigrade ever certified by USAC as used for championship racing.

Finally, after more than 35 wins and 80,000 race-engine miles without a failure, CAM2 is now available to drivers who change their own. No matter where or when the Penske Team races today, the oil in the crankcase is CAM2.

And now that you can get it, you ought to change your oil.

YOU OUGHT TO CHANGE YOUR OIL.

Veteran Billy Vukovich put his machine in the race easily, but impressive rookie Bobby Olivero got bumped on the last day despite a superb effort by mechanic, John Capels, left, and owner, Gil Morales.

Indy...
a Mallory tradition.

Cars equipped with Mallory Ignition have been
consistent Indy winners for years. And
the rain-soaked 1976 Indy was no exception as Johnny Rutherford won
with Mallory. In fact, 30 of the 33 qualifiers were equipped with
Mallory Ignition. So you can see the builders of these sophisticated machines have
made Mallory their unanimous choice. Mallory believes racing "improves the breed." That's why we have supported
Indy and the entire USAC program over the years. And Mallory has been a regular winner throughout the USAC
circuit. □ You can win with Mallory too. See the full line of Mallory race-proven products at your dealer. Send $1.00
for your Mallory decal and embroidered jacket patch. The new full-color Mallory catalog is $2.00.

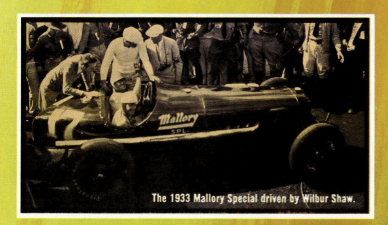

The 1933 Mallory Special driven by Wilbur Shaw.

MALLORY ELECTRIC · DIVISION OF W. R. GRACE & CO. · 1801 OREGON STREET · CARSON CITY, NEVADA 89701 · (702) 882-6600

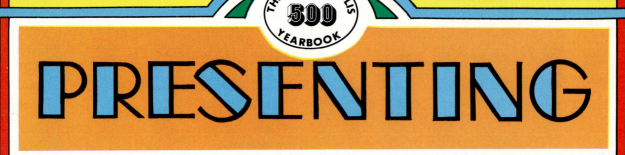

PRESENTING

THE INDIANAPOLIS 500 YEARBOOK

The Month of May

DAY BY DAY

Editor's note: Our thanks once again to the folks at Gilmore Racing Team who annually supply the press with a complete daily report of Speedway activities and the Indianapolis STAR and NEWS newspapers for their assistance in helping us to compile our day-by-day record.

By Jack Fox
(and assorted others)

Gordon Johncock tried out his new Wildcat March 31 even before it was painted.

May 8th, Saturday

"THE TRACK IS NOW OPEN FOR PRACTICE!" With these traditional words from the Chief Steward, Tom Binford, the Indianapolis Motor Speedway's 60th practice period officially began.

Until the ridiculous race to see who would be the first car on the track resulted in serious injuries to Steward Walt Myers in 1974, the honor used to be hotly contested for its minimal publicity value. Since the unfortunate accident, the opening day has been much more relaxed. The opening ceremonies and symbolic ribbon cutting went off as usual and when the track was opened to practice, Larry "Boom Boom" Cannon was unopposed in his bid for first-on-track honors.

Rolla Vollstedt, who was one of the hottest contenders to see his car make the first official practice lap, had another publicity gimmick this year and it was a good one! Earlier in the year Rolla had sent in his entry with Ms. Janet Guthrie listed as the driver.

Little had been heard of Guthrie in championship racing circles but a creditable job in the Trenton race had served notice that she could handle a race car at least well enough to make the starting field and run as well as the car was capable. Her debut at Indianapolis received more "ink" in the racing (and other) press than any other facet of the Speedway's opening. It would all month. She was good copy and graciously gave reporters factual and unassuming answers. The "ladies of the press" assigned to her were perhaps less racing-oriented but they did turn up the fact that her favorite recipe

was an eggplant dish. Paul Scheuring, sports director of WXLW remarked "I don't care how good a race driver she is, she'll never get me to like eggplant!"

Janet's heralded appearance failed to come off as her car developed an oil leak while Dick Simon was shaking it down for her. The leak couldn't be fixed in time for her to get on the track. To add to her disappointment, an airline lost her helmet and driving equipment and she had to borrow a crash hat and suit from the most vocal male chauvinist. . .Bill Vukovich.

Binford had imposed a speed limit of 180 for veteran drivers and 160 for the rookies, but this was waived the case of Midget driver Bobby Olivero who did such an expert job of handling his Alex Foods Special that he was allowed to take the entire four phases of his drivers test in one day. This was the first time that a rookie had completed his entire test on the track's opening day. The veteran drivers who watched and judged his performance were in agreement that he had performed flawlessly and he was allowed to remove the three tape rookie stripes from his car. Alex Morales, his car owner, and one of the country's most successful purveyors of frozen and packaged Mexican food and recently extended part of his line into the Indianapolis area and the region which curiously refers to bell peppers as "mangos" is now developing a taste for burritos.

Only one car turned anything like a fast lap on this opening day and that was the No. 6 Cam2 Motor Oil Special

driven by Mario Andretti. This is his first departure from the Vel's-Parnelli operation in several years--a period filled with mechanical frustrations. Mario's best lap was 178.077, not too far from the speed predicted to qualify for the race. Unfortunately Mario will be racing in Europe on the first qualifying weekend so he will have no chance for the pole unless the weather gives him a break and washes out the first two days.

Both Roger McCluskey and young Spike Gehlhausen blew engines in their cars and Steve Krisiloff had an oil pump break on the No. 8 Routh Meat Packing Eagle which shut down the track. A total of 13 cars were on the track with second fast time being recorded by Olivero on the last lap of his test.

The weather was cool but sunny.

May 9th, Sunday

Tom Binford, the Speedway's Chief Steward who triples as a president of DePauw University and of a local bank, lifted his 180/160 speed limit and a group of former winners—Mario Andretti, Johnny Rutherford, Gordon Johncock and A.J. Foyt-as well as Tom Sneva, Wally Dallenbach and and Roger McCluskey all exceeded that barrier. Rutherford was fastest of the group and ran one lap at 187.698 before a goodly Mother's Day crowd.

Spike Gehlhausen took all four phases of his drivers test and passed with ease. The 21-year old Jasper, Ind. driver is a graduate of the Midget ranks in which he has been competing since he was a teenager. Olivero, who

Edmund Strauss has been selling newspapers at the Speedway for many years.

passed his test yesterday likewise came from the small cars, driving with USAC, USRC and BCRA on the Pacific Coast. Gehlhausen's bright yellow car is one of the most attractive on the track.

Janet Guthrie is still waiting to make her debut as the No. 17 Bryant Heating and Cooling Special is still having trouble. Dick Simon is shaking

Fran Derr has the year-long task of filling ticket orders. The day after the race she begins working on next year. Despite the heavy demand she keeps the tickets flowing.

down the dark blue car and has experienced nothing but trouble. Just before noon, Simon burned a piston and the Vollstedt crew had to work all afternoon installing another engine. The car was back on the track shortly before 6:00 and Simon got in a few more laps but there was no chance for Guthrie to take a ride.

For the first time in the track's history red lights will be installed so that the race can be stopped should an emergency situation develop. The red will inform the entire field of the situation at the same time rather than have them drive to the starting line to see the red flag.

May 10th, Monday

Janet Guthrie finally became the first woman driver to turn a wheel officially on the Indianapolis Motor Speedway but her appearance was short-lived as after seven practice laps, a piston blew coming down the front stretch and she coasted into the first turn without power. She had not actually started her drivers test and was just getting acquainted with the track and her car. Despite her good showing at Trenton, many railbirds feel that if she qualifies for the race it will have to be in another car as the Vollstedt to which she is assigned is considered marginal. With all of the trouble it has encountered so far, some people are betting that she will not even be able to pass her test. For the second straight day Johnny Rutherford had fast-time honors in his Mc-Laren No. 2 Hy-Gain. The sponsor is one of the largest makers of CB radios and they entered racing with a win (Trenton). Johnny's speed was 188.363. Fast speed of the day pays off with two free dinners at the Classic Motor Lodge (formerly the Speedway Holiday Inn) located just across 16th Street from the track's southwest turn.

Al Unser was close to Rutherford when he turned a lap in 188.048 just before the track shut down for the evening. Al was in the Cosworth-powered Parnelli. It has taken months to make the Cosworth competitive but it finally gives promise of racing with the highly-touted Offys and the remaining Foyts.

Tom Sneva, Mario Andretti, Roger McCluskey, Gordon Johncock, and Wally Dallenbach were all over 180.

Almost as many cars had engine trouble as ran over 180. Besides Guthrie's problems, Bill Vukovich blew an engine of the Alex Foods No. 5

and Bobby Unser had the Offy come apart on Bob Fletcher's Cobre Tire Eagle. Mike Hiss blew Lindsey Hopkins' red No. 11 and Steve Krisiloff again had trouble with the red and white Routh No. 8. This time the supercharger blew and the track had to be shut down for almost an hour while pit crews searched the track for pieces of the disintegrated blade.

It was a warm, sunny day-no rain so far this year-and 29 of the 48 cars now quartered in Gasoline Alley were on the track taking practice runs.

May 11th, Tuesday

After almost four days of accident-free practice, the Speedway had its first crash of the year and it was one of the most spectacular in the track's 60-year history. Few people witnessed it, however, although those who did had a perfect ringside seat.

Rookie Eddie Miller, unknown to most people at the track but with some Formula titles to his credit persuaded Fred Gerhardt to give him a ride in the Thermo-King No. 46, Gary Bettenhausen's back-up car. Reportedly the ride cost Mr. Miller $15,000 plus a sizable insurance policy on the

The Star's Ray Marquette and Bobby Unser.

Grant King and J. C. Agajanian combined to successfully field a three-car team.

Winning racing's biggest single event. Again.

For the 37th time, a car sparked by Champion spark plugs has won the richest, most prestigious auto race in the world—the Indianapolis 500. This year Johnny Rutherford cinched the victory driving a McLaren-Offy. And celebrated the second time in three years that he has won this giant racing classic.

Nailing down the second spot was three-time winner A. J. Foyt in a Coyote-Ford.

Also sparked by Champion.

Next time you buy spark plugs, specify the brand that has proved its performance at Indy. Year after year. Specify Champion. World's No. 1 selling brand.

CHAMPION ®

Fill 'er up with Champions.

Toledo, OH 43661

What's in it for you?

You get closer to racing, that's what! A lot closer. As close as anyone gets, without wearing a helmet. Here's how it works and what the Goodyear Motor Sports Club membership card will mean to you:

1. The Club was formed to offer dedicated racing fans some of the same advantages and facilities as those enjoyed by drivers, car owners, sponsors, promoters and the media.

2. The Club will have a special, private hospitality area at over 26 major races during the coming year.

3. The hospitality area is a special nerve center for members. Everything is included . . . visits from drivers, race reports, and press information. For your convenience there are bulletin boards, PA loudspeakers, additional rest rooms, even free Coca-Cola®.

4. There are guided tours of the garages on our special people-mover. You can ask questions and actually see what's new in racing, firsthand.

5. Away from the track, we keep you in touch with a twice-a-month newsletter, and CHALLENGE, a full-color magazine that comes to you four times a year (plus a special year-end issue!).

6. You get a unique racing portfolio which includes a lap-speed calculator, a track locator map and racetrack directory.

7. You get discounts on race admission tickets, car rentals through Hertz, accessories from AUTO WORLD, and wholesale prices on Club merchandise.

8. There are Club competitions at the track or through the mail, special prize drawings at Club hospitality areas and other special privileges. (Just ask the members who were in the Winner's Circle with Niki Lauda, at Watkins Glen!)

9. You get the small things you'd expect from a club like a quality membership certificate, illustrated portraits of your Club advisors, a Club cap, a bumper sticker, decals and jacket patch that show you're a member.

10. With your full membership, inexpensive annual associate memberships are available to the entire family.

11. Finally the Club is composed of racing enthusiasts just like yourself. And it's advised by 18 of the finest racing drivers in the world.

Here's your pass.

Membership application. Please enroll me as a member of the Goodyear Motor Sports Club and rush my complete membership kit.

NAME_____
(PLEASE PRINT)

ADDRESS_____

CITY_____STATE_____ZIP_____

_____
Signature

ANNUAL FULL MEMBERSHIP $15.00
Please check method of payment:
☐ Check or money order payable to Goodyear Motor Sports Club.
Please charge to my credit card account:
☐ Master Charge   ☐ BankAmericard
☐ American Express

CREDIT CARD NO.   EXP. DATE

INTERBANK NO. (Master Charge only) Located above your name.

NOTE: Associate memberships are available to immediate family of Full Member. You will receive full information on this with your membership kit.

GOODYEAR Motor Sports Club

2101

Insert payment in envelope with this application. Mail to the Goodyear Motor Sports Club. P.O. Box 66. Akron. Ohio 44316.

Eddie Miller

Eddie Miller had the closest brush with disaster during the month when he got in trouble during the second phase of his rookie test. His Thermo-King Eagle drifted high in turn one and Miller slid into an infield drainage ditch. His car rolled and flipped over two fences before coming to rest upside down just feet away from infield bleachers and the main tunnel. Miller suffered two fractured vertebrae and his car was demolished.

Wick photos

4 great high performance machines

Ever drive a $25,000 automobile? Did the mere feel of fit and finish ruin you forever for anything less? Did you, perhaps, wonder that any gears made of metal could be as silky as that five speed? That anything as quiet, as beautiful as that engine could press you back in your seat like that? Were the tightest curves in your favorite road suddenly made straighter?

If you know what we mean, you know why we put a Nikon Camera with three of the world's great cars. What those cars are to cars, Nikon is to cameras. Except that it's neither as expensive nor as hard to get.

One look around the spectators at any automotive event tells our story. Nikons everywhere. And Nikkormat, the moderately-priced camera that's part of the Nikon System.

Because these cameras equip you for every creative effect in the magical realm of photog-

raphy. There are over 50 interchangeable Nikkor Lenses, 6mm through 2000mm, famed for their sharpness. There are hundreds of other elements of the most complete system in 35mm photography. For the Nikon, there are even motor drives, and interchangeable finders.

But you don't have to be a master mechanic to make great photographs. Exposure control, with the Nikon center-weighted through-the-lens meter system, is fast, simple and accurate. Every control is designed for fast, sure, fumble-free operation. And we do more than just sell you the camera. We'll also provide instruction: The new Nikon Owner's Course, traveling to more than 150 cities. Ask your dealer how you can attend this exciting $10 Course free. Or write for Lit/Pak 10. Nikon Inc., Garden City, New York 11530. Subsidiary of Ehrenreich Photo-Optical Industries, Inc. EPOI (Canada: Anglophoto Ltd., P.Q.)

Nikon. A high performance photographic machine
OFFICIAL CAMERA OF UNITED STATES AUTOMOBILE CLUB

car with Lloyds of London. Miller was on his test when he got out of shape coming out of the first turn. It appeared to observers that he overcorrected when he got too high and the car slid down toward the infield a distance of of 325 feet. Once on the infield grass, the car hit a drainage ditch and flipped end-over-end, over two fences, barely missing one of the huge maple trees which remain in the short stretch. The car finally came to rest just a few feet short of the tunnel which leads to the new Hall of Fame and a similar distance from the front row of the infield bleachers where a few startled spectators really got their money's worth.

It is almost inconceivable that a driver could come through such an accident without critical or even fatal injuries, but Miller remained conscious through all of the gyrations and his removal from his battered car and the report from Methodist Hospital indicated that while he had fractured two vertebrae in his neck, he is not seriously injured and should be released in a few days. The car, while extensively damaged, was not quite as bad as one would imagine after such a spectacular crash.

Miller was taking the second phase of his drivers test and had just run a lap at 167.380.

At long last Janet Guthrie got going on her test and got her first 20 laps out of the way in spite of an intermission after the first seven when she once again experienced engine problems. It might have been possible for her to go through the second phase (165 plus) but USAC officials decided that it would be best to wait until the morrow so as not to interfere with the fast boys who usually take

Eddie Miller preparing for his fateful run.

over the track between 5:00 and 6:00. These boys dropped their speed of the previous two days and Tom Sneva had only to run 185.109 to pick up the free dinners and best the 29 other cars which made practice runs. Sneva's teammate was only slightly slower with 184.843 and Johnny Rutherford ran 183.708 in his back-up car.

Pancho Carter made his first run in Dan Gurney's light blue Eagle and did a creditable 180.650. Gordon Johncock was the only other driver over 180.

Railbirds have begun to note a less-than-frantic attitude among the drivers. Possibly the Trenton race, which gave a lot of them some actual racing practice only a week and a half ago, may have taken the usual edge off things or the lack of really competitive drivers could be the reason. The desire to win the pole is still there, but almost everyone has conceded that honor to either Rutherford or Foyt. Whereas there used to be some fifty or sixty good drivers shooting for one of the 33 starting spots

Carl Cindric, top Offy builder for Herb Porter, seems to be pondering a problem.

there now are barely enough to round out the field unless some come in at a late date. It appears that any driver running reasonably well will, barring mechanical or other difficulties, have a pretty good chance of qualifying.

May 12th, Wednesday

Johnny Rutherford set himself up as the favorite to win the pole position no matter which McLaren Hy-Gain Special he drives. The handsome, talented Texan ran a lap in No. 2 at 189.833 and then just before closing time he drove the No. 15 at 189.633. Al Unser was close behind Rutherford's fast run with 189.743 and A.J. Foyt ran just a tick of the watch

Goodyear boss Leo Mehl and George Walther discuss the race prospects.

Indianapolis Attorney Donald R. Bringgold was an interested visitor to the pits.

Three-time winner Mauri Rose and former driver Duane Carter, Sr. recall the past.

[23]

Laurie Schwartz is the busy manager of the Speedway Motel.

Roy Grugel has manned a Gasoline Alley post for the last 49 years.

Billy Scott's crew Chief Jim Wright got No. 28 in the race.

Jerry Eisert is a car builder and heads Dan Gurney's mechanics.

Bob Clidnst is a master car builder but his are the scale model type.

slower at 189.693.

Dan Gurney came up with another leadfoot to help Pancho Carter replace the departed Bobby Unser. Vern Schuppan, an Australian who learned to love auto racing by watching the late Bob Tattersall wheel a Midget "down under" passed his driver's test in Carter's No. 48. Schuppan has done an excellent job in Formula 5000 racing for the Gurney stable. He will be assigned to Dan's No. 9 when it is ready.

Two more engines bit the dust with Larry Cannon's Hoffman and Olivero's Alex Foods coming unglued during the afternoon. Eldon Rasmussen lost a half-shaft on his yellow No. 58 which caused the track to shut down.

It was another beautiful, sunny day with nary a cloud in the sky. This, so far, has been one of the most perfect months, weatherwise, in years and rather unseasonal of Indiana in May.

Agriculture Secretary Earl Butz, Don Foltz, press room assistant and Speedway grounds superintendent Clarence Cagle visit in the pits.

Publisher Ray Mann's efforts to help George Bignotti use a timing gun seem to be amusing to driver Mike Mosley and his wife Alice.

Young

1975 National Championship but not a digit A.J. particularly likes. No matter which car he qualifies, undoubtedly he will carry No. 14 in the race.

Spike Gehlhausen became the year's first driver to run afoul of Chief Steward Tom Binford. He had something apparently wrong with his car but failed to come in for consultation after being given the black flag...three times! His penalty was minimal and amounted to only an hour "rest period".

Drivers running over 180 were both Al and Bobby Unser, Foyt, Dallenbach, Johncock, McClusky and Mike Mosley.

Superintendent Clarence Cagle aroused ire from some of the drivers after he erected a 346-foot long catch fence in the short south chute in order to prevent an accident similar to Eddie Miller's which saw his car go almost into the bleachers. It was felt that the fence might cause more problems than it would prevent. Cagle stated that he, too, would have preferred to use steel guard rails similar to highway barriers but such rails were unavailable in such short notice. You can be sure that once they become available the hard-working Cagle will have them in place.

Thirty-four cars, a record so far, were on the track and 56 are now signed into Gasoline Alley although not all of them have been certified for practice.

May 13th, Thursday

With but one day remaining before the opening day of qualifications, the track had its first shutdown due to weather when it clouded up and rained at 4:17 after 32 cars had already made practice runs. Wind earlier in the day held speeds down below normal and Al Unser had the best of it with a 186.259 in his backup Cosworth/Parnelli. Tom Sneva was second with a 186.181 and then Unser has third with his primary car, No. 21, 185.989. Janet Guthrie's car seemed in better shape than it has all month and she was working on finishing her driver's test when the rains shut down the track. Her fast lap was 168.2, not bad considering the trouble the car has been encountering. The fact that she has not finished her test will rule out any possibility of a weekend qualifying attempt since officials want all rookies to have at least two days of high-speed practice before taking a green flag. This is a long-standing rule and a very wise one.

Like Unser and Rutherford, A.J. Foyt has been practicing with both his first-line car and his backup and making good speeds with both. He was over 182 in No. 1 which is his official number emblematic of winning the

May 14th, Friday

The drivers who have been shunning the track all week suddenly got frantic in their quest for speed but the elements failed to accommodate them and rain allowed the track to be open

deBrier

Merle Bettenhausen shares some stories with former 500 mechanic Johnny Pawl.

Mahoney

Jo Quinn, safety director, and David Cassady, concession manager visit in the pits early in the month. The 1976 race was to be Quinn's last as he died a few weeks later.

[26]

for only an hour and a quarter. Thirty-eight cars, however, did get out to try their hotter setups. Rutherford was fastest once again with a lap of 188.877 in his No. 2.

Al Unser, who seemingly has displaced A.J. Foyt as the most likely candidate to win the pole from Rutherford, was second fast with 188.066 but Foyt could only register 183 plus on the electric eye. Either Supertex is having trouble or he is not worried about his ability to set fast time Saturday. Since he had yet to turn in a really torrid lap the evidence would seem to point to the former reason. Johnny Parsons got into the exclusive 180 mph circle for the first time as did Bill Vukovich. Other drivers practicing in that bracket were Pancho Carter, Tom Sneva, Mike Mosley, and George Bignotti's drivers, Dallenbach and Johncock.

At 6:15 the traditional drawing for qualification positions was held in front of the soggy Tower. Larry Cannon appeared to be the first com-

George Snider and friend Debbie Plemmons seem happy that he is driving for the Leader Card team.

petitive driver in the line with a No. 2 draw. Dick Simon's No. 44 Lan Hairpiece Spl. drew No. 1 but it has no driver assigned and has not seriously practiced. Bobby Unser drew 3, Salt Walther, 4, Johncock, 7, Parsons, 8, Dallenbach, 13, Rutherford, 15 and Foyt, 20. Al Unser will have time to see what he must shoot for as he drew 29 for his No. 21 and 43 (and last) for No. 25.

One particularly interested (and interesting) arrival at the track was Belgian Andre Pillette who came in with photographer Bruce Craig.

Andre was making his first visit to Indianapolis where his father, Theodore, finished fifth at the wheel of a

Mercedes-Knight in 1913, and it is doubtful if there has ever been a more enthusiastic foreign spectator since Donald Davidson arrived from England with his purple pants, green sweater and pointy shoes back in 1964. Pillette and Davidson immediately hit it off when they were introduced at the USAC office.

While you would expect a foreign ex-Grand Prix driver to be road race oriented, this apparently is not the case with Pillette who conducts an International Racing School in Hasselt, Belgium where young men are taught to drive road races. After watching an Eastern Sprint Race with Craig, Andre

USAC Executive Director Dick King takes a break from his busy May schedule.

Howard Gilbert builds the V-8 Foyt engines for A.J. and makes the Coyotes howl.

Midget champ Sleepy Tripp checked out the Speedway and hopes to have a ride in 1977.

These early arriving fans were ready for a day of qualifying but had to wait seven hours.

area was quite good this year with a number of Marion County Sheriffs mounted on horseback. This enabled them to move rapidly and efficiently through the masses of humanity and parked cars. It looked like a chapter from the Old West when some idiot kicked one of the horses and then took off on foot across the infield with half a dozen riders in full pursuit. The chase was over in little more than 100 yards and the miscreant was removed from the scene to the Sheriff's holding van parked across the road from the Hospital near the police helicopter pad. It appears that this year the uniformed gentlemen are being more selective in their arrests. One bloody fight between two young men in a large mud puddle was stopped and then the officers determined who started the altercation and only the bad guy was taken in. It wasn't an

was high in praise of a form of racing where the drivers are still visible to the public. He was also highly critical of the overly-safety conscious grand prix drivers who, he feels, would prefer not to go too fast. "Everywhere they have long straightaways where you can get up high speeds," stated the former Gordini and Ferrari driver of the Fangio, Moss, Ascari era "They want to start adding chicanes to slow everybody down!"

In his several weeks at the track, Andre made many friends and did what he could to promote a championship ride for his son, Teddy, European Formula 5000 Champion. The only deal he could come up with was an offer by Al Loquasto's father to put Teddy in their backup car for only $55,000. Andre, not-reluctantly, replied "Non!"

May 15th, Saturday

The week which started out with such beautiful weather deteriorated rapidly toward the weekend and Saturday was no better than Thursday and Friday.

The morning found the skies still leaden and a light rain was falling. The packed grandstands which usually greet the first qualifying day were only partially filled and after the traditional ceremonies everyone settled back to await a cessation of the moisture and drying of the track. The infield roads which had to be re-oiled earlier in the week to keep down clouds of dust had been turned into muddy rivers and the green grass of Wednesday was now a quagmire, particularly in the area adjacent to the "snake pit."

Crowd control in that infamous

Arizona Senator Barry Goldwater was a popular first qualifying day visitor.

Snakepit residents are never at a loss for something to do but this year they were under constant observation from mounted police.

Spike Gehlhausen

Rookie Spike Gehlhausen missed a chance to qualify on the first day when he spun and hit the wall coming out of turn one during a practice run. His extensively damaged car slid 500 feet after impact into the path of another rookie Billy Scott (number 28) who finally spun to avoid a collision. Both cars and drivers eventually made the race.

Wick and Ellis photos

Larry Bisceglia, first in line for the 28th year, checks the turn one action.

Ken Pollitt signals a car's position. He is an official all along the USAC trail.

Gary Bettenhausen relaxes along the pit wall.

vehicle which would meet with no opposition from the contestants or fans.

The usual half-hour practice period opened shortly after 2:00 but it was shut down at 2:39 when Bobby Unser's car blew an engine and dumped oil all over the track. At 3:17 Salt Walther was waved away on his qualifying run. His first lap was quite slow since Salt likes to wave to his fans and some wave back. His first lap on the clock, 49.42 (182.113) is creditable but not particularly remarkable. His next lap is much better, a 183.524 but the third drops considerably to a low 180 and as Salt heads into the front stretch and Pat Vidan's green flag his crew whips out their yellow bunting and his run is called off. The first incomplete run of the year.

Bill Puterbaugh followed Walther in Lee Elkins' McNamara Motor Express Eagle but after three laps of trying to get up to speed he gave up and pulled back into the pits without taking the green flag.

Gordon Johncock, who some people thought could capture the pole position awakened the soggy crowd with his first lap. The 1973 winner's first timed lap was announced as 47.46 (189.633) and there were cheers throughout the rest of his run which found the day-glo red Sinmast/Wildcat slowing down each lap but not critically. His second was 189.195, the third 188.166 and the final a safe 187.149. The announced average was 188.531 which is faster than almost all of the other cars had practiced under ideal conditions.

When interviewed over the PA sys-

easy matter of identification as both combatants were totally covered with mud.

The parking of cars in the area formerly reserved for spectators has helped dilute the rowdyism and the most serious danger results from being hit by errant frisbies and footballs. The consumption of beer is always high particularly on qualifying days, but you rarely see or smell people smoking those funny cigarettes.

The sun began peeking out around noon and the pickup trucks went out to try and dry the asphalt aided by a heat-producing turbine-powered

tem, Gordon gave full credit to George Bignotti's crew. "Well, it's a lot better speed than we really expected yesterday. We were having our problems. We couldn't get over 181 yesterday. The crew worked all night putting in a new engine and it really felt better. People really don't realize how hard these crews work getting these cars ready."

While Johncock was speaking Mel

Lindsey Hopkins, long time Indianapolis entrant fielded what many observers felt was his best car ever with Roger McCluskey driving.

Bob Fletcher hired Bobby Unser for the 1976 season but engine trouble slowed the car.

Elmer Hoffstetter keeps drivers, crews and fans nourished. He manages the cafeteria.

Phil Casey headed the Gerhardt crew for the Thermo-King team and Gary Bettenhausen.

Kenyon had been pushed out on the track in the orange Dave McIntire Eagle/Kenyon/Coyote Foyt which indicates that it is a thoroughly reworked chassis with parts from two different cars shuffled around by Mel's brother, Don.

Mel has long used No. 61 on his Midgets-he is the winningest driver of the small cars in the business-and this number was supposed to bring him good luck at the Speedway, but it was not to be.

On his third practice lap Mel got high coming into the backstretch and lost control. He made a half spin, slid 350 feet and hit the wall with his left rear before sliding down the wall an additional 650 feet. The car was badly damaged and Mel took a trip to Dr. Hanna's Emporium of Cuts and Bruises. Nothing more than a bad shaking up was discovered and Mel was later released.

Twenty minutes later the track was ready for re-opening and Duane "Pancho" Carter took off in Dan Gurney's Jorgensen Eagle/Offy. The former Midget and Sprint Car champ did a fine job and turned in an average speed of 184.824. Safely in the show, but not quite the front row performance Bobby Unser used to clock. "We got it up to speed rather quickly I thought. The first lap was pretty good but I had a problem from then on."

Bill Vukovich ran 181.433 which some railbirds felt might be a little shaky and others thought quite secure basing their opinion on the relatively slow practice speeds of all but the superstars.

Bill was followed by Wally Dallenbach in George Bignotti's No. 40 but he didn't come near to his teammate Johncock's speed and logged a disappointing 184.445.

"You're never satisfied but we're pretty pleased considering the problems we had. The crew worked three days around the clock getting the car together. I told George I would settle for 184 and we got 184.4. We've got a lot of work to do yet during the next week."

Tom Bigelow came in after taking his three practice laps in the Leader Card No. 24 which this year, is painted yellow and black instead of the usual white, blue and red.

The interest of the crowd which has been lagging for the past hour is immediately revived when Tom Carnegie announces that the next driver

Joe Fitzsimmons is a long time racing fan who is known at "Joe Fitz" at the track.

Fans come ready for rain or sunshine.

Stan Worley, USAC's chief registrar checks the medical records of all the drivers.

on the track will be Johnny Rutherford. The McLaren roars to life and popular John starts his warmup laps. The crew finally gives Pat Vidan the GO signal and the green flag starts him on his way.

The fans still remaining in the stands and infield-and there are noticably fewer than in recent years-cheer him on and erupt into huzzahs as his first lap time and speed is announced. FORTY-SEVEN AND TWENTY-SEVEN ONE HUNDREDTHS! One hundred NINETY POINT THREE NINE SIX! Only A.J. Foyt or Al Unser can keep him from the valued pole. John's next three laps are slower since his speed average is well ahead of Johncock's-47.57 (189.195); 47.69 (188.719) and 47.99 (187.539) The average speed works out to 188.957 from an elapsed time of 3:10.52.

The elated Rutherford, always an interesting interview tells the fans "We had hoped we could run a little bit quicker but it didn't happen. It just kept getting slicker and slicker. I don't know if it will stand up. There are a couple of guys back there named A.J. Foyt and Al Unser and they're kind of lurking in the weeds. You never can tell. I wish I could have gone quicker but we'll see how we stand up at the end of the day."

After Rutherford's blistering run, Larry McCoy suffers the humiliation of having his car stall trying to leave the line. He, disgustedly, is pushed to the rear of the long line which, if the normal number of cars take the

Marv and Pappy Webster got their No. 76 car qualified early but later were bumped.

normal amount of time attempting to qualify will not see him coming back up until sometime Sunday afternoon. It is obvious that today's line will hold over for another day. Under the new rules, the pole position will not offically be decided until all of the cars in the original draw for position have had a shot at the green flag in unbroken sequence.

John Martin is next away in the Grant King-J.C. Agajanian No. 98. This is the traditional Aggie Number which he has held since Johnny Mantz first drove his Kurtis-Kraft 2000 in 1948. Martin's first lap is a very disappointing 179.784 and his second not too much better at 180.687. The third is back to 179.892 and out comes the yellow flag from his crew.

The next big question about to be answered is "Has A.J. Foyt been 'sandbagging' this month or has he really been having troubles which have held his speed down" The orange Coyote, one of the most attractive and low-slung cars on the track, is rolling and all eyes are on Supertex. He is on his second qualifying lap when the time and speed for his first circuit is announced. Forty-eight and four one hundredths! (187.344) not bad but nowhere near fast enough to seriously challenge either Rutherford or Johncock. The second lap is worse-a mile an hour slower-186.258. The third, 184.578 and a final tour of 182.927! You can bet that the voluable Texan is fuming under his nomex head stocking. Jim Phillippi has the ticklish job of interviewing him when he is confronted with the timing card which shows a four-lap average of only 185.261. Not bad for an average driver but not what one would expect from a three-time winner.

"It's absolutely a disgrace," sputters the red-faced man who some believe is the greatest race driver in the history of the sport, "to me, my car, and my crew! The damn thing wasn't handling. It you were watching you could see." After Phillippi expressed the hope that the car will handle better on race day, Foyt tersely snaps "If it don't, I'll park it!"

With Foyt's threat out of the way college-bred Tom Sneva is next away in the Norton Spirit McLaren. He is another of the front runners although not many people feel that he can seriously challenge Rutherford's speed. His run is creditable and a mile an hour better than Foyt's (186.355) but far from the necessary 189 average.

Pat Vidan flags the race from the three-year-old tower. He flagged his first 500 in 1962 when Rodger Ward was the winner.

Both Bobby Olivero, the handsome Midget driver from Lakewood, California and Roger McCluskey, the grizzled veteran of hundreds of speedway encounters both fail to take green flags nor does Steve Krisiloff who follows them in the Routh Meat Packing No. 8. No attempts were charged to any of these drivers.

Al Unser, the only other driver believed capable of winning the pole

Sam Hanks retired from racing after winning the 1957 race but remained active. He is now the Speedway's Director of Racing.

is pushed off in Parnelli Jones and Vel Miletich's blue and white Cosworth sponsored this year by American Racing Wheels. His run is extremely consistant but not in Rutherford's class. His four laps vary only .19 of a second (48.37, 48.36. 48.18, 48.37) for an average of 186.258. The fact that three of his laps varied only .01 is almost unbelievable! With all of the wind factors and the hundreds of problems which can beset a driver on a qualifying run there are only two answers. Either Unser is driving the car just as fast as it will run or he is so accustomed to the two and a half mile track that his "groove" varies by only a few inches.

After the Unser run, everything was an anti-climax. Five straight cars took warm-up laps but none attempted to make an official run. The group included Billy Scott in the No. 28 Spirit of Public Enterprise Eagle/Offy; Al Loquasto in his No. 86 yellow and white Frostie Root Beer McLaren-Offy prepared by old master Clint Brawner; Bill Simpson in his own No. 38 Nikon Eagle/Offy which stalled on the backstretch; Sheldon Kinser in another Grant King-Agajanian car sponsored by THEBOTTOMHALF an Indiana pants emporium; and Dick Simon, in the silver Bryant Vollstedt/Offy.

As the little anonymous man in the tower extended his pistol out of the northwest window and shot the 6:00 gun there were still eight cars in line from the original draw which will still have a technical shot at the pole although their prospects of out-qualifying Rutherford appear slim at best.

First out Sunday noon (weather permitting) will be Johnny Parsons followed by Larry Dickson, Jan Opper-

man, Jim McElreath, Mike Mosley, Al Unser in his backup car, Eldon Rasmussen and Gary Bettenhausen.

For those who qualified there will be an evening of celebrating and for those who haven't its back to the garage and a lot of frenzied night work.

May 16th, Sunday

In contrast to Saturday's wet morning, the Sunday gathering was greeted by sunny skies although the Weather Bureau predicted a possibility of rain by mid-afternoon. The infield is drying somewhat but yesterday's mud remains in a number of places.

The 10:00 o'clock practice session saw no particularly remarkable speeds with Roger McCluskey and A.J. Foyt both slightly over 185. Foyt was taking some laps in his already-qualified No.

Jerry Grant prepares for a practice run in his AMC powered California-Oklahoma Spl.

Frank DelRoy, USAC technical chief and assistant Jack Beckley visit with A. J. Foyt.

Eula Hannon, left, and Shirley Trusnik see little of the race cars but many of the fans as they run the gift shops near Gasoline Alley.

Diana Watson is one of the Hostesses in the Buick Pace Car Room.

Pam Parsons' main interest at the track is the success of Johnny.

[33]

Busy ticket office workers are from left: Suzie McGuire, Gene Fox, Marge Weyland, Linda Price, Lucille Raehn, Catherine Cooper, and Gina Hazelwood. These ladies process ticket orders from all over the world.

Marty Hoyer, Peggy Swalls, Jan Binford, June Swango and Mary Lou Beaudry keep the IMS office running smoothly.

Carol Denton, Kay Eddleman and Judy Hicks are familiar faces to visitors of the gift shop in the new museum building.

Racing film maker Dick Wallen and his wife Luann are Speedway regulars.

Jo King, Nancy King, Harriet Beckley and Jan Meyers work in the USAC hospitality room.

14 and it seemed to be running little faster than when he turned in his disappointing qualifying speed.

A few minutes after noon, Tom Binford opened the track for qualifications with the first two cars in line the end of the original line. Jim McElreath was out first in Marvin Webster's black Eagle/Offy. The elderly car owner from Mill Valley and the veteran driver have not been successful in the last few races. Webster's cars never made the race and Jim was nursing Sprint Car injuries in '75.

McElreath makes a consistant run, but his average is only 179.122 which raises a number of eyebrows. The educated guessers have figured that a 180 average would be just about minimum to make the race but obviously, Webster feels that he is safe. Gary Bettenhausen runs 181.791 in the navy blue and red Thermo-King despite an all but useless left arm, also the result of a sprint car tilt several years ago.

Johnny Parsons makes a nice, though unspectacular run in Tassi Vatis Ayrway/WIRE Eagle/Offy, a white, black and hot pink creation. Vatis, a shipping tycoon is a veteran car owner who manages to keep in the background and let chief mechanic Bill Finley take the credit for the success of their operation. Parsons' speed was 182.843. Lee Elkins' McNamara Motor Express is next out with Bill "Putt Putt" Puterbaugh at the controlls and the chunky local driver does an easy 182.002. Elkins is another who has long supported racing having owned Speedway, Dirt Championship, Sprint and Midget cars despite years of ill health, personal and business problems ...a real racer.

Tom Bigelow settles for a 179.991 and with A.J. Watson masterminding the operation you begin to get the feeling that those in the know have figured out the possible combinations of speed, cars and drivers and decided that the high 170's will get the job done. Just how many others they can psyche into the feeling will determine if they will stay in the race or not.

Both Larry McCoy and John Martin leave the line but come in without taking the flag and then Bobby Olivero becomes the first rookie to complete his run as he tours the Alex Morales "Tamale Wagon" at 180.288; a little on the shaky side.

A surprise fast qualifier was Roger McCluskey who brought cheers from a crowd which has found little of interest so far this afternoon. Roger awakened one and all with a first lap of 186.181 and a fast lap of 187.071. His average was 186.500 in the No. 7 owned by Lindsey Hopkins who has been entering cars at Indianapolis since before some of the modern drivers were born.

With the fans once more feeling racy, Bobby Unser took the Fletcher Eagle/Offy out and burned up the pavement with an average of 187.520. Back in the minds of many railbirds was the fact that A.J. Foyt was being pushed back still further on the overall qualifying speed list. His fifth starting spot was secured but with McCluskey's and Unser's runs he was now seventh fastest in the field and there were several other hot cars unqualified.

The blue and yellow City of Syracuse with Sprint star Larry Dickson was next away but it was a futile effort and he didn't take the green.

Billy Scott, the 27-year old San Bernardino rookie had three laps in the 178 bracket and got the yellow from the crew but Jan Opperman completed his run in the orange Spirit of of Truth, No. 42, but his average was only 180.045. The Noxon, Montana driver is much more potent on dirt Sprint Car tracks but seems to adapt well to the IMS's Kentucky Rock Asphalt.

Following Opperman was Bill Simpson, of safety equipment fame. He accepted a 180.406 for his Nikon sponsored No. 39.

Australian Vern Schuppan was the last driver in the qualifying line to make a run on the clocks, but after

Road racing rivals Sam Posey and David Hobbs in different roles. Hobbs is oval racing and Posey is writing.

three laps under 180 Dan Gurney flagged him in for some adjustments.

It was two o'clock and the drivers who had not gone fast enough were itchy to urge a little more speed out of their mounts so the practice session which followed Schuppan's abortive run was most welcome.

A half hour later John Martin pushed his dark red No. 98 to the line and went out to qualify with a 182.417. A safe bet to remain in the starting field. Aggie was happy to once again see his No. 98 in the race. Aggie

Tom Carnegie gets a shy response during an interview with Tom Sneva's daughter.

[35]

has been battling cancer for the past several years but you wouldn't know it as he looks in fine fettle. Few people on the racing scene have done more for the sport and the smiling Armenian with the Stetson has more followers and fans than all but a handful of superstar drivers.

The track was again opened for practice but there was a flurry of activity around the starting line toward 4:30 when Mike Mosley indicated that he was ready in Jerry O'Connell's Sugaripe Prune Eagle/Offy. Jerry is a personable though low key car owner who's inlaws own one of the largest fruit packing houses in the Santa Clara Valley. The adjacent Shamrock Truck Lines (which hauls the dried prunes) is Jerry's baby and his big green trucks are familiar sights all over northern California.

Mosley proves he isn't driving any truck when he runs a blazing and consistant 187.588. Mike is quiet to the point of non-communication and "retired" temporarily last season. The urge was too great this year and he once again returned to the Flying Prune.

It was clouding up as Vern Schuppan again went out for a try and this time he was successful with a good, safe 182.011. He became the second rookie to qualify and the twenty-second driver to make a successful (for the present, anyway) run.

The rain clouds were gathering when the next practice session started and in a few minutes the yellow light was flashed. It was raining on the course. Not hard, but you can't take chances. With five minutes remaining before

Clint Brawner ended a dry spell as he got Al Loquasto's Frostie McLaren in the race.

the closing gun, Binford certified the track as dry and Dick Simon headed out on a run. The popular driver who is under contract to wear his Lan Hairpiece this year, also qualified safely with 182.343 as the gun sounded. was a happy moment for Simon who has spent most of his time during the past week trying to help Janet Guthrie up to speed.

The scoring tower shown brightly in the cloudy dusk with twenty-three orange number which indicates a pretty productive weekend...as well as a safe one.

May 17th, Monday

While many of the cars which qualified during the weekend were in various states of repair in their garages, the big news and a milestone for Indianapolis competition was the passing of the rookie test by Janet Guthrie.

Rolla Vollstedt finally got the less-than-competitive blue No. 27 running long enough for Janet to get 20 good laps out of the twenty she ran. Her fastest of the group was a 171 and the jury of drivers sent out to watch her performance gave her top marks for a consistant run. Tom Bigelow, Gary Bettenhausen, Graham McRae, and Al Loquasto were her jury, all having driven the race but Loquasto who has been trying with little success for a number of years. In past years it has been standard procedure that only experienced drivers served on the jury but possibly Al was the only other driver available.

Rain in the morning made things get a little bunched up when the green light finally flashed at 2:30. Nine cars in all made practice runs on a traditionally-slow afternoon. Al Unser was fast for the day working his qualified No. 21 at 187.304.

Midget racing star Billy Englehart and relatively unknown Ed Crombie were working on their tests although Crombie's Zombie (as WXLW's Paul Schuring has named it) couldn't come near the speed required to start his test. The car is an old Vollstedt chassis.

Last year's four rookie drivers were honored at the annual Monroe Auto Equipment Rookie Recognition Dinner. Rookie of the Year Bill Puterbaugh, Sheldon Kinser, Larry McCoy and Eldon Rasmussen were the first year men receiving the honors and a few fine gifts.

NASCAR photographer D. Lynn Justice takes a busman's holiday with his instamatic.

May 18th, Tuesday

A day when there was little actual action was punctuated by two accidents: one to rookie Ed Crombie who was in the process of taking his driver's test. Sheldon Kinser looped out the No. 97 King-Agajanian car a little later but, unlike Crombie, made no contact with the wall.

Crombie was on the first phase of his test running approximately 160 mph when he lost control in the northwest turn and slid 450 feet to the inside wall which he hit with his right rear wheel. He slid 225 feet along the wall, hit the wall again and finally stopped near the pit entrance. Crombie was uninjured but his chances for passing his test evaporated since all tests must be completed on Wednesday and there is no way his car could be fixed by that time should officials allow him to continue, which is doubtful.

Kinser "lost it" in the first turn while he was running in the 177 bracket. He slid 750 feet through the short chute and then made a half spin. Shortly before Kinser spun, Tom Bigelow had blown an engine and there is a possibility that some oil got on Kinser's tires causing the mishap.

Bill Engelhart, in contrast to Crombie, was a very happy rookie as he passed his test in Dick Simon's light brown No. 44 Eagle.

Only 15 cars practiced and Gordon

Sheldon Kinser

A chassis adjustment proved to be too much on Sheldon Kinser's THEBOTTOM-HALF Dragon as he lost control exiting turn one and slid about 750 feet through the south short chute. He returned to the track after a change of tires.

Johncock was running his qualified car at 186.994. A.J. Foyt ran only 182 in trying to work out the Coyote's handling problems which have plagued him for the past week.

Mario Andretti returned to the Speedway after a weekend sojourn driving the Belgian Grand Prix, one of the stops on the World Road racing title. Mario started working with his red CAM2 No. 6 and easily hit 183.449. He will attempt to qualify on Saturday although he will have no shot at the pole which is locked up for Johnny Rutherford. The best Mario can start the race is behind the slowest Sunday qualifier remaining in the race after bumping.

Lloyd Ruby was pleased to hear that Mike Devin, his former chief mechanic, has decided to bring his No. 51 to the track for the popular Texan. Devin had declined to operate the car without the aid of a sponsorship and Ruby, despite his experience, talent and popularity had been unable to line up a competitive ride. Since the Firestone-Goodyear big buck operations have shriveled, the small race car owner has had to pay a lot more of the bills himself. It has made it necessary for drivers in some cases to help finance their rides with cash outlays which would astound the layman. Poor Ralph Ligouri walked around all month with over $10,000 which had been collected to help him get a ride and his results were...zilch! This could indicate that the going rate is over $10,000 or that Liguori's Speedway reputation precludes his being hired for any amount. Once, years ago, a Phoenix businessman offered a car owner $5000 to give Donny Davis a ride in a local Championship event. The car owner made him a counter proposal, "Make it $7000 and I'll sell you the car and YOU put him in it!"

Late in the afternoon the few spectators on hand were cheered by the appearance of Jim Hurtubise in his front-engined Mallard. While it has no hope of making the program the fans love to see Herk and his neat car and let him know it. Through the years Herk's cars have had more engine than

[37]

Rookie Ed Crombie's hopes ride the hook back to Gasoline Alley after meeting the wall.

chassis problems, so the chassis really hasn't had a fair chance although in the past few years it would have taken a mircle to qualify the car.

Changes in car assignments found Steve Krisiloff deserting the Routh No. 8 in favor of Tassi Vatis' No. 92 Fleagle and Jerry Karl lining up a ride in the Routh in the wake of Krisiloff's departure.

May 19th, Wednesday

It is either feast of famine for Lloyd Ruby. With the news that Mike Devin was on his way from Phoenix with an Eagle for Rube to drive the 48-year old driver had to turn down a ride in Al Unser's No. 25, the backup Cosworth. Mike and Lloyd have been together for a while and the team looks sure to make the race. This will be Ruby's 16th consecutive start and there isn't a soul at the track who thinks he will be among the missing at the start of the 60th 500.

Once again, Al Loquasto, who has seen more concrete walls than green flags in his unrequited romance with the 500, ran his No. 86 into the south chute wall after spinning and sliding 400 feet while exiting the tricky first turn which seems to be the bad luck

corner this year. The rear of the car was dinged up a bit but Al was un-injured. Clint Brawner will have a lot of work to do getting it ready for Saturday's trials but feels that it can be accomplished in time. Clint and Joe Scalzo have a fine book on the stands about Brawner's many years as a chief mechanic and the many frus-trations which go with the job. Fortunately the book ends with the '73 season as from that point things REALLY got bad.

John Rutherford took his qualified McLaren out and ran over 189 with what he claimed was his race day setup. Were this the case, and if the other cars perform as they did last weekend, John could be taking a shower while the other boys are still fighting for second.

Mario Andretti, who is given the only chance to match or top Ruther-ford's qualifying speed, had his CAM

2 McLaren running at 187.5 and with three more practice periods before the Saturday afternoon trials he just might find two or three miles more.

John Mahler, who qualified for the 500 several years ago only to be re-placed in the starting field by his bumped car owner, Dick Simon, took a refresher test in Spike Gehlhausen's No. 19 McLaren. He will drive the other Gehlhausen car, the No. 91 Kingfish. Lee Kunzman replaced Larry Dickson in the City of Syracuse and Bob Harkey found a ride in the third King-Agajanian car, the No. 96 King-fish. "Harkey Bob" is one of those drivers like the late Eddie Johnson who can get a car in the race with a minimum of practice time.

Jim Hurtubise was still taking laps in his Mallard and while running far below qualifying speed he was only slightly slower than Janet Guthrie who could get only 168 out of her Vollstedt.

The decision to run all of the King-Aggie cars makes one wonder why some of the other teams with highly competitive cars fail to take a shot at the race with them. With Ruby out of the picture, the second Cosworth is sitting without a chauffeur although, Al Unser has run it in the high 180's. Certainly there are several drivers walk-ing the pits who could not only get it in the race but who might just be around longer than the primary car. It always gives Unser (or whoever) another shot at the race as a relief driver should his No. 21 (or whatever) encounter trouble.

Popular Jim Hurtubise' roadster was back.

A de-feathered Eagle in Gasoline Alley. In this case Bobby Olivero's car. It was bumped.

[38]

Al Loquasto

Rookie Al Loquasto spun for 400 feet at the end of turn one before riding the short chute for 220 feet to the entrance to turn two. Both car and driver finally made the race.

Wick photos

May 20th, Thursday

Eighteen of the now-qualified cars were on the track taking practice runs but none of them seemed to do anything particularly spectacular. Jim McElreath's "bubble" speed, while still shaky, begins to look better when you look down the list of possible weekend qualifiers. If he is to be bumped, the unqualified combinations will have to start showing more speed than they have been. Ten positions remain to be filled in the starting field before bumping starts.

Mario Andretti is the one driver seemingly cruising above the 185 mark with ease and the question is not IF? but HOW FAST?

One of the more interesting cars is Jerry Grant's No. 73 California Oklahoma Eagle powered with an AMC stock block engine. Dave Klym has been working out the bugs at Ontario and the car was a late arrival. Grant, a particularly good qualifier seemingly has no trouble getting speed out of a car. Fred Carrillo, the car's owner will be remembered for running afoul of USAC officials for trying to re-qualify an already bumped car under a different number. Sharp-eyed technical men caught the deception aborning and found that a supposed legal Eagle was in reality an illegal Eagle.

Ol' Clint Brawner worked a minor miracle and had Al Loquasto's mangled McLaren back on the track although Al was running six or seven miles an hour slower than before the accident yesterday noon.

Janet Guthrie continued to have problems and had to be towed in with a stuck gearshift. She had been running around 168, five miles an hour slower than Dick Simon who was again helping her get up to competitive speed. It would appear that if she is to make the starting field she will have to switch rides as it is doubtful that even a Johnny Rutherford could make the race in No. 27. Her troubles have begun to get even her most vocal critics on her side. She has worn all these setbacks with a particular grace although you just know she would like to start heaving wrenches around.

One of the better veterans getting into the 178 bracket was "Ziggy" Snyder who, like Bettenhausen has been suffering from a "Sprint Car Arm." Ziggy landed a ride in the Leader Card No. 23 and, like Harkey, is one of those drivers who doesn't need a week to work up bravery.

May 21st, Friday

With less than 24 hours left to get ready for the last qualifying trials, a number of cars are slowly crawling up toward racing speed. There were no particularly fast runs except for Mario Andretti's 188.088 and a phenominal lap of 190.880 by Foyt in his un-assigned No. 1 Coyote. While A.J.'s No. 14 has to strain to run the low 180's the other car zipped around with apparent ease...if running 190 can be called easy.

Salt Walther, who performs on a day-at-the-track show on a local TV station, will be first in line with his navy blue, red and white McLaren and he should have little trouble quali-fying.

With Janet Guthrie unable to get any speed out of her assigned car speculation was rife that she might step into one of the hot team cars such as Foyt's No. 1 or Parnelli's No. 25. When asked Foyt replied, "As of now, no. No one has even talked to me about it." Rolla Vollstedt indicated that she was still under contract to his team although it would seem un-likely that he could, or would, hold her to a car which is obviously slow. Certainly he has received all of the publicity value from her name and any attempt to keep her out of a competi-tive car would have an adverse effect.

Jerry Grant ran 180 in the AMC, Ziggy Snider 180.6 in the Leader

Mike Devin again gave Lloyd Ruby a ride. Starter Pat Vidan welcomes them to the field.

Card/Hubler/Chevy Eagle/Offy; Bob Harkey, 180.1 in the No. 96 Kingfish and Walther a good 183.187 for the second fastest time for an unqualified car of the day.

May 22nd, Saturday

Any cars which fail to qualify for this year's 500 will not be able to lay the blame on the weather as they might have had last weekend's climatic conditions prevailed. It was a beautiful day with weather in the high 70's and only light winds.

The practice period was trouble free and as had been predicted, Mario Andretti served notice on Johnny Rutherford that although the latter might hold the pole position, that was no guarantee that he would be the fastest car in the race. Mario's best practice lap was 189.473, over six miles an hour faster than the second fast practicer, Jerry Grant's 183.336. Bob Harkey and Salt Walther both ran 182's, Krisiloff a 181 and Ziggy Snider and Lloyd Ruby, now sponsored by Fairco Drugs, 180's. Walther was the first driver away to start the third qualifying period and he did not disappoint with a 182.797.

Al Loquasto, after many years of trying, safely qualified at 182.002 and joined Bobby Olivero and Vern Schup-pan as the third rookie in the field.

Sheldon Kinser could do no better than two laps at 178 and 177 in No. 97 and was called in but Andretti kept the ball rolling when he pushed off in his gleaming Roger Penske CAM2 Motor Oil McLaren/Offy.

Photographer Mark Wick about to get a look at the Speedway from the WIBC helicopter.

Tom Carnegie elicits cheers when he announces that Mario's fast lap was 47.21, .06 faster than Rutherford's best lap. The three following circuits drop slightly, 47.45 (189.673); 47.59 (189.115) and a "slow" lap of 188. 206. The tension builds as the timers figure his average speed. Will he be faster than Rutherford? HE IS! and the final average comes down as 189.404 almost a half mile and hour faster!

Mario was being interviewed ("the group-Penske, Jim McGee and their pit crew-worked together wonderfully all month and never had a cross word"), as Jerry Grant roared by on his run. The AMC performed flawlessly and Jerry was in the race with a 183.617.

John Mahler and mechanic Larry Burton couldn't find speed in the second Spirit of Indiana.

[40]

A Goodyear-blimp's-eye view of the Speedway from above the first turn during qualifying.

City Travelers Checks Eagle/Offy. The banking concern has recently been exhibiting a strong interest in auto racing and is continually widening the scope of their race-oriented publicity campaign.

Larry McCoy had worked back up in the qualifying line by this time after his abortive run an hour ago and now he is successful with a 181.388 to become the 31st car in the field. He is the last qualifier and the track is opened to practice.

The green was on for only 20 minutes when Billy Scott spun in the north short stretch but was able to regain control and drove around to the pits.

Activity was not as feverish as might be expected with only a few cars taking the track at one time. It was announced late in the afternoon that Janet Guthrie has set an unofficial closed course record for women when she clocked a practice lap at 173.611. A record maybe, but certainly not fast enough to make the race. The rumors are still heard that she will get a better car but none are forthcoming with the afternoon's deadline approaching.

Along about 5:15 there is some qualifying activity when Billy Scott announced his intention of making another run. Several cars immediately get in line behind him and a "happy hour" seems to be shaping up.

Scott is successful-quite impressively so-with a run of 183.383 and one hot lap of 184.615 to become the fourth rookie to qualify.

Sheldon Kinser records a 181.114 in the red No. 97 THEBOTTOMHALF

Instead of being elated, Grant labled his run "Very disappointing. The car has a lot more potential. We had a little trouble, but outside of that, the stock-block American Motors V-8 runs like a million dollars."

"Foyt told me that the right foot controlled the speed." was Ziggy Snider's comment after apologizing for

not going faster than his logged 181. 141 in the A.J. Watson-prepared Eagle/ Offy. The yellow and black car didn't have too much practice, but it appears to be in the show. Ziggy's run was a model of consistency with only .11 separating his four laps. The next half hour was one of frustration with no checkered flags. Larry McCoy was flagged in after three laps just over 180 and David Hobbs was running 178 when his Dayton-Walther split a radiator and Eldon Rasmussen's first lap of 177.235 immediately brought out the yellow flag. This was applauded as good sportsmanship as the time was obviously too slow and the flag after the one lap gave the other cars in line additional time to run...not that it appears there will be any weather problem. This year there can be no question of the cars getting enough time to qualify as has been the charge in the past.

Veteran Bob Harkey, who has only had a few days of practice in the third red King Aggie car did a good 181.141 and Steve Krisiloff ran 182. 131 in the Tassi Vatis First National

Al Loquasto and Clint Brawner enjoy their favorite root beer to celebrate qualifying.

Car builder and driver Eldon Rasmussen ponders a problem with his car.

[41]

Dragon/Offy...all three of the Aga-janian-King cars have now qualified, and the field is full. With over a day left, bumping will now start and Jim McElreath has the unenviable position of sitting on the "bubble."

Twenty-one year old Spike Gehlhausen bumps the aging McElreath to become the youngest driver in a 500 since Mike Mosley was a rookie. His speed in the pretty yellow McLaren is 181.717 and Tom Bigelow is next on the hot seat. He doesn't have to stay there long as Eldon Rasmussen bumps him five minutes later. Rasmussen's speed is a none-to-secure 180.650.

The final car on the track just before 6 o'clock is Mike Hiss in Lindsey Hopkins' red No. 11. It is a good car and really looks racy but Hiss just can't get it running fast enough to take the flag and dejectedly pulls in.

As the last cars are being towed back to Gasoline Alley Paul Scheuring unearths some hot news. A.J. FOYT'S CREW IS SETTING UP NO. 1 FOR JANET GUTHRIE.

In an hour or so, the story is picked up by the media. The car has already run 190 so here is her chance after a month of the worst kind of luck. Sunday might have some drama after all, even though the field is already full and two cars have already been bumped. Tony can order more hot dogs as the crowd will undoubtedly be larger than it would be normally.

May 23rd, Sunday

Shortly after the opening of the pre-qualifying practice session, Janet Guthrie gets out in the No. 1. The stories were true and she is certainly running faster than in the Vollstedt. She gets one lap at 180.796 which, if nothing else, ups her women's closed course record by almost seven miles an hour.

A little later Foyt announces that despite her practice speed, he has decided not to run the car. It would just cause too many problems with his pit organization and his previously-planned race strategy. There are, of course, other factors. The car will be used for other championship races and if Foyt can't see it finishing high up in the field there is no real reason to wear it out. Miss Guthrie's practice lap, while near qualifying speed, was still 10 mph slower than the car was capable of running as proved by A.J.

Tom Bigelow, who was bumped by Eldon Rasmussen got back into the

field when he drove the Wilke No. 29 Eagle/Offy at 181.965, bumping Jan Opperman who immediately went out looking for another ride and hooked up with the No. 8 Routh Meat Packing Eagle.

Mike Hiss, who was on the track when the gun went off yesterday, ran the No. 11 three laps in the low 181's and high 180's and was greeted by the yellow flag from his crew. He pulls back in the pits for some additional

adjustments. This was his first official attempt.

The man everyone wanted to see in the race not only qualified but did it with a VERY hot average...186. 480. Rube guided the yellow car on a most consistent run after only two days of practice...a great tribute to the Wichita Falls, Texas driver who has had so much bad luck in his sixteen past races. The veteran has bumped rookie Bobby Olivero who was the

Celebrating after a short but successful week, Lloyd Ruby looks forward to race seventeen.

Jim McElreath accepts Ayr-Way Stores' Almost Made It award after qualifying time ran out.

[42]

Mike Hiss

Mike Hiss's second attempt to make his sixth 500 ended in the south short chute infield grass after this 440-foot slide on his first lap. It was the only accident during an official qualification attempt.

Wick and Hunter photos

[43]

Pole position was good enough for Hy-Gain McLaren crew until race day which was OK too.

first rookie to get up to qualifying speed.

Hiss, whose ex-wife drove the Devin car in the championship race at Phoenix so ineptly that her 500 ambitions -for the present anyway-were brought to a screeching halt, took his second flag but looped out coming out of the first turn. He slid 400 feet backwards but made no contact with the wall and there was no damage to the car. He will have only one more shot at the checker.

David Hobbs took out the No. 33 Dayton-Walther but after a first lap of 183.711 he slows down abruptly with a broken throttle.

Forty-five minutes later the throttle is fixed and he makes a good run with an average of 183.580 bumping Bill Simpson.

The happy hour line has formed, but it isn't particularly long as most of the unqualified cars have already given up. Eldon Rasmussen is going through the agonies of the damned as both Opperman and Mel Kenyon are in line. Kenyon, despite his earlier accident had made a lot of races and is a seasoned 500 driver. Opperman has one of the heaviest right feet in all auto racing.

At 5:39 Opperman goes out but after three warmup laps he pulls in. Obviously he hasn't been running fast enough.

Now it's Kenyon's turn in the orange No. 61.

Those people on the front stretch with stop watches know it before the official announcement is made and are shaking their heads. Kenyon's first lap is 179.247 too slow but maybe a 183 could average things higher. The second lap is slower! The yellow is displayed and although he pulls back into line there will just not be enough time to work back up to the front.

Billy Engelhart, the classy Midget driver, is off with but six minutes remaining before the gun. Opperman is back to the front of the line and has his engine ready to fire up. Engelhart's first lap is only 177.690 and the dejected Dick Simon crew hang out the yellow.

The little man with the gun is just sticking it out the tower window when Opperman's crew shoves him off. He has to beat Rasmussen's 180.650. Can he do it?

He is in the second turn on his second lap when Tom Carnegie breaks into the description of his run. "Here is his time and IT'S FAST ENOUGH! FORTY-NINE AND SIXTY-SIX ONE HUNDREDTHS. ONE EIGHTY-ONE POINT TWO THREE TWO!"

Opperman's subsequent laps are faster 49.49 (181.855), 49.50 (181.818) and his last lap is his fastest ...49.46 (181.965) not only successful run but a very consistant one. Opperman is IN and Rasmussen is OUT!

The field average is 183.785. There are four rookies in the field; Mario Andretti is the fastest, at 189.404 and Sheldon Kinser at 181.114 is slowest.

For the first time in the history of the 500, three groups of drivers have had identical speeds: Bill Puterbaugh and Al Loquasto with 182.002, Jan

Sometimes the heat is too much to take.

Jim Hurtubise and Tom Sneva share a joke in the pits during practice.

Opperman and Spike Gehlhausen with 181.717 and George Snider and Bob Harkey with 181.141. Wonder what the odds are for this happening?

George Snider got the award for the most consistant run and Jim McElreath and his City of Syracuse won a check for $2,000 for being the next in line when the final gun went off.... the Almost Made It Award, sponsored by the local Ayr-Way Stores.

May 24th, Monday

With the track closed until Thursday, the action was relegated to teardowns in Gasoline Alley and the gathering of the 500 Oldtimers Club. All day the veterans of another era

This guardrail and level ground replaced the ditch which flipped Eddie Miller.

gathered in the club's trailer behind the Press Building where they greeted each other and compared aches and even re-ran a race or two. The Club is limited to drivers, riding mechanics, car owners, chief mechanics, press representatives, Speedway employees and officials who were active at least 20 years ago. Oldest member on hand was Lee Oldfield who was a member of the original Mason (Duesenberg) team in 1912 and whose motor racing career goes back to 1904. The evening barbeque took place in a large tent behind the Tower and George Robson's 1946 winning Thorne-Sparks No. 16 was on display. Awards and plaques were presented and the recipients are reported elsewhere in this volume.

May 27th, Thursday

Thirty-three cars appeared for "Carburetion Day" and the month's final three hours of practice.

Tom Sneva in the No. 68 Norton Spirit set fast time with a 188.166 effort and was followed closely by Johnny Rutherford in the No. 2 Hy-Gain McLaren at 187.931. Sneva's teammate, Mario Andretti, pushed his No. 6 CAM2 McLaren to 187.266.

Rutherford experienced trouble in

Golf obviously is all business for A. J.

Peter DePaolo, 1925 winner, and friend Howard Scharffin enjoyed playing in the golf tourney. The May 24 event provided those closely associated with the race a chance to relax and show their golf skills or lack of them on the Speedway course.

[45]

Andy Granatelli visits with Dave Laycock, retired car builder and chief mechanic.

A cowboy hat too big for a Texan? Johnny Rutherford received this one from Buffalo Beer.

Betty Packard, right, presents the Jim Pack-ard Memorial Award to June Swango for "tireless dedication" to racing and its fans.

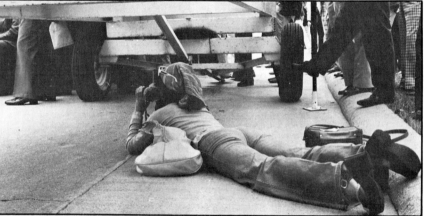

Photographers will go anywhere to get pictures at the Speedway. This one is under the drivers' platform during the drivers meeting the day before the race.

Mechanic Darrell Soppe applies the air jack to Mario Andretti's car during pit practice.

turn four, barely brushing the wall and placing an auspicious black mark where his right rear tire touched the concrete. There was no damage to the car.

Three-time winner A. J. Foyt and double winner Bobby Unser turned laps in the 186 range and teammates Wally Dallenbach and Gordon John-cock put their new Wildcats into the 185 area along with Salt Walther.

Johnny Parsons was the only starter not taking practice laps. His No. 93 Ayrway/WIRE Eagle was undergoing engine work. First alternate Eldon Rasmussen practiced but second alter-nate Bill Simpson left his No. 38 Nikon Special in the garage.

Rookie Spike Gehlhausen oil-ed down turn three when his No. 19 Spirit Of Indiana threw a rod early in the practice session.

Al Unser had his No. 21 Parnelli/ Cosworth into the 183 range joining Mike Mosley in the No. 12 Sugaripe Prune Eagle, Pancho Carter in the No. 48 Jorgensen Eagle, and Roger McCluskey in the New No. 7 Hopkins.

The Indianapolis Press Club's Last Row Party sees, from left, writer Art Harris, Tom Bigelow, a lovely lady, Jan Opperman and sportscaster John Totten having a good time at the annual bash.

Tony Hulman and one of his most dedicated employees, Al Bloemker, director of publicity, at the Speedway at the annual driver's dinner.

The State of Indiana honors the 33 starting drivers each year. Secretary of State Larry Conrad, center, was host. He's flanked by former governor Ed Whitcomb, right, and Sid Collins along with his pretty wife.

The Thermo-King party is another fun night in May. Vice-president Bill Snyder, left, and mechanic/builder Wally Meskowski shown here.

Miss Cindy Moore helps Renner's Express President Ron Renner with a name tag during the Indianapolis Transportation Club luncheon.

Indianapolis 500 Yearbook publisher Carl Hungness accepts a cash award from STP's Paul Tippett during the American Automobile Racing Writers & Broadcasters breakfast. The 500 Yearbook won an award in the STP contest.

The American Red Ball company has been sponsoring a scholarship award since the late Eddie Sachs was killed. The latest recipient is Gary Bettenhausen shown accepting a trophy from Sachs' son.

PORTRAIT OF A WINNER

Bryant Air Conditioning made Speedway history when owner-designer-builder Rolla Vollstedt, right, brought Janet Guthrie out for practice. Although she didn't qualify, she more than showed her ability. Teammate Dick Simon spent much time helping others, but easily made the field and even received an award for his cooperation within the racing fraternity.

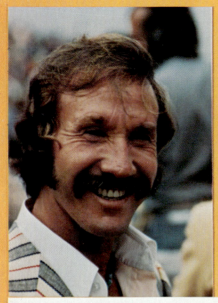

Pace Car pilot Marty Robbins

Bryant's Phil Hedback

Winner Johnny Rutherford

Owner Jim Gilmore

Rookie Janet Guthrie

Chuck Looper

Veteran Mel Kenyon

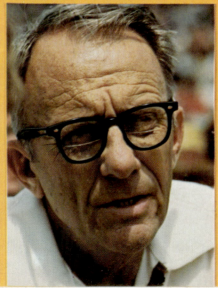

Owner Bob Fletcher

Driver Rick Muther

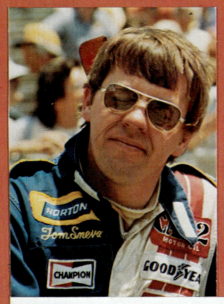

Tom Sneva is the Norton Spirit

Gary Bettenhausen

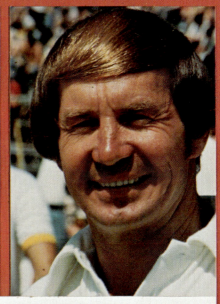

Owner Parnelli Jones

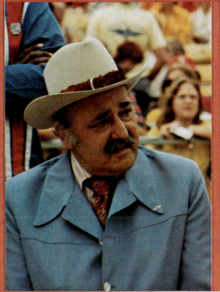

Traditional J.C. Agajanian

Steady George Snider

Impressive Salt Walther

Racer Johnny Parsons

CAM 2 driver Mario Andretti

Owner Lindsey Hopkins

Racing Cars

A brand new auto racing publication is coming your way in January of 1977: Racing Cars Magazine will be dedicated to the oval track fan and is being produced by Carl Hungness Publishing, the same folks who publish the world-famous Indianapolis 500 Yearbook. Published quarterly. Send $2.50 for a sample or $10 for a year subscription. Racing Cars, Box 24308-Y, Speedway, IN 46224.

Our name is what we're all about.

Wheel Horse.

It's a well known name in the lawn and garden tractor industry. Respected for its engineering, quality control and trouble-free performance.

We first developed "the horse" in 1946 in a backyard garage. Now, with major expanding manufacturing facilities and an extensive dealer network, we annually produce and sell Wheel Horse tractors and attachments to thousands of homeowners throughout the U.S., Canada and abroad.

Our garden tractors and riding mowers range from 19.9 HP to 5 HP. And, in an era of fuel conservation and emission control, we have become one of the leading producers of battery-powered models. Our mowers, snowblades, lawn sweepers, tillers and other attachments provide year-round convenience and service.

Matching the right tractor to your lawn and garden needs has been our job for over 31 years. And that's why we continue to say, year in and year out, "Get a horse. Wheel Horse, of course."

WHEEL HORSE
lawn & garden tractors

Wheel Horse Products, Inc., 515 West Ireland Road, South Bend, Indiana 46614

Favorite A.J. Foyt

GMC's John Moran

USAC's Shim Malone

'500' Faces

It takes a wide variety of people to make the Indianapolis 500 a race. Here are just a few who took part the 60th annual classic.

Driver's Gordon Johncock and Al Unser

Colorful David Hobbs

Champion's Freddie Agabashian

Mechanic Danny Jones

Chief Steward Tom Binford

For a big thirst!

Mark Stainbrook

Jan Opperman and daughter, Jay Lou

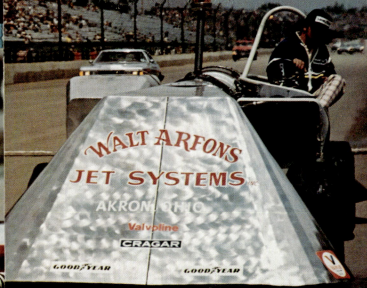
Craig Arfons at work

Hurst's June Cochran, Linda Vaughn, and Eloise Coulter

"500" Queen Rebecca Tippy

What's In A Name?

Although you cannot see them from the grandstands, the little things on Speedway cars reflect the exacting details and bits of humor. From the top left: the Ill-Eagle of Lindsey Hopkins' new anti-Eagle car, the mark of Grant King's new cars, appropriately named Dragon; the standard Parnelli Jones/Vel Miletich team emblem, a toy Coyote in A. J. Foyt's machine which carries the same name, the emblem for Jan Opperman's Spirit of Truth, and Jim Hurtubise used this emblem.

Larry McCoy showed a lot of confidence and put his Shurfine Racer solidly in the field for his second Indianapolis 500. With backers like Bob Bidwell, lower left, Jim Bidwell, center, and mechanic Shorty Mosley, right, we know he would have finished higher if the rains had stayed away from the Speedway.

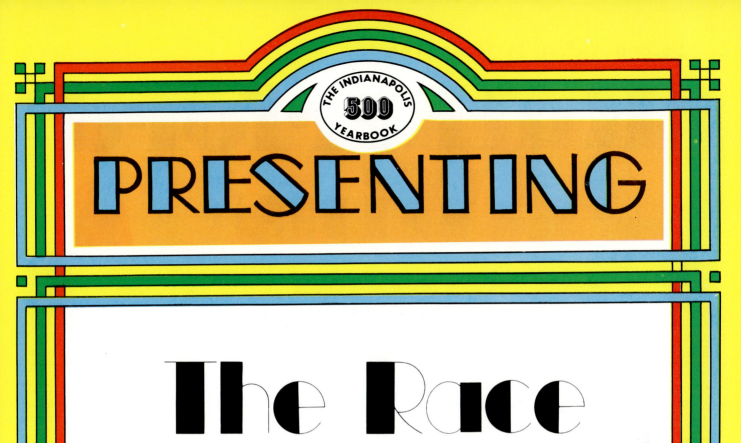

THE INDIANAPOLIS 500 YEARBOOK

500

PRESENTING

The Race

Rutherford Wins

The National Weather Service changed its forecast of the possibility of rain from 30 percent to 60 percent some 30 minutes before Pat Vidan waved the green flag to start the 60th running of the Indianapolis 500-Mile Sweepstakes.

And they were right. For the third time in the last four years, fans have not seen 500 miles of racing. The last race they remember where a man went the distance, Johnny Rutherford gave them their money's worth as he charged from 25th position to first. When he pulled into Victory Lane in 1974 he was considered one of the most popular "500" winners ever. Then, he showed a few of the affects of running the distance: his face was a little grease-smudged, his cheeks lined from the tight Nomex sock he had worn under his helmet, and a look of jubilation that only a winner can show.

This year, John and his pretty wife, Betty, took a walk in the rain after John had cleaned up a bit and waited for the crew to push the Hy-Gain McLaren into the winner's circle. They had been anticipating their walk for over two hours after the red flag had been waved when 102 laps were completed, just 255 miles. John waved to the multitude of photographers once again as he wore the victory wreath, smiled and flashed the victory sign. But it wasn't the same. Even John said, "I'm proud and happy to win–but I would have liked to race for it."

Then someone asked him if he thought the fans got their money's worth and he rightfully replied, "If they didn't like the racing when we were going, they don't know what racing is about. We had some great racing going on out there. It was like on a dirt track."

Rutherford was right. If, for some official reason, the race had been scheduled to run only 255 miles, it would go down in history as being one of the most competitive ever run in the 60-race history of the famed speed plant. When the event was called, some 27 of the original 33 starters were still running -- the largest number since 1954 when there were 31. The lead had changed eight times among six drivers and side by side racing was the order of the day. Johnny Rutherford knew what he was talking about, the fans got their money's worth. And by all estimations there were more fans here than ever before, between 350,000 and 400,000.

They were given a preview of things to come early in the event when A.J. Foyt made a daring pass to take the lead from polesitter Rutherford on the fourth lap. John had pulled his 32 competitors in nice formation through the first three circuits when Foyt went by Rutherford.

The fans had already seen three drivers leave the race before the two leading Texans brought them to their feet. Talented rookie Spike Gehlhausen suffered mechanical ailments and failed to make a full circuit around the plant he's been dreaming of racing in for many years. Then hardworking Dick Simon broke a connecting rod in his Bryant Heating and Cooling entry after registering only one lap and brought out the first yellow on lap four. It lasted two laps. Consistent high-finisher Billy Vukovich experienced the same problem after only two circuits. While Vuky was back in the garage area changing to his Levi's and T-shirt, Roger McCluskey was experiencing good and

The Great Race Is Wet Again

bad luck that would bring out the second yellow flag. He hit an oil slick and spun his Hopkins No. 7 into the third turn wall.

"It was the best ride I've ever had here," Roger would later say of his Roman Slobodynskyj designed Hopkins car. The veteran Tucson, Ariz. racer was indeed fortunate that damage to himself was not severe as he received only a shaking up after slamming into the immovable concrete with tremendous force. After qualifying 13th at a speed of 186.500 mph, McCluskey was chosen by many as a dark horse to win the race. Quiet car owner Lindsey Hopkins, who has poured several fortunes into this sport, graciously accepted a position other than first once again and said that he would be back for another year. Lindsey is a true Southern Gentleman who's other hobby is magic: but in over two decades of entering cars at the Speedway, he's never been able to pull a win out of the hat.

While the yellow for McCluskey was on, both Rutherford and Foyt ducked into the pits. John was first to go on the 12th circuit, and he picked up a fuel load in only a dozen seconds. A.J. only stopped for six seconds but exited with a long pole hanging off the back of his car that nearly caused him to be black flagged. His crew had designed a special wrench, about six feet in length, that was merely a piece of tubing with a socket attached to the end and utilized by a man who would not have to jump over the pit wall to adjust Foyt's rear wing. They were making a trial fit of the wrench when it became lodged on a bolt and A.J. made

his exit. The pipe refused to fall off until Foyt was through the first turn and starter Vidan was instructed to display the black flag to the familiar Gilmore No. 14 as soon as it came down the front straight. Fortunately, the apparatus dislodged itself and a track safety man retrieved it without incident.

Although A.J. returned undaunted by the addition to his car, alert fans knew that his position could be in jeopardy as his one time rival, Mario Andretti, had rocketed from 19th starting position to seventh in the space of two laps at the beginning of the race. Mario's first pit stop, also on the 12th lap, virtually cost him any chances of victory however, as it lasted 44 seconds. His competent CAM2 crew experienced problems with an air hose and a wheel nut. Rutherford has proven in 1974 that starting position isn't as important as it's cracked up to be and when Mario had to miss the first weekend of qualifying due to a Formula 1 commitment, he was automatically relegated to the rear of the field. He proved that he was still polesitter material when he logged the fastest qualifying time for the 1976 race with a 189.404 mph average. After several dry years at Indianapolis driving for Parnelli Jones and Vel Miletich (and usually arriving with a new, untested car), Mario was glad to be once again considered a contender. We speculate that the personable little Italian would like to notch his belt with another "500" win but isn't so obsessed with the fact that he'll continue racing much past his 40th birthday.

While the leaders were all making their first pit stop, second generation driving star Pancho Carter inherited the number one spot and held it until Wally

Race '76

BACK ISSUES

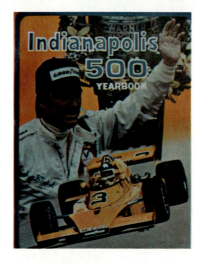

1973
Regular 4.00
Hardbound 8.50

1974
Regular 5.00
Hardbound 9.50

1975
Regular 5.75
Hardbound 11.00

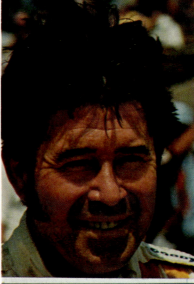

Back issues of each Carl Hungness Indianapolis 500 Yearbook are still available. See our Index in the rear of this book for content of each prior year.

1976
Regular $5.75
Hardbound 11.95

1977 "500" YEARBOOK
Advance Order
(offer expires May 30, 1977)

Regular $5.75
Hardbound 11.95

Send Orders To:
Carl Hungness Publishing
P.O. Box 24308-Y
Speedway, IN. 46224
(317) 244-4792

Indianapolis 1976
A good day for
Johnny Rutherford
A good day for Goodyear

Pole to checkered flag, Johnny wins his second Indy 500.

Staving off a determined challenge from three-time Indy winner A. J. Foyt, Johnny Rutherford kept his bright orange McLaren out front to win the rain-shortened 60th running of the greatest spectacle in racing.

Averaging 148.725 mph over 102 laps, the soft-spoken 38-year-old Texan registered his second career victory at the Indy 500 . . . and his second Indy win on Goodyear racing tires.

Rutherford also won the 1976 pole position,

qualifying his McLaren at 188.957 mph.

Rutherford's other Indy win came in 1974, also following a duel with A. J. Foyt. Last year, Rutherford finished a close second to Bobby Unser when rain halted the race after 133 laps.

All three of these outstanding Rutherford efforts were made on Goodyear racing tires.

Goodyear proudly congratulates Gentleman Johnny Rutherford, his crew and the entire Hy-Gain McLaren team for proving once more that . . .

WINNERS GO GOODYEAR

Marty Robbins, singer and stock car driver anticipates pacing the race in the Buick.

Vocalist Tom Sullivan leads "Up With People" in singing the National Anthem.

Bill Vukovich was one unhappy driver when his Alex Foods racer quit on the first lap.

Young Spike Gehlhausen's first 500 ended before the green flag fell.   No oil pressure.

David Hobbs ducks under a wrench deposited on the track by A.J.   Foyt's Coyote.

A track worker eyes oncoming traffic while removing the wrench in world record time.

Steve Krisiloff turned to people power when he ran out of fuel.

Bobby Unser's new ride gets service as Pancho Carter passes in Unser's old car.

Rutherford returns to racing while the Penske crew services Andretti's car.

Johnny Parsons had just left his pit when he suddenly became a tricycle driver.

Larry McCoy takes a very low groove while Bill Puterbaugh passes using racetrack.

Lloyd Ruby's crew covers his car while waiting for a restart.

A.J. Foyt eyes the darkening sky as he enters his car for the aborted restart he so desperately wanted.

The Buick Pace Car was the only car which completed its appointed rounds race day.

The short race made no difference for cleanup crews. The mess was just soggier.

Roger McCluskey

Many knowledgeable followers of the happenings at the Speedway over the years felt Roger McCluskey had his best chance ever to win the 500 this year in his new Lindsey Hopkins creation but his 15th race ended with this ninth lap accident in turn three. The car was seriously damaged and McCluskey shaken. Tom Sneva had his windshield and helmet visor broken by a suspension part from McCluskey's car.

Yzenbaard photos

Dallenbach breezed by him on the backstretch. Dallenbach had been the class of the field during last year's race only to be robbed by mechanical failure. His George Bignotti prepared Sinmast/Wildcat wasn't handling up to his expectations, but was close enough to make him another prospective winner as was his teammate Gordon Johncock.

Johncock, and what seemed like 30 other cars, pursued Dallenbach down the front straight on the 20th lap and Gordon came out the leader. For a moment, who was leading was not the important question, but "do you think they'll all make it?" was asked by many. Announcer Tom Carnegie was having a heyday describing the action and up in the scoring tower Sid Collins was telling the truth when

he told his millions of radio listeners to, "Stay tuned for the greatest spectacle in racing."

At the end of 20 laps there had been some significant position changes that are, as always, difficult to detect because of the number of cars running. Johnny Parsons clipped off seven spots in his bright Ayr-Way/WIRE radio car in his drive from 14th to seventh; Andretti was up to sixth from 19th; Krisiloff from 23rd to 10th; Salt Walther from 22nd to 13th; Lloyd Ruby from 30th to 18th.

Johncock continued his pace for the next 10 circuits with Rutherford less than a second behind him when they crossed the traditional yard of bricks at the start/finish line on the 30th lap. When he pitted on the 38th circuit, he handed the lead to Tom

Sneva, the college educated throttle-stomper who had survived the most horrendous crash ever seen at this facility when he catapulted through the second turn last year. The ever-calculating Roger Penske team called him in on the 39th lap for a pit stop that ultimately took some 36 seconds. Tom's crew was delayed somewhat inasmuch as they had to make repairs to the windshield of his McLaren. During the first yellow flag, Rutherford ran over a coil shock-absorber spring that had been torn from McCluskey's car, and kicked it up into Sneva's path. The errant heavy steel coil crashed through the windshield and into his face, destroying his radio microphone (located inside his helmet) and winding up in his lap. Sneva suffered some minor cuts inside his

Hunter

Stringer

An extra touch to this Foyt pit stop nearly cost A.J. a black flag stop. The crew man (top left) adjusting the rear wing from behind the pit wall lost his grip on the wrench and A.J. pulled the tool to the back stretch with him.

Gary Bettenhausen leads Jerry Grant and Steve Krisiloff through turn one during early race action. All three later stalled on the course but only Bettenhausen was not running when rain stopped the race.

mouth but said later, "If we had been running at speed, it would have knocked my head off."

After the event, when Rutherford was informed that he had run over the spring and the damage it had done he said, "Thank God for those BELL helmets we wear--those full face jobs. Probably saved his life." Rutherford is one of those thoughtful individuals who is constantly giving credit where due. Bell helmet founder Roy Richter and his hard-working field man Jimmy Coughlin were in attendance as usual

and they were justifiably proud that their product had performed as designed.

Rutherford took up where Sneva left off and led Foyt on the 40th lap by two and a half seconds. A.J. was only a tick of the watch ahead of Johncock, just over a second, who in

turn had a six second lead on an impressive Johnny Parsons, the handsome second-generation charger who paid his dues for many years in the midwestern bullrings running Sprint cars and Midgets.

Both Rutherford and Foyt had made their second pit stops in the mid-thirties lap count and were set for a couple dozen laps of flat-out racing. Rutherford's consistency was unquestioned and he collected first place money for laps 39 through 60 when he pitted. As we watched the action from the first turn we spied a casual-looking Billy Vukovich and asked him, "Who's it gonna be?" to which he quipped, "Not me. Don't want to talk about it. I think I just lost about 20 grand." Vuky and close friend Merle Bettenhausen were busy timing Gary B's laps when Vukovich noted, "He'll be in the top five--the top three, if he keeps running like that all day." Bettenhausen's drive ended on the 52nd lap when he too suffered mechanical ailments and he would be credited with a 28th place finish. A Bettenhausen likeness would not be installed on the traditional Borg-Warner trophy in 1976 either, although Gary's father had tried for 15 years and Gary himself has been chasing the elusive "500" win since 1968.

By the time Gary went out of the event, most were certain that either Foyt or Rutherford would log another Indianapolis win. Although Ruther-

Hunter

The rain delay looked like a Godsend for Foyt as it gave his crew a chance to fix his broken sway bar. The problem would have forced A.J. from the race had it not been repaired.

Gordon Johncock watches a crewman make an adjustment in the rain.

Fans covered up and waited or just waited until the race was called.

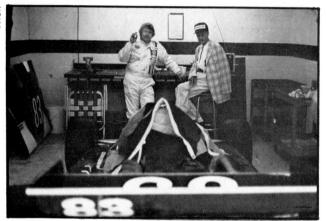

1975 Rookie of the Year Bill Puterbaugh and his car owner Lee Elkins were safely in their garage discussing the race........

when a third deluge drenched crews waiting in the post-race technical inspection line through which the first 10 cars are required to pass.

ford had a nine second lead over Foyt at the 50 lap mark, A.J. was running comfortably. Johncock was just behind Foyt but far ahead of Pancho Carter in his newly-landed Jorgensen Eagle ride. Pancho's car owner, Dan Gurney, was proud of his new driver's performance: he was ahead of Gurney's '75 winner, Bobby Unser, by a full 13 seconds.

Unser's change of teams for the 1976 event, to the Bob Fletcher owned stable, hadn't proved as successful as he had hoped, even though he brought chief mechanic Wayne Leary and assistant Butch Wilson with him. Leary and Wilson (along with Dean Williams) had been Gurney mainstays for nearly a decade and the combination seemed to have been broken. It was evident that Bobby was not Victory Lane material under present circumstances: He was running laps some two miles per hour slower than the leading three. Fletcher had cut his Indianapolis entries from his usual three to one in order to concentrate on a win with Bobby. Considering the talent he has corralled, he'll most likely be in contention for the 1977 event--or know the reason why. Fletcher is a car owner who doesn't treat his hobby like a set of golf clubs

that are put aside when not on the course. In the concern department, he comes close to Johncock and Dallenbach's owner Pat Patrick who has a fine faculty for amassing the necessary ingredients to win races. At 50 laps, Patrick had Johncock in third ready to take advantage of any slip that might occur in the first two positions. Gordon later said that the weight-jacker on his car had broken and he wasn't nearly as competitive as he could have been.

The suspense started once again as first Rutherford came in for a fuel load and a left front tire on the 60th lap, then Foyt for fuel and both front tires. Foyt's crew, headed by Jack Starnes and A.J.'s father, had him back out in 15 seconds compared to Rutherford's 17 and the three-time winner came out leading on the 61st lap, the same lap he pitted on. He too was taking advantage of a yellow flag caused by Johnny Parsons. Parsons had lost his right front wheel, but continued driving on the hardened brake disc, a feat that looks much more dangerous than it actually is.

One reason that Parsons lost his wheel is that his crew did not replace a pin known as a wheel lock after his third pit stop: it takes extra time to

insert the device and it is extremely popular among crews to leave it off. No less than nine teams were fined by the sanctioning body, the United States Auto Club, for wheel lock violations. Parsons continued in the event after replacing the wheel but was never again in contention for a top spot.

Foyt though, was running right where he wanted to be, first-- nine to 14 seconds ahead of Rutherford. He had traffic aplenty to contend with during his leading laps as no one dropped out after Bettenhausen on the 52nd circuit. While Rutherford was behind, only he and Foyt were running consistently in the 148 mph average range. But the difference in just a few hundreths of a second around the two and one-half mile distance can mean feet at the finish line which are turned into yards as the laps roll by. In the early stages Foyt appeared to be clearly faster. The only question asked, and it's the same of a leader each year was, "Do you think his car will hold out?"

In Foyt's case the answer was no, but we didn't know it until the rains came. He was slowing and the ever-present Rutherford was consistent. Foyt wasn't slowing much though:

maybe a tire had worn a little and he was being cautious. There was no evidence of the dreaded smoke or oil. For a man who sometimes seems to have such a quick temper, a person who will say things he doesn't mean when things don't go his way, Foyt never loses his composure on the race track. He never puts himself in a compromising position that forces him to take uncalculated risks. He won't keep driving his car hard unless it feels comfortable. Maybe he's seen too many of his peers drive their last race when they begin believing that they can make up for mechanical malfunctions.

A.J. would have to bow to Rutherford on the 79th lap but John was forced to pull what the racing writers call a "dramatic pass" in the third turn in order to get by the seemingly ageless veteran. Rutherford could see that Foyt was having handling problems and slipped by the world's most famous racer with no remorse.

Foyt made a pit stop for fuel and right side tires on the 81st lap and in the process was one of the ones who violated the wheel lock rule. Neither he nor his crew knew that his Coyote needed something else other than tires to cure its handling problems. Rutherford pitted five laps later and took on the same things that Foyt did--in the same fashion. His crew violated the wheel lock rule too.

A.J. held on to second through his next stop on the 92nd lap, which was during the yellow flag for a stalled Jerry Grant. This time he changed left side tires in an attempt to make the car handle. At the end of 90 laps he was only 1.99 seconds behind Rutherford, but fell steadily back from there on. And that was it. The rain drops came on the 100th circuit, out came the yellow flag and then the red on the 103rd lap. Half the race had been completed: it could officially be over. But then again, it could be re-started, it was only 12:48 and hours of daylight were left.

Foyt came in, his crew popped the nose off his car and the veteran exclaimed, "Whooee, I was lucky. No wonder the damned thing wouldn't handle!"

The front sway bar, an integral suspension part had broken and the general comment by all those who saw the situation and understood it was, "How did he drive that thing as fast as he did?" Then the conjecture started.

He would have lost anyway, because it would have taken too much time during a regular pit stop to replace it. How do you know they would have even taken the nose off in the first place to find the broken sway bar-- maybe they would have kept changing tires all day long."

And then the speculation of, "Who would have won if they had replaced the sway bar and re-started the race?" Once again, we'll never know. Rutherford was man enough to concede the fact that, yes, Foyt just might have gone out and re-passed him if the race had been re-started. And Johnny would have been happier if he'd gone 500 miles and beat the second-place man fairly and squarely. But he knew he could do that too. He'd already proven it. In more than one kind of racing vehicle too. It was a good race, one of the best ever. One man suffered a little bad luck and maybe another had some good luck. Either way, those who consider themselves Indianapolis 500 fans had one to talk about for a long time. What would have happened if Andretti wouldn't have....That's Indianapolis, a never ending saga of "What if?"

TOTAL PRIZE MONEY EACH YEAR OF THE TONY HULMAN REGIME

1946	$ 115,450
1947	$ 137,425
1948	$ 171,075
1949	$ 179,050
1950	$ 201,135
1951	$ 207.650
1952	$ 230,100
1953	$ 246,300
1954	$ 269,375
1955	$ 270,400
1956	$ 282,052
1957	$ 300,252
1958	$ 305,217
1959	$ 338,100
1960	$ 369,150
1961	$ 400,000
1962	$ 426,162
1963	$ 494,030
1964	$ 506,575
1965	$ 628,399
1966	$ 691,808
1967	$ 734,634
1968	$ 712,269
1969	$ 805,127
1970	$1,000,002
1971	$1,001,604
1972	$1,011,845
1973	$1,006,105
1974	$1,015,686
1975	$1,001,321
1976	$1,037,776

USAC CHAMPIONSHIP BOX SCORE -- INDIANAPOLIS, INDIANA -- MAY 30, 1976

Track: Indianapolis Motor Speedway	Avg. Speed: 148.725 mph	Basic Purse: $ 850,500
Type Track: 2.5 Mile Paved Oval	Time: 1:42:52.48	Lap Prize: $ 40,000
Organizer: Anton Hulman	Distance: 500 Miles	Accessory: $ 147,276
Weather: Overcast, Hazy, Rain	Event No. 3	TOTAL: $1,037,776

FIN. POS.	ST. POS.	DRIVER	CAR NAME/ NUMBER	PTS. WON	MONEY WON	LAPS COMP.	RUNNING/ REASON OUT
1	1	Johnny Rutherford	Hy-Gain McLaren (2)	1,000	$256,121	102	Running
2	5	A. J. Foyt	Gilmore Racing Team (14)	800	$103,296	102	Running
3	2	Gordon Johncock	Sinmast (20)	700	$ 67,676	102	Running
4	7	Wally Dallenbach	Sinmast (40)	600	$ 38,049	101	Running
5	6	Pancho Carter	Jorgensen (48)	500	$ 33,777	101	Running
6	3	Tom Sneva	Norton Spirit (68)	400	$ 30,960	101	Running
7	4	Al Unser	American Rac. Wheels (21)	300	$ 27,441	101	Running
8	19	Mario Andretti	CAM2 Motor Oil (6)	250	$ 28,331	101	Running
9	22	Walt Walther	Dayton-Walther (77)	200	$ 23,728	100	Running
10	12	Bobby Unser	Cobre Tire (3)	150	$ 23,992	100	Running
11	30	Lloyd Ruby	Fairco Drugs (51)	100	$ 23,039	100	Running
12	14	Johnny Parsons	Ayr-Way/WIRE (93)	50	$ 21,215	98	Running
13	27	George Snider	Hubler Chevrolet Co. (23)		$ 20,718	98	Running
14	32	Tom Bigelow	Leader Card Racers (24)		$ 20,193	98	Running
15	11	Mike Mosley	Sugaripe Prune (12)		$ 20,954	98	Running
16	33	Jan Opperman	Routh Meat Packing (8)		$ 18,943	97	Running
17	10	Larry Cannon	American Financial (69)		$ 18,060	97	Running
18	17	Vern Schuppan	Jorgensen (9)		$ 17,605	97	Running
19	29	Sheldon Kinser	THEBOTTOMHALF (97)		$ 17,179	97	Running
20	28	Bob Harkey	McIntire Chev/Ford Ctr. (96)		$ 16,782	97	Running
21	15	John Martin	Genesee Beer (98)		$ 16,713	96	Running
22	18	Bill Puterbaugh	McNamara Motor Express (83)		$ 16,072	96	Running
23	21	Billy Scott	Spirit of Public Ent. (28)		$ 17,859	96	Running
24	23	Steve Krisiloff	1st Nat. City Trav. Ck. (92)		$ 15,775	95	Running
25	24	Al Loquasto	Frostie Root Beer (86)		$ 15,420	95	Running
26	26	Larry McCoy	Shurfine Foods (63)		$ 14,993	91	Running
27	20	Jerry Grant	California-Oklahoma (73)		$ 15,594	91	Running
28	8	Gary Bettenhausen	Thermo-King (45)		$ 15,623	52	Waste gate
29	31	David Hobbs	Dayton-Walther (33)		$ 15,281	10	Water leak
30	13	Roger McCluskey	Hopkins (7)		$ 15,468	8	Accident
31	9	Bill Vukovich	Alex Foods (5)		$ 15,283	2	Rod
32	16	Dick Simon	Bryant Heat. & Cool. (17)		$ 14,426	1	Rod
33	25	Spike Gehlhausen	Spirit of Indiana (19)		$ 14,197	0	Oil pressure

FAST QUALIFIER: Mario Andretti (No. 6) -- 3:10.07 (189.404 mph)

LAP LEADERS: Laps 1-3, Rutherford, Laps 4-13, Foyt; Laps 14-16, Carter; Laps 17-19, Dallenbach; Laps 20-27, Johncock; Lap 38, Sneva; Laps 39-60, Rutherford; Laps 61-79, Foyt; Laps 80-102, Rutherford.

YELLOW FLAGS: Laps 4-6, Simon stalled; Laps 10-13, McCluskey accident; Laps 14-16, Debris on track; Laps 60-64, Parsons lost wheel; Laps 91-94, Grant stalled; Laps 101-102, rain; RED FLAG on lap 103.

WINNERS

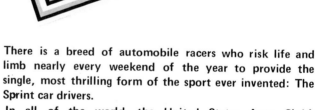

Here's the greatest argument solver we've ever produced. Our Indianapolis 500 Winners wall poster has an official Speedway photograph of every winner from Ray Harroun through Johnny Rutherford's second victory.

It's more than a simple documentary of all the winners too. Up on top we've headlined the three time winners and put the two-timers right beneath them.

Then we bordered our 2' x 3' work in two colors which makes it more than your personal log of who won when...it's nice just to look at and compare the evolution of the Indianapolis 500 racer over the years.

When ordering specify
Winners poster
or
USAC sprints
poster

There is a breed of automobile racers who risk life and limb nearly every weekend of the year to provide the single, most thrilling form of the sport ever invented: The Sprint car drivers.

In all of the world, the United States Auto Club's (USAC) Sprint car division is considered the ultimate proving ground for the Sprint driver who terms himself a professional. The competition is so torrid and the action so frightening that the USAC Sprints are popularly termed the "Thunder & Lightning" division.

For the first time in the history of USAC Sprint racing a collector's edition full color wall poster has been produced by Carl Hungness Publishing to honor these rugged gladiators. Our color reproduction and the quality of the action photographs allow you to feel the excitement the USAC Sprinters generate.

Mail $3.50 for each poster to:

Carl Hungness Publishing
Box 24308-Y
Speedway, IN   46224

[72]

Starting Field

Row 1

#02 Johnny Rutherford
Hy-Gain McLaren/Goodyear
Qual: 5/15 @ 4:29

3:10.52	188.957
47.27	190.396
47.57	189.195
47.69	188.719
47.99	187.539

#20 Gordon Johncock
Sinmast-Goodyear Wildcat
Qual: 5/15 @ 3:27

3:10.95	188.531
47.46	189.633
47.57	189.195
47.83	188.166
48.09	187.149

#68 Tom Sneva
Norton Spirit
Qual: 5/15 @ 5:00

3:13.18	186.355
48.18	186.800
48.10	187.110
48.25	186.528
48.65	184.995

Row 2

#21 Al Unser
American Racing Wheels Spl.
Qual: 5/15 @ 5:27

3:13.28	186.258
48.37	186.066
48.36	186.104
48.18	186.800
48.37	186.066

#14 A. J. Foyt, Jr
Gilmore Racing Team
Qual: 5/15 @ 4:52

3:14.32	185.261
48.04	187.344
48.32	186.258
48.76	184.578
49.20	182.927

#48 Duane Carter, Jr
Jorgensen Eagle
Qual: 5/15 @ 3:55

3:14.78	184.824
48.42	185.874
48.59	185.223
48.98	183.748
48.79	184.464

Row 3

#40 Wally Dallenbach
Sinmast-Goodyear Wildcat
Qual: 5/15 @ 4:14

3:15.18	184.445
48.69	184.843
48.88	184.124
48.78	184.502
48.83	184.313

#45 Gary Bettenhausen
Thermo King Eagle
Qual: 5/16* @ 12:10
(*1st Day Pole Line Qual)

3:18.03	181.791
49.36	182.334
49.57	181.561
49.49	181.855
49.61	181.415

#05 Bill Vukovich
Alex Foods Spl
Qual: 5/15 @ 4:05

3:18.42	181.433
49.36	182.334
49.51	181.781
49.89	180.397
49.66	181.232

Row 4

#69 Larry Cannon
American Financial Spirit of Cinti
Qual: 5/15 @ 2:26

3:18.47	181.388
49.78	180.796
49.80	180.723
49.32	182.482
49.57	181.561

#12 Mike Mosley
Sugaripe Prune Special
Qual: 5/16 @ 4:24

3:11.91	187.588
47.96	187.656
47.98	187.578
47.91	187.852
48.06	187.266

#03 Bobby Unser
Cobre Tire
Qual: 5/16 @ 1:11

3:11.98	187.520
47.93	187.774
47.98	187.578
48.01	187.461
48.06	187.266

Row 5

#07 Roger McCluskey
Hopkins Spl.
Qual: 5/16 @ 1:04

3:13.03	186.500
48.34	186.181
48.11	187.071
48.21	186.683
48.37	186.066

#93 Johnny Parsons
Ayr-Way/WIRE Spl.
Qual: 5/16 @ 12:20

3:16.89	182.843
49.33	182.445
49.11	183.262
49.10	183.299
49.35	182.371

#98 John Martin
Genesee Beer Dragon
Qual: 5/16 @ 2:16

3:17.35	182.417
49.16	183.076
49.33	182.445
49.28	182.630
49.58	181.525

Row 6

#17 Dick Simon
Bryant Heating & Cooling
Qual: 5/16 @ 5:53

3:17.43	182.343
49.08	183.374
49.05	183.486
49.37	182.297
49.93	180.252

#09 Vern Schuppan
Jorgensen Eagle
Qual: 5/16 @ 4:52

3:17.79	182.011
49.34	182.408
49.09	183.337
49.76	180.868
49.60	181.452

#83 Bill Puterbaugh
McNamara Motor Express Spl.
Qual: 5/16 @ 12:28

3:17.80	182.002
49.46	181.965
49.34	182.408
49.52	181.745
49.48	181.892

Row 7

#06 Mario Andretti
CAM2 Motor Oil Special
Qual: 5/22 @ 11:23

3:10.07	189.404
47.21	190.638
47.45	189.673
47.59	189.115
47.82	188.206

#73 Jerry Grant
California-Oklahoma Spl
Qual: 5/22 @ 11:32

3:16.06	183.617
48.87	184.162
48.93	183.936
49.16	183.076
49.10	183.299

#28 Billy Scott
Spirit of Public Enterprise
Qual: 5/22 @ 5:23

3:16.31	183.383
48.75	184.615
49.00	183.673
49.12	183.225
49.44	182.039

Row 8

#77 Salt Walther
Dayton-Walther Special
Qual: 5/22 @ 11:00

3:16.94	182.797
48.98	183.748
49.17	183.038
49.39	182.223
49.40	182.186

#92 Steve Krisiloff
1st Natl City Travelers Checks
Qual: 5/22 @ 12:17

3:17.66	182.131
49.23	182.815
49.35	182.371
49.57	181.561
49.51	181.781

#86 Al Loquasto, Jr
Frostie Root Beer
Qual: 5/22 @ 11:08

3:17.80	182.002
49.48	181.892
49.17	183.038
49.34	182.408
49.81	180.686

Row 9

#19 Spike Gehlhausen
Spirit of Indiana
Qual: 5/22 @ 5:38

3:18.11	181.717
49.20	182.927
49.53	181.708
49.59	181.488
49.79	180.759

#63 Larry McCoy
Shurfine Foods Special
Qual: 5/22 @ 12:30

3:18.47	181.388
49.57	181.561
49.57	181.561
49.60	181.452
49.73	180.977

#23 George Snider
Hubler Chevrolet Co. Spl.
Qual: 5/22 @ 11:40

3:18.74	181.141
49.75	180.905
49.66	181.232
49.69	181.123
49.64	181.305

Row 10

#96 Bob Harkey
Dave McIntire Centers - Ford & Chev
Qual: 5/22 @ 12:10

3:18.74	181.141
49.56	181.598
49.58	181.525
49.73	180.977
49.87	180.469

#97 Sheldon Kinser
THEBOTTOMHALF Dragon
Qual: 5/22 @ 5:29

3:18.77	181.114
49.66	181.232
49.44	182.039
49.82	180.650
49.85	180.542

#51 Lloyd Ruby
Fairco Drug Spl.
Qual: 5/23 @ 2:06

3:13.05	186.480
48.31	186.297
48.29	186.374
48.28	186.413
48.17	186.838

Row 11

#33 David Hobbs
Dayton-Walther Special
Qual: 5/23 @ 4:50

3:16.10	183.580
49.10	183.299
49.78	184.502
48.94	183.899
49.28	182.630

#24 Tom Bigelow
Leader Card Racer
Qual: 5/23 @ 12:00
(renumbered from #29)

3:17.84	181.965
49.32	182.482
49.45	182.002
49.60	181.452
49.47	181.928

#08 Jan Opperman
Routh Meat Packing Special
Qual: 5/23 @ 5:58

3:18.11	181.717
49.66	181.232
49.49	181.855
49.50	181.818
49.46	181.965

The average speed of the 33 cars that started the 1976 race was 183.785 MPH.
The average speed of the 1975 starters was 185.057 MPH.
Information courtesy of Dick Sauer, Indianapolis Motor Speedway Timing and Scoring.
(Qualifying date and time of day listed under car name.)

10 LAP RUN DOWN

LAP NO. 10

POSI-TION	CAR NO.	DRIVER
1	14	A. J. Foyt
2	2	Johnny Rutherford
3	20	Gordon Johncock
4	68	Tom Sneva
5	40	Wally Dallenbach
6	48	Pancho Carter
7	6	Mario Andretti
8	93	Johnny Parsons
9	21	Al Unser
10	3	Bobby Unser
11	12	Mike Mosley
12	45	Gary Bettenhausen
13	73	Jerry Grant
14	92	Steve Krisiloff
15	69	Larry Cannon
16	77	Salt Walther
17	9	Vern Schuppan
18	23	George Snider
19	98	John Martin
20	86	Al Loquasto
21	96	Bob Harkey
22	8	Jan Opperman
23	24	Tom Bigelow
24	97	Sheldon Kinser
25	51	Lloyd Ruby
26	28	Billy Scott
27	83	Bill Puterbaugh
28	63	Larry McCoy
29	33	David Hobbs

LAP NO. 20

POSI-TION	CAR NO.	DRIVER
1	20	Gordon Johncock
2	40	Wally Dallenbach
3	2	Johnny Rutherford
4	68	Tom Sneva
5	48	Pancho Carter
6	14	A. J. Foyt
7	93	Johnny Parsons
8	3	Bobby Unser
9	6	Mario Andretti
10	92	Steve Krisiloff
11	12	Mike Mosley
12	21	Al Unser
13	77	Salt Walther
14	45	Gary Bettenhausen
15	73	Jerry Grant
16	23	George Snider
17	96	Bob Harkey
18	51	Lloyd Ruby
19	28	Billy Scott
20	69	Larry Cannon
21	97	Sheldon Kinser
22	8	Jan Opperman
23	24	Tom Bigelow
24	98	John Martin
25	86	Al Loquasto
26	83	Bill Puterbaugh
27	9	Vern Schuppan
28	63	Larry McCoy

LAP NO. 30

POSI-TION	CAR NO.	DRIVER
1	20	Gordon Johncock
2	2	Johnny Rutherford
3	14	A. J. Foyt
4	40	Wally Dallenbach
5	48	Pancho Carter
6	68	Tom Sneva
7	3	Bobby Unser
8	6	Mario Andretti
9	93	Johnny Parsons
10	21	Al Unser
11	77	Salt Walther
12	12	Mike Mosley
13	45	Gary Bettenhausen
14	51	Lloyd Ruby
15	23	George Snider
16	73	Jerry Grant
17	28	Billy Scott
18	69	Larry Cannon
19	97	Sheldon Kinser
20	24	Tom Bigelow
21	8	Jan Opperman
22	92	Steve Krisiloff
23	98	John Martin
24	86	Al Loquasto
25	96	Bob Harkey
26	83	Bill Puterbaugh
27	63	Larry McCoy
28	9	Vern Schuppan

LAP NO. 40

POSI-TION	CAR NO.	DRIVER
1	2	Johnny Rutherford
2	14	A. J. Foyt
3	20	Gordon Johncock
4	93	Johnny Parsons
5	77	Salt Walther
6	48	Pancho Carter
7	3	Bobby Unser
8	40	Wally Dallenbach
9	68	Tom Sneva
10	21	Al Unser
11	6	Mario Andretti
12	12	Mike Mosley
13	51	Lloyd Ruby
14	92	Steve Krisiloff
15	23	George Snider
16	73	Jerry Grant
17	45	Gary Bettenhausen
18	96	Bob Harkey
19	69	Larry Cannon
20	24	Tom Bigelow
21	28	Billy Scott
22	97	Sheldon Kinser
23	8	Jan Opperman
24	98	John Martin
25	86	Al Loquasto
26	83	Bill Puterbaugh
27	9	Vern Schuppan
28	63	Larry McCoy

LAP NO. 50

POSI-TION	CAR NO.	DRIVER
1	2	Johnny Rutherford
2	14	A. J. Foyt
3	20	Gordon Johncock
4	48	Pancho Carter
5	3	Bobby Unser
6	40	Wally Dallenbach
7	68	Tom Sneva
8	21	Al Unser
9	6	Mario Andretti
10	93	Johnny Parsons
11	77	Salt Walther
12	12	Mike Mosley
13	51	Lloyd Ruby
14	92	Steve Krisiloff
15	73	Jerry Grant
16	23	George Snider
17	45	Gary Bettenhausen
18	96	Bob Harkey
19	69	Larry Cannon
20	24	Tom Bigelow
21	28	Billy Scott
22	8	Jan Opperman
23	97	Sheldon Kinser
24	98	John Martin
25	86	Al Loquasto
26	83	Bill Puterbaugh
27	9	Vern Schuppan
28	63	Larry McCoy

LAP NO. 60

POSI-TION	CAR NO.	DRIVER
1	2	Johnny Rutherford
2	14	A. J. Foyt
3	20	Gordon Johncock
4	48	Pancho Carter
5	40	Wally Dallenbach
6	68	Tom Sneva
7	6	Mario Andretti
8	21	Al Unser
9	93	Johnny Parsons
10	77	Salt Walther
11	3	Bobby Unser
12	51	Lloyd Ruby
13	12	Mike Mosley
14	73	Jerry Grant
15	23	George Snider
16	24	Tom Bigelow
17	28	Billy Scott
18	8	Jan Opperman
19	97	Sheldon Kinser
20	96	Bob Harkey
21	69	Larry Cannon
22	86	Al Loquasto
23	98	John Martin
24	83	Bill Puterbaugh
25	9	Vern Schuppan
26	92	Steve Krisiloff
27	63	Larry McCoy

LAP NO. 70

POSI-TION	CAR NO.	DRIVER
1	14	A. J. Foyt
2	2	Johnny Rutherford
3	20	Gordon Johncock
4	48	Pancho Carter
5	40	Wally Dallenbach
6	68	Tom Sneva
7	21	Al Unser
8	6	Mario Andretti
9	77	Salt Walther
10	3	Bobby Unser
11	51	Lloyd Ruby
12	93	Johnny Parsons
13	12	Mike Mosley
14	73	Jerry Grant
15	23	George Snider
16	24	Tom Bigelow
17	8	Jan Opperman
18	96	Bob Harkey
19	97	Sheldon Kinser
20	69	Larry Cannon
21	83	Bill Puterbaugh
22	86	Al Loquasto
23	9	Vern Schuppan
24	28	Billy Scott
25	98	John Martin
26	92	Steve Krisiloff
27	63	Larry McCoy

LAP NO. 80

POSI-TION	CAR NO.	DRIVER
1	2	Johnny Rutherford
2	14	A. J. Foyt
3	20	Gordon Johncock
4	48	Pancho Carter
5	40	Wally Dallenbach
6	68	Tom Sneva
7	6	Mario Andretti
8	77	Salt Walther
9	3	Bobby Unser
10	21	Al Unser
11	51	Lloyd Ruby
12	12	Mike Mosley
13	73	Jerry Grant
14	23	George Snider
15	93	Johnny Parsons
16	24	Tom Bigelow
17	8	Jan Opperman
18	69	Larry Cannon
19	97	Sheldon Kinser
20	83	Bill Puterbaugh
21	86	Al Loquasto
22	9	Vern Schuppan
23	96	Bob Harkey
24	98	John Martin
25	28	Billy Scott
26	92	Steve Krisiloff
27	63	Larry McCoy

LAP NO. 90

POSI-TION	CAR NO.	DRIVER
1	2	Johnny Rutherford
2	14	A. J. Foyt
3	20	Gordon Johncock
4	48	Pancho Carter
5	40	Wally Dallenbach
6	68	Tom Sneva
7	21	Al Unser
8	6	Mario Andretti
9	77	Salt Walther
10	3	Bobby Unser
11	51	Lloyd Ruby
12	93	Johnny Parsons
13	23	George Snider
14	24	Tom Bigelow
15	8	Jan Opperman
16	12	Mike Mosley
17	69	Larry Cannon
18	97	Sheldon Kinser
19	9	Vern Schuppan
20	96	Bob Harkey
21	98	John Martin
22	83	Bill Puterbaugh
23	28	Billy Scott
24	92	Steve Krisiloff
25	86	Al Loquasto
26	63	Larry McCoy
27	73	Jerry Grant

LAP NO. 100

POSI-TION	CAR NO.	DRIVER
1	2	Johnny Rutherford
2	14	A. J. Foyt
3	20	Gordon Johncock
4	40	Wally Dallenbach
5	48	Pancho Carter
6	68	Tom Sneva
7	21	Al Unser
8	6	Mario Andretti
9	77	Salt Walther
10	3	Bobby Unser
11	51	Lloyd Ruby

Pit Stop Report

FIRST PLACE Johnny Rutherford   Hy-Gain McLaren/Good year

2	1	12	Fuel Only	12 seconds
	2	35	Fuel, R/F & R/R Tires Changed	18 seconds
	3	60	Fuel L/R Tire Changed	17 seconds
	4	86	Fuel, R/F & R/R Tires Changed (Violated Wheel Lock Rule)	16 seconds
			TOTAL TIME	63 seconds

SECOND PLACE A. J. Foyt, Jr.   Gilmore Racing Team

14	1	13	Fuel & Adjusted Wing with Remote Wrench which Hooked on to Car Leaving Pits	6 seconds
	2	37	Fuel Only	14 seconds
	3	61	Fuel, R/F and R/R Tires Changed	15 seconds
	4	81	Fuel, R/F and R/R Tires Changed (Violated Wheel Lock Rule)	16 seconds
	5	92	Fuel, L/F & L/R Tires Changed	15 seconds
			TOTAL TIME	66 seconds

THIRD PLACE —Gordon Johncock Sinmast Goodyear Wildcat

20	1	12	Fuel, R/F & R/R Tires Changed	16.4 seconds
	2	38	Fuel, R/F & R/R Tires Changed	14.6 seconds
	3	62	Fuel, R/R & L/R Tires Changed (Violated Wheel Lock Rule)	21 seconds
	4	85	Fuel, R/F & R/R Tires Changed (Violated Wheel Lock Rule)	14.7 seconds
			TOTAL TIME	66.7 seconds

FOURTH PLACE —Wally Dallenbach Sinmast Goodyear Wildcat

40	1	12	Fuel Only	11 seconds
	2	37	Fuel, R/F & R/R Tires Changed	21 seconds
	3	62	Fuel Only (Found Wheel Lock Violation)	13 seconds
	4	86	Fuel Only	15 seconds
			TOTAL TIME	60 seconds

FIFTH PLACE —Duane Carter, Jr.   Jorgensen Eagle

48	1	33	Fuel, R/F & R/R Tires Changed	19 seconds
	2	61	Fuel, R/F & R/R Tires Changed	16 seconds
	3	89	Fuel, R/F & R/R Tires Changed	15 seconds
			TOTAL TIME	50 seconds

SIXTH PLACE —Tom Sneva   Norton Spirit

68	1	13	Fuel & Repaired Cracked Windshield	28 seconds
	2	39	Fuel, R/F & R/R & L/R Tires Changed. Also more repairs to Windshield	36 seconds
	3	62	Fuel Only	17 seconds
	4	88	Fuel, R/F, R/R & L/R Tires Changed	28 seconds
			TOTAL TIME	109 seconds

SEVENTH PLACE —Al Unser   American Racing Wheels Special

21	1	11	Fuel & Adjusted Front Wing	19 seconds
	2	36	Fuel, R/F & R/R Tires Changed	27 seconds
	3	55	Fuel Only	17 seconds
	4	79	Fuel & R/F Tire Changed (Found R/F Wheel Lock Missing)	15 seconds
	5	90	Fuel, R/F & R/R Tires Changed	27 seconds
			TOTAL TIME	105 seconds

EIGHTH PLACE —Mario Andretti   CAM2 Motor Oil Special

6	1	12	Fuel, R/F, R/R & L/R Tires Changed	44 seconds
	2	39	Fuel, Engine Stalled and Restarted	33 seconds
	3	60	Fuel, R/F, R/R, & L/R Tires Changed	25 seconds
	4	87	Fuel, R/F & R/R Tires Changed (Violated Wheel Lock Rule)	21 seconds
			TOTAL TIME	123 seconds

NINTH PLACE —Salt Walther   Dayton-Walther Special

77	1	16	Fuel & Adjusted Turbo/Charger Waste Gate	21 seconds
	2	40	Fuel, R/F & R/R Tires Changed	24 seconds
	3	59	Fuel & R/R Tire Changed	23 seconds
	4	83	Fuel & R/F Tire Changed	23 seconds
	5	99	Fuel, L/F & L/R Tires Changed	32 seconds
			TOTAL TIME	123 seconds

TENTH PLACE —Bobby Unser   Cobre Tire

3	1	10	Fuel Only	4 seconds
	2	33	Fuel, R/F & R/R Tires Changed	19 seconds
	3	58	Fuel, R/F & R/R Tires Changed	25 seconds
	4	87	Fuel, R/F & R/R Tires Changed	21 seconds
	5	89	Fuel, L/F & L/R Tires Changed	18 seconds
			TOTAL TIME	87 seconds

ELEVENTH PLACE —Lloyd Ruby   Fairco Drug

51	1	15	Fuel Only	16 seconds
	2	40	Fuel & R/F Tire Changed	24 seconds
	3	62	Fuel & R/R Tire Changed	20 seconds
	4	87	Fuel Only	17 seconds
			TOTAL TIME	77 seconds

TWELFTH PLACE —Johnny Parsons Ayr-Way/WIRE Special

93	1	16	Fuel Only	23 seconds
	2	40	Fuel, R/F & R/R Tires Changed	18 seconds
	3	59	Fuel, R/F & R/R Tires Changed	28 seconds
	4	60	To Replace Lost Front Wheel (Wheel Lock Violation)	70 seconds
	5	79	Fuel, R/F & R/R Tires Changed	38 seconds
	6	87	Fuel & R/R Tire Change	21 seconds
			TOTAL TIME	198 seconds

THIRTEENTH PLACE —George Snider Hubler Chevrolet Co Special

23	1	12	Fuel Only	10 seconds
	2	36	Fuel Only	15 seconds
	3	59	Fuel, R/F & R/R Tires Changed (Violation-No Gloves on Rear tire Changer)	40 seconds
	4	83	Fuel Only	15 seconds
			TOTAL TIME	80 seconds

FOURTEENTH PLACE —Tom Bigelow Leader Card Racer

24	1	11	Fuel Only	9 seconds
	2	37	Fuel Only	16 seconds
	3	58	Fuel Only	14 seconds
	4	87	Fuel, R/F & R/R Tires Changed	19 seconds
			TOTAL TIME	58 seconds

FIFTEENTH PLACE —Mike Mosley Sugaripe Prune Special

12	1	12	Fuel & R/F Tire Changed	12 seconds

	2	38	Fuel, R/F & R/R Tires Changed	16 seconds
	3	59	Fuel, R/F & R/R Tires Changed (Engine Stalled Leaving Pit & Restarted)	52 seconds
	4	86	Fueled & Restarted Engine (Was Out of Fuel When Pushed into Pit)	24 seconds

TOTAL TIME 104 seconds

SIXTEENTH PLACE—Jan Opperman   Routh Meat Packing Special

8	1	15	Fuel Only (Violation-6 men over the wall)	15 seconds
	2	38	Fuel & Adjusted Wing	43 seconds
	3	59	Fuel, R/F & R/R Tires Changed	23 seconds
	4	82	Fuel only	17 seconds

TOTAL TIME 98 seconds

SEVENTEENTH PLACE—Larry Cannon   American Financial Special

69	1	12	Fuel Only	14 seconds
	2	36	Fuel Only	17.5 seconds
	3	56	Fuel, R/F & R/R Tires Changed	35.2 seconds
	4	84	Fuel Only	17.2 seconds

TOTAL TIME 83.9 seconds

EIGHTEENTH PLACE—Vern Schuppan   Jorgensen Eagle

9	1	16	Fuel Only	26 seconds
	2	21	Fuel & R/R Tire Changed	22 seconds
	3	45	Fuel Only	15 seconds
	4	58	Fuel, R/F & R/R Tires Changed	21 seconds
	5	87	Fuel Only	28 seconds

TOTAL TIME 112 seconds

NINETEENTH PLACE—Sheldon Kinser   THEBOTTOMHALF Dragon

97	1	15	Fuel Only	13 seconds
	2	40	Fuel & R/F Tire Changed Also Restarted Stalled Engine	50 seconds
	3	59	Fuel & R/R Tire Changed (Violated Wheel Lock Rule)	60 seconds
	4	87	Fuel Only	16 seconds

TOTAL TIME 139 seconds

TWENTIETH PLACE—Bob Harkey   Dave McIntire Centers Ford & Chevy

96	1	26	Fuel Only	19 seconds
	2	52	Fuel, R/F & R/R Tires Changed	33 seconds
	3	80	Fuel & L/R Tire Changed	36.5 seconds

TOTAL TIME 88.5 seconds

TWENTY-FIRST PLACE—John Martin   Genesee Beer Dragon

98	1	11	Fuel & Adjusted Turbo/Charger Waste Gate	27 seconds
	2	38	Fuel & Adjusted Turbo/Charger Waste Gate	31 seconds
	3	57	Fuel, R/F & R/R Tires Changed	63 seconds
	4	69	Fuel Only	15 seconds
	5	98	Fuel & Adjusted Turbo/Charger Waste Gate	16 seconds

TOTAL TIME 152 seconds

TWENTY-SECOND PLACE—Bill Puterbaugh   McNamara Motor Express Special

83	1	9	Fuel & L/R Tire Changed	67 seconds
	2	33	Fuel, R/F & R/R Tires Changed	25 seconds
	3	58	Fuel Only	19 seconds
	4	83	Fuel Only	18 seconds

TOTAL TIME 129 seconds

TWENTY-THIRD PLACE—Billy Scott   Spirit of Public Enterprise

28	1	10	Fuel Only	7.5 seconds
	2	37	Fuel Only	13.5 seconds
	3	58	Fuel, R/F & R/R Tires changed	27.5 seconds
	4	68	Fuel, R/F & R/R Tires changed (Violated Wheel Lock Rule)	36 seconds
	5	86	Fuel Only	14 seconds

TOTAL TIME 98.5 seconds

TWENTY-FOURTH PLACE—Steve Krisiloff   First National City Travelers Checks

92	1	30	Fuel & R/R Tire Changed	25 seconds
	2	56	Fuel & R/R Tire Changed	44 seconds
	3	78	Fuel, R/F & R/R Tires Changed	25 seconds

TOTAL TIME 94 seconds

TWENTY-FIFTH PLACE—Al Loquasto, Jr.   Frostie Root Beer

86	1	12	Fuel Only	17 seconds
	2	34	Fuel & R/R Tire Changed	22 seconds
	3	55	Fuel, R/F & R/R Tires Changed	27 seconds
	4	83	Engine Stalled, Fuel & Restarted Engine	52 seconds

118 seconds

TWENTY-SIXTH PLACE—Larry McCoy   Shurfine Foods Special

63	1	7	Fuel Only	30 seconds
	2	8	Tire Inspection Only	26 seconds
	3	33	Fuel Only	22 seconds
	4	55	Fuel & Adjusted Turbo/Charger Waste Gate	70 seconds
	5	58	Fuel & L/F Tire Changed, Tried to Remove R/R Wheel but could not get nut off	65 seconds
	6	82	Fuel & R/R Tire Changed	35 seconds

TOTAL TIME 248 seconds

TWENTY-SEVENTH PLACE—Jerry Grant   California-Oklahoma Special

73	1	11	Fuel & R/R Tire Changed	22 seconds
	2	33	Fuel, R/F & R/R Tires Changed	22 seconds
	3	59	Fuel & L/R Tire Changed, Also Adjust L/F Wing	24 seconds
	4	87	Pushed into pit, Fuel & R/F Tire Changed, Also Adjusted Rear Stabilizer Bar, Restart Engine	85 seconds

TOTAL TIME 153 seconds

TWENTY-EIGHTH PLACE—Gary Bettenhausen   Thermo King Eagle

45	1	12	Fuel Only	12 seconds
	2	38	Fuel, R/F & R/R Tires Changed	22 seconds
	3	53	Discovered Broken Turbo/Charger Waste Gate Out of Race	24 seconds

TOTAL TIME 34 seconds

TWENTY-NINTH PLACE—David Hobbs   Dayton-Walther Special

33	1	2	Tighten Water Hose Clamp & Added Water	638 seconds
	2	7	Fuel & Water Added	478 seconds

TOTAL TIME 1,116 seconds

THIRTIETH PLACE—Roger McCluskey   Hopkins Special

7	1	5	Fuel & R/F Tire Changed	11 seconds

TOTAL TIME 11 seconds

THIRTY-FIRST PLACE—Bill Vukovich   Alex Foods Special

5		3	Out of Race Lap No. 3 (Connecting Rod)	

THIRTY-SECOND PLACE—Dick Simon   Bryant Heating and Cooling

17			None (Engine Failed)	

THIRTY-THIRD PLACE—Spike Gehlhausen   Spirit of Indiana

19			None (Engine Failed)	

"Turn one at Indy isn't much. It's just gettin' through it that's hard."

By A. J. Foyt

"To a race driver, it sometimes seems like everybody in the world has something to say about the Indy '500.' Which is all fine. Except, you can't really know that race until you've driven it. And you don't know what driving it is like until you move into that first turn.

"Now, to look at it, turn one at Indy isn't much. It's just gettin' through it that's hard. Particularly on the first lap when all the cars are coming down like a herd of longhorns tryin' to get position.

"You drive into it hearin' everything. The crowd. The

gears. Even the tires wearing. Now, at the end of the pit wall, you turn the wheel to the left until the nose comes around and you get a good line on the inside of the track. Then you hit the throttle, turn right, and wait for the torque to catch up with you. You're drifting a little, and the strain is tremendous.

"Halfway through the turn, you stand on the throttle again and drive back down toward the infield. You come out of it running 170, 180, maybe, and you settle the nose.

"Don't let anybody dog you that it's easy. It's not. And, you've got 199 more times to do it that afternoon. But, the point is, with all that to think about, you want your engine running like heavy cream. That's the last thing you want to think about. And that's why I do all my racing on Valvoline® Racing Oil. Because I know it's going to protect that engine."

Valvoline is one motor oil that can take the punishment of racing. That's one reason why pros like A. J. Foyt run on it. (Foyt has used it exclusively for years.) And why more pros at Indy, on major drag strips and on road race courses run on Valvoline Racing Oil than any other brand.

Your engine needs the same kind of protection. Because everyday driving can be just as hard on a motor oil as racing. There's a quality Valvoline Motor Oil for every kind of car, every kind of driving. Choose Valvoline. The motor oil the pros run on.

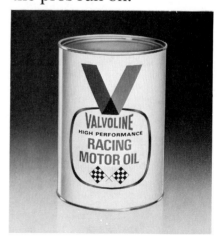

speedway miscellaneous

Jerry Sneva, Tom's younger brother who is a well-qualified oval track racer in his own right, showed up on the first day of practice and was heard to say,

"I don't know too many people back here and I've never been able to walk up to a car owner and tell him how great I am."

Unfortunately for both Jerry and an owner seeking a promising rookie, Jerry didn't secure a ride for Indianapolis 1976.

Lee Kunzman, left, and a talented Jerry Sneva sharing a joke in the pits.

If you were a basketball fan visiting Indianapolis on Mother's Day (May 9) you could have witnessed the greatest assemblage of Hoosier hardwood heroes ever presented on the same floor. Names like Billy Keller, Oscar Robertson, George McGinnis, Jon McGlocklin, etc. put on a bash that saw proceeds go to Muscular Dystrophy. It was a fine idea.

***

After lambasting Arlene Hiss' debut into Championship racing at Phoenix, Billy Vukovich did an about face and and showed his real mettle when he complimented Janet Guthrie on her performance at Trenton.

Janet's racing togs didn't arrive at the Speedway when she needed them and Vuky promptly loaned her his spares. Although it sometimes appears as though he doesn't want you to know it, Vukovich can be one of the most humorous and pleasant drivers around.

Janet Guthrie held up well amidst the barrage of jokes made about Vuke's uniform.

Last year, when a driving rainstorm hit the track with 26 laps to go, the lack of a red light system was blamed for cars slipping and sliding into one another until they could reach the main straight and see the red flag displayed. Red flag (or light) of course, means the race is stopped immediately.

At the request of Tom Binford, chief steward, track Superintendent Clarence Cagle had a complete red system installed for the '76 event.

***

The meanest, toughest and bravest drivers of them all, the USAC Sprint car racers, practiced at the Dayton, Ohio high-banked asphalt track on May 8 after a several year lapse. The following day Pancho Carter won the 40 lap feature.

***

Bill Simpson, the multi-talented businessman, race driver debuted a new driving uniform. It resembles a quilt and has wax treated stitches that expand under heat and thereby provide an air cushion for additional protection.

Bill also spent a bit of time pursuing his continuing search for Cord L-29's while in Indy. He has an impressive collection of antique cars.

Indianapolis Star writer John Bansch interviewed cooperative Jan Opperman about the race driver's new church and a few of his quotes are worth listening to:

"I want to help young people from 12 to 20—help the druggies, give them a chance to get their heads straight. I teach them about love and God and when they begin to understand their attitude begins to change. . .they're insecure, looking for someone or someone or something to say 'I love you', and when they discover God is love, they no longer will be insecure."

Jan has opened what amounts to a rehabilitation center in the mountains of Montana. He'll handle about a dozen young people at a time, and plans to continue spreading the good word throughout the racing circuits he follows.

You're a good man Jan Opperman.

***

About his Formula 1 involvement, Mario Andretti says, "I plan to give it two or three years to see what I can accomplish. Then I'm going to come back here (Indianapolis) and pick up where I left off."

***

Bill Simpson took time out in Indy to try and locate his favorite car, a Cord L-29.

After Eddie Miller managed to get his Thermo-King sponsored entry upside down during the second phase of his rookie test, garage talk centered around the requirements necessary to obtain a Championship license. While Miller may very well be a capable driver he lacked experience in ultra-high horsepower equipment.

***

Although general admission to time trials was raised from $2 to $3 this year, you can't find a better bargain in sports. There's six hours of trials, 90 minutes of practice and the best girl-watching vantage point this side of the Mississippi River.

***

Ever wonder what goes on inside all those little offices under the Tower Terrace? Most are occupied by accessory companies and are utilized as hospitality rooms where members of the racing fraternity can gather for a few minutes relaxation. We dropped in on Champion Spark plug's Freddie Agabashian, whose racing exploits could well fill a book and heard him tell of the time he was a mechanic working on Cord automobiles. He was a crackerjack mechanic and his reputation for making the cantankerous Cords perform like Swiss watches spread all the way from his native Northern California down the coast to Los Angeles.

Two characters of questionable background appeared and asked Freddie's boss:

"We understand youse guys got a guy who's good at makin' these things run. We wanna see him right now."

Agabashian's boss attempted to explain that Freddie had a full schedule for the day, but Freddie intercepted and offered to take the car for a test drive. It was indeed sick. Agabashian talked them into bringing the car back another day and he performed a few of his specialties on it and became an instant hero.

"Listen, we got a whole bunch of these things down in L.A.," one of the gentlemen noted. "We want you to come to work for us," he continued. "You can even bring that thing with you and we'll give you enough money to finish it first-class."

The thing was Freddie's first Midget race car he was painstakingly fabricating from scratch in his spare time. Agabashian would ultimately turn out to be one of the finest Midget racers the country has ever seen, but he wouldn't allow his new-found friends

Mario Andretti just might have been the 1976 Indianapolis 500 pole sitter if he hadn't taken time out to qualify for a Formula 1 race. The popular little Italian looked good in his Penske-prepared equipment.

to help him along his journey.

"It was a teriffic offer, more money than I'd ever heard of," Agabashian said. "But could you imagine what would've happened if some day, say outside a bank, one of my tune-ups decided to go sour and the car didn't start?"

Agabashian has come a long way from his wrench-turning days. Now, the Speedway's radio broadcast wouldn't be the same without him as a color man. He hasn't lost a bit of the old moxie that made him a successful racer. The racing clan should be glad that he joined the right mob.

***

Clay Ballinger, a USAC technical crew member and auto racing stawart in general, recalled that half a century ago a gal named Alfreda Mais and her spouse Johnny were the scourge of International Motor Contest Association (IMCA) racing.

"They could run 1-2," Clay said. "Alfreda could run against the best of 'em."

Whenever something new arrives at the Speedway, you can count on a knowledgeable oldtimer telling you how new the concept isn't.

***

Rookie Vern Schuppan arrived at the Monroe Rookie Recognition banquet a little late, but had a solid excuse for his tardiness. He was spending time with the kids at the Indiana School for the Blind.

***

Last year we printed a section titled "Wives and Loved Ones."

Eddie Miller and wife look over a sequence of his horrendous accident. He's a lucky boy.

Gordon Johncock's companion Linda insisted she be listed as Linda Johncock. This year she and Gordon took out a marriage license. We guarantee the Indianapolis 500 Yearbook to be accurate unless swayed by female decisions.

***

No one ever asked Janet Guthrie (or Tony Hulman) how the traditional "Gentlemen, Start your Engines," phrase might change if Janet had made the program. J.C. Agajanian said, not too convincingly, at the Phoenix race where Arlene Hiss made her debut: "Championship drivers, start your engines." Somehow, even with all of Aggie's charisma, that didn't do much for us.

Freddie Agabashian shares the announcing tower with Sid Collins on race day, but spends the rest of the time as a representative of Champion Spark plug company.

Dr. Harlen Hunter, a St. Louis doctor and race fan who helped revive the Indianapolis 500 Yearbook, became friends with Sid Collins, right, and diagnosed a serious back problem the famed announcer had.

Wally Dallenbach is one driver the sport can be proud of. He helped his hometown obtain a badly needed ambulance and took time out in May to deliver it 1,300 miles.

Wally Dallenbach, the man for who all intents and purposes virtually had the field whipped for the 1975 race, didn't let the hectic month of May conflict with his civic spirit.

Wally moved his family from the east to a ranch near the town of Basalt, Colo. about three years ago and has taken on a pioneering attitude.

"Our area in the central high Rockies is about 7,000 feet above sea level and the roads are all two-lane highways. There aren't enough guardrails in the entire country to protect all the curves on the mountain roads so no one has bothered to put up any.

"What this means is that when there is an accident, it's likely to be serious, yet emergency equipment is nonexistent."

One of the first things a race driver looks for at a given track is the ambulance, and the curves around Basalt must have reminded Dallenbach of a treacherous situation. He rounded up 18 volunteers from the surrounding area and formed a rescue team last winter. Trouble was, they didn't have a vehicle, an ambulance to use when the need arose.

After qualifying his Sinmast Wildcat on the inside of the third row Wally kept his promise to the men back home and continued his search for a rescue vehicle. He found one up in Knightstown, Ind. that cost $20,000 properly outfitted. Then he made arrangements for a note to be issued to he and his fellow rescue men.

A week before the race he hopped in the ambulance and drove it home, 1,200 miles.

"I'm taking the ambulance back now," he said, "because we want the rescue service in operation as soon as possible. If we save just one life, it's worth the effort."

Nice guy that Wally Dallenbach.

***

Dr. Harlen Hunter, the St. Louis doctor who is credited with supplying the backing necessary to revive our Indianapolis 500 Yearbook in 1973 should be thanked by race fans worldwide who have ever enjoyed the annual radio broadcast narrated by Sid Collins.

One of Doc Hunter's ambitions was to meet some of his racing heroes and and get to know them on a first name basis. He built a particularly good rapport with Collins, the famed Voice of the 500 and after watching Sid limp around after the '75 event, Harlen suggested that Sid see a neurosurgeon.

Sid explained that he had already seen three doctors and they all pretty much agreed his problem was a fairly simple one that proper exercise would correct. Harlen disagreed and convinced Sid to enter a hospital for testing.

Sid's condition was serious. They told him if he'd gone much longer he would be paralyzed. The cure scared him even worse, he would require a spinal disc fusion immediately. But the operation would not begin on his back: they had to enter his neck from the front and go periously close to his larynx to reach the spine. There was a chance that his voice would be gone.

As we know now, the operation was a complete success and although Sid found it painful climbing to the top of the Speedway tower in '76, he's well on the road to recovery.

"Isn't that something," he notes. "Three doctors for five months tell me I have a slight muscle problem and then a doctor walks out of the Speedway crowd and tells me what's wrong. If I hadn't been associated with the Speedway, I probably would have gone along and eventually been paralyzed. I'm a very lucky man."

[81]

Jim McKay--ABC Sports.

Lou Palmer and Paul Page of WIBC.

Media and Accessory People

Here are a few of the dozens
who annually make up part
of the Speedway scene.

Link, Hunter, Wick, Stringer photos

Artist Ron Burton, driver Larry Rice and publisher Don Rackemann, sitting, look over a copy of Rackemann's paper, Motorsports Weekly.

Bob Funcannon is the P.A. voice from the south end of the pits.

Jackie Stewart and Peter DePaolo, former drivers, chat on ABC TV.

The Sears Die-Hard battery shop in Gasoline Alley is essential.

Sportscasters Chet Coppock and Don Hein dwarf Mario Andretti.

P.R. man Bill Marvel visits with two-time winner Rodger Ward.

Jack Mackenzie is trophy guard.

Mechanic Ed Bauie and Premier's Ray Mello.

John Serbin and Dick Ward from Monroe.

John Fugate, Speedway publicity.

Race writer Crocky Wright.

Robin Miller-- writer/racer.

Statistician Dick Jordan.

George Moore-- Indianapolis Star.

Paul Scheuring-- WXLW radio.

Ray DeLaRoche-- Sunnen

Ralph Salvino-- STP

Roger Phillips-- Cam2

Bob Braun-- 50-50 Club host.

Dick Ralston-- Goodyear

Pat Cronin-- pace car room

Van Steenwyk and Jack Brandt, Indiana Oxygen.

ABC's Chris Schenkel and Harlan Fengler.

Jim Coughlin and Roy Richter, Bell helmets.

Ayr-Way President Dave Kinney chats with P.R. man Jim Kohlmeyer.

[83]

Missed The Show

The official Indianapolis Motor Speedway program lists 71 entries for the 1976 Indianapolis 500. Now you might think that means 71 cars will be fighting for the 33 starting spots, not so.

There is a lot of mystique and heartbreak with those that don't make the show. The last minute qualifying adventures can make sleepless nights worthless in a bump situation. But, that same effort can be made especially meaningful when a car makes it at the last second.

"Whew, our prayers were answered."

Some cars never arrive, some are entered to provide garage space and others go into reserve status. Those "backup" cars enter service if an accident wipes out the number one ride or if an owner feels he can support another driver.

We include cars that represented possible qualification. And that is not everybody. Could you tell the difference between Johnny Rutherford's No. 2 and his backup.

They both had the same number! How about the No. 41 ICP-2 machine, did you ever see it? Neither did we.

Some of the entries change colors or numbers and it is a game trying to figure them out. No. 75 turned out to be the No. 8 entry Jan Opperman drove in the race. Herb Porter had two entries, No. 80 and No. 89. Ever see them? I didn't think so.

How about the No. 87 Jim Robbins car? It hasn't been raced since 1971 and it is entered annually based on a will request.

What about the entries you never saw or heard about? Where was the No. 36 Shurfine Foods car, the No. 35 Cobre Tire special, the No. 52 stock block entered by Kenny Moran, or the No. 54 Schlitz Special for Woody Fisher? Additional A. J. Foyt entries can be traced to the No. 84 and No. 82 cars. Where were they?

So look closely. The cars on the track represent serious efforts while the cars on the entry list may be there for other reasons.

Janet Guthrie almost got the ride of her life in A.J.'s backup.

Mike Hiss had the speed but not the luck to make the race.

Tom Bigelow got bumped and then made the race in his backup car.

Al Unser's backup traveled many miles but never got a driver.

Janet Guthrie's car was the most photographed but too slow.

Bill Simpson did everything right then was bumped out of the race.

Jan Opperman knew he'd make the race but not in his primary car.

Billy Englehart and Dick Simon just couldn't find the speed secret.

Eddie Miller's incredible accident destroyed the No. 46 car.

Jim Hurtubise pushed the roadster over 173, still too slow.

Eldon Rasmussen became the last qualifying victim of 1976.

Mel Kenyon tried so hard he spun but never got enough speed.

The unique Moser stock block couldn't go quick enough.

Larry Dickson, Lee Kunzman tried, Jim McElreath was left in line.

Ed Crombie's hopes ended when his ride crashed in turn four.

Jim McElreath's car number was right, then it was bumped out.

Bobby Olivero drove a record rookie test then was also bumped out.

John Mahler returned but his Spirit of Indiana was too slow.

A bad engine doomed Rick Muther's qualifying efforts this year.

WINNER'S COMMENTS

Editor's Note: Soon after the "500" winner takes his victory lap around the track, he is shuttled into the Speedway's press room where a post-race interview is conducted. Johnny Rutherford is one of the press favorites. He's articulate, humorous and cooperative. Chet Coppock and Chuck Waggoner of Indianapolis' WISH-TV provided us with a tape of the Rutherford interview. We present it below in its entirety (unedited) for your reading enjoyment.

QUESTION: What's your reaction to winning your second 500?

J.R.: "The anxiety of waiting for the race to restart was a new ordeal for me," "Still victory is sweet any way you can get it. We were in the right place at the right time when the rains came. I feel sad for A.J. who most certainly would have put a charge on had we re-started. His car was fixed and he was loaded for bear.

"I think had we gotten another green flag he would have most certainly have been gone and we would have had to race very hard to keep up with him. I think we woulda had a heck of a race. I'll put it that way.

"Of course Gordon Johncock is always very tough so any time you get those guys face to face it's a race."

"I do feel sorry that it stopped this way but we still won it. But like I say we just happened to be number one when the rains came."

QUESTION: A.J. made the complaint that you were cheating on the Pacer.

J.R.: "Well, A.J. had made some verbal abuse to me (for lack of a better word)" "He said that I had cause his team had told him we had gained some 20 seconds. I'm not sure what exactly the figure was, 23, 18, OK, 18 seconds. A.J., failed to find out from his team that he had made one more pit stop than we had and that's where his 18 seconds went.

"So. . . I wasn't cheating on the yellow out there, I was keeping in line with everybody else and everybody

slowed down I slowed down. So it was virtually the same as the old system, the honor system, just drifting in on the car in front of you while everybody gets slowed down to Pacer speed then that's what it was and I don't feel like by any stretch of the imagination we were cheating on the yellow."

QUESTION: Do you know that the timers and Scorers found nothing . . . .

J.R.: "Yes, I would certainly hope that there wasn't, because I wouldn't go out there and try to cheat any more than Bobby Unser of A. J. Foyt or . . . (laughter form press corps.)

QUESTION: A. J. said he would have done it (cheat under the yellow) if he could get away with it."

J.R: I suppose so - -you do everything you can out there but by the same token, you could get caught and if you get caught it's a lot worse. It's best just to swing along with everything and take it easy."

QUESTION: Can you compare your feelings now with the other victory?

J.R.: "Well, its a whole different set of circumstances. I'm proud to be a winner and of course I've kinda created a situation that may be hard to live with in-as-much as Hy-gain came with us at Trenton-we won Trenton, we came here, sat on the pole, and now we've won the race.

"I'm afraid they'll get mad if I lose one!"

QUESTION: What about your personal feelings?

J.R.: "My personal feelings is a - - - I'm really kinda relieved,- - it's been a hectic month, a pressure month to more or less being out front, and getting recognition for what you do puts a great deal of demand cause you guys all write nice stories about us and we gotta live up to 'em. So now that's it over with it's kinda a relief and let's get ready for Milwaukee."

QUESTION: Did you work on your car during the delay? A. J. and Gordy were. . . .

J.R.: "No, we were working well enough before that we left the car alone virtually. I think we made some tire changes, nothing mechanical.

"A.J. had a broken front sway bar, roll bar, and as a result they had to change that--that's why he would have been back in the hunt."

QUESTION: You were a little upset that he was able to do that . . .

J.R.: "No, I was concerned because I did not know what the rule was personally. Some years you couldn't touch the car on a red light and I was just making sure they could work on it."

QUESTION: What were you told about the rule?

J.R.: "In '67 did it happen? I think they made the change in the interest of safety--I think it's good cause A. J. was struggling . . . maybe it's not good . . . .maybe they should. . .(chuckle)."

QUESTION: When you last passed A.J. did you think you would win the 500?

J.R.: "Well, I thought there might be a possibility cause after the second pit stop we changed tires (right side) and my car came to life as far as handling and I was surprised at the guys I could catch and pass I thought would normally be a tussle..

"Of course, when I caught A. J. it didn't take me but one turn to realize that he had trouble cause he was slowing way down in the turns. It was just a matter lining up to get him."

QUESTION: Did you see the rain coming in No. 4?

J.R.: "No, we were on yellow I thought I noticed rain on the windshield but they get very dirty with rubber, oil and grit and I thought I saw rain but that could have been something loose flapping. Then the yellow came out again and were slowed and I saw rain on my visor."

QUESTION: Did you have a pit stop planned if the rains came?"

J.R.: "Tyler told me we could get 16 laps without a stop."

QUESTION: At what stage did your car come to life?

J.R.: "After the second pit stop."

QUESTION: Did you pit during the last yellow before the rain to make sure of your position?

J.R.: "We didn't want to get in a situation like last year and be in the pits when it all stopped and lose first place so we decided to stay out till the rain stopped or we could get back and make a stop so we wouldn't get badly penalized for it."

QUESTION "Do you feel that the paying customer got his money's worth today?

J.R.: "I'll tell you what, if they didn't like the racing that was goin' on while we were racing then they don't know what racing's about. There was some fantastic situations. I forget how many cars were in that gaggle down the main straightaway.

"I'm sure glad somebody didn't open the gate cause we would have wiped out half the field!"

QUESTION: During the two hour interim what were your personal feelings? Did you want to get out there again?

J.R.: "The man is asking me to define mixed emotions.

"Mixed emotions is watching your mother-in-law drive over a cliff in your new Cadillac."

QUESTION: How'd you feel when the second wave of rain came?

J.R.: "Again--you'r asking me to define mixed emotions, Jep. I think probably when it did rain I wanted to get out there and race. You know I thought, by golly, A.J. is ready now let's go out and test him and see what they can do and run the rest of the way.

"If we could have, it would have been good. I could also visualize making a couple of pace laps and getting green, have A.J. catching up and going ahead and have it rain again. A.J. wants that fourth one awful bad but I'm sure glad I got my second one today."

QUESTION: Did you know what lap it was when it was raining and you were leading?

J.R.: "That's what my first thought was--have we got 51 percent in? We had gotten it in.

"We would like all of you to meet ANDY ANDROS, head man at Hy-Gain, who made it all possible for us to get together. They are one of the biggest suppliers of CB radios and antennas.

Dave Overpeck of the INDIANAPOLIS STAR had a ringside seat for the interview.

"We've had a very good time with 'em--Just don't get mad when we finish second some time."

QUESTION: Fuel consumption?

J.R.: "We had a very good fuel consumption. Actually with the valve on the car you're strapped, you can't run anymore, that's it--75 inches was on my gauge so we would have run steady and straight all day and hope for the best.

"There was a reason why I was suddenly in the lead so in the second '250' we would have tried to do it again."

QUESTION: "Did A.J. almost hit the wall?

J.R.: "He almost did right in front of me when he passed me early in the race. I took off in the lead and in a minute here came that 'ol orange Coyote bustling up through there.

"He caught me going down the backstretch into the third turn and passing me inside all of a sudden I had to back off very abruptly because his car slid right across in front of me and I thought it was gonna hit the wall.

"Didn't know what happened but it obviously was the oil and water dumped by David Hobbs' car just a few laps earlier. A. J. had a very anxious moment there I'm sure, cause it was for me watching him--I passed him back and we went around the track and he passed me again and took off."

QUESTION: When you passed was there any signal between you?

J.R.: "Oh, I waved at him."

QUESTION: Did it develop into a two man race?

J.R.: "Well, I really don't know. Gordon Johncock was not to be denied --he was figuring in there probably thinking about the end of the race not the middle. It's one of those things that just happens. As it was boiling down it was A.J. and myself."

John's pretty wife Betty helps scoring.

QUESTION: Was anything said on your radio significant or significantly help particularly with the weather?

J.R.: "No, the two-way radio was just for keeping posted as to what was going on and I relayed information to the pit. If the yellow comes on I immediately shout it in but they usually see it at about the same time. But its just a matter of being able to talk back and forth and keep alert. They do help watching for the green flag."

QUESTION: Did you see McCluskey's accident?

J.R.: "No, I didn't see anything but the aftermath I ran over one of his springs lying in the middle of the race track. It broke the fiberglass on the left radiator shell."

PRESS COMMENT: "That must be the one that wound up in Sneva's Car."

J.R.: "It might have but I. . . .I'll bet that's what it was cause I remember glancing in the mirror immediately after that and he was right behind me at some distance."

PRESS COMMENT: "It landed in his lap."

J.P.: "Is that right?" Thank God, for these Bell Helmets we wear, those full face jobs."

QUESTION: Do you think you could have held off A.J.?

J.R.: "That's kinda like me saying I would have won last year's race. If it hadn't rained you know . . . .we'll never know.

"I would like to think that we were probably one of the few that could have given A.J. a tussle and it would have been interesting to see I'm sure."

QUESTION: "You and A. J. are pretty good friends. Did you have any conversation with him during the delay?

J.R.: "Yes,-just a very brief conversation about the third turn incident, in fact just before we went to try to start the race again. Guys say something about something you saw out there to somebody and they'll grab it and blow it out of proportion.

"I'm sure that his comments about us cheating on the yellow were nothing more than "How can we lose that much time?'

"Everybody's done it in competition and it was probably distorted and when he found out we had made one fewer pit stop to that point than he had then it was over and gone with.

QUESTION: Did he say anything about that?

J.R.: "No. In fact it wasn't even mentioned."

QUESTION: Did he out race you early in the race?

J.R.: "When he caught me and passed me--yes. But my car was not handling well at that time and it was pushing (understeering) very badly and I was slowing down through the turns quite a bit and I think had I been handling as well as he had--we'd put on quite a show."

QUESTION: Prior to McLaren your best finish was 18th. How do you account for that?

J.R.: "Probably the reason for never finishing better than 18th before McLaren is that I never finished until I joined McLaren.

"I had never, in fact the year I won was the first time I had ever gone the distance here and in '73 it rained. (1st year at McLaren)

"The circumstances surrounding my joining Mclaren were the fact that the Patrick Team now used to be the Mitchner Racing Team from Jackson, Michigan. Patrick and Mitchner are business associates and Mitchner had to get out of racing or felt he had to pull back so Patrick took over the team and started building and making it as big as it is now."

"Well, we were under-manned and tried to do too many things and the whole team kinda split up as far as mechanics and myself.

"So, I had a chance to go with the Thermo King team, Fred Gerhardt's team, they were without a driver. That was the year Malloy was killed. So I went with them and had driven

for them all year and ended up seventh in the national standings.

"Um, their mechanic quit, the team disorganized as I looked. The same time McLaren was looking for a driver and it just seemed to kind of fall in place and we got together and Teddy Mayer of McLaren made me an offer I couldn't refuse and I joined and you know what it's been ever since."

QUESTION: How could a tire change bring your car to life?

J.R.: "These things are very technical and very hard for me to explain to you what's taken me 16 years of professional racing to learn. But it's nothing more than those little black things that fit on the wheels and are probably the key ingredient that makes the car handle or not handle unless the car is mechanically off."

QUESTION: Which tires, the right side?

J.R.: "Well, we changed right side-yes, and it becomes very technical in that it can mean a great deal as to whether or not the right rear is two or three tenths bigger than the left rear.

"That's how close it is, that's how fine a line it is, whatever change we made whatever characteristics of the tire we put on were, were better."

QUESTION: What laps did you pit stop?

J.R.: "You'd have to check with somebody here who was keeping count. I don't it's hard for me to keep count in the car, I dunno."

QUESTION: Have you learned about the rain and how to prepare for it?

J.R.: "Well, no. It's one of those things if you worried about then you probably would forget something more important. If it rains you can't drive in it, impossible.

"Tyler told me to take it easy and don't get out of shape or loose it and so as it turned out I took his advice and we won it."

QUESTION: Do you feel your luck is turning?

J.R.: "I'd rather be lucky than good any day."

QUESTION: "Did you think the speed was about what you'd thought it would be or could you have gone quicker?

J.R.: "I'd have to say it was about what I thought it would be. I think I had some laps at 183. I'm not sure. A.J. probably was running that fast or faster maybe. I don't know what the statistics are. It felt about right because I was holding a very comfortable pace that I could have kept all day."

QUESTION: Last year you said you wanted to win three in a row, you've come awfully close."

J.R.: "That's true, I'll say this: I would like to be the first three in a row winner and the first four time winner. I could do that if I could win the next two"

QUESTION: Any concern on the pit stop you made under green and went yellow right after. Did you fear it would put you in a hole you couldn't get out of?"

J.R.: "Yes, some concern, we just completed a stop when the yellow goes on. You're always wanting a yellow light to pit on because the field slows down and you don't lose as much ground and of course Tyler was on the radio saying, 'Foyt's done it again. He's on the yellow and we just pitted on the green Blah, Blah (meaning expletives).

"But that's the breaks of the game and I won it in the rain and that's the breaks of the game I guess."

QUESTION: Did you get any warning when the green comes back on?

J.R.: "You have to kind of pay attention and watch the track crews and see where all the trucks are, where they are headed to and that's one of the things you pay attention to around here in May is where everything is located when you go out on slow laps.

"When the race starts you begin to put these things back into place and on a yellow if the trucks aren't there you know it will stay yellow till they get back.

"So you gotta look at all the terrain and figure everything out, and as it turned out, we were I think I only got caught once. I think Gordy in turn two. When it went green he anticipated it and got by me going into two before I could get up to speed."

QUESTION: When you came this month, everything seemed to fall into place, were you confident about the race?

J.R.: "Probably, to the point it was a little bit scary because everything was happening right. I had been in racing long enough to know that when it all happens like that before a race you better make sure you got everything together in the race."

QUESTION: How many engines did you use during the entire month?

J.R.: "In the car I raced in we had two engines. The practice and qualifying engine and the race engine. And the race engine was the same engine out of the other car and we sent it back to Detroit and had it rebuilt and that's the engine we won Trenton with, the late style Drake."

QUESTION: With so many problems with the new Drake, yours performed flawlessly.

J.R.: "What problems? We didn't have any problems."

QUESTION: Why?

J.R.:"McLaren engines. Detroit Michigan. That's the only thing I can say. Gary Knutson and Don Bartose are the engine builders in Detroit and they. . .I don't know what they did but it was right."

QUESTION: A secret in the webbing?

J.R.: "Right, for us to know and for them to find out."

QUESTION: When did you see that A.J. had problems?

J.R.: "When I caught him and passed him. He was still going pretty quick for having a broken front sway bar."

QUESTION: Was he pretty loose?

J.R.: "No, he wasn't because that's I think the mark of a true veteran. He wasn't driving the car hard enough to let it jeopardize his situation. He knew he had a problem and he slowed down to where he could handle the car and that's all he could do."

QUESTION: Do you feel USAC restrictions make for good racing?

J.R.: "I definately think so, that's a fact. A forgone conclusion. The racing we've had since these rules have been in effect has been fantastic. Trenton was hammer and tong. Several cars in the same lap nose and tail racing very hard for the lead.

"That's the kind of racing you're gonna see in USAC National Champion ship racing for this season. Now that we have the new series sponsor, Citicorp, the first National City Travelers Checks-"Ta Daaaa," then I think you're gonna see more cars cause with the series sponsor. There will be more money and be more enticing to bring back more race cars. I think we'll see some fantastic racing this year."

QUESTION: Are you planning to do what you did in 1974, go right to Milwaukee and win that?

Team manager Tyler Alexander was happy.

J.R.: "I sure would like to and then Pocono and Michigan, and Texas and so on and on. We'd like to put 'em all together-But I think probably the biggest goal I have right now is to win the National Championship. This will give me a big leg up on it today and if we can keep it all together we're gonna be right there.

"That's one of the things about the McLaren Team, they're very professional and everyone here knows the way they operate. As long as we keep everything going I hope we can keep doing very well."

QUESTION: Would you like to see the Pace car or the Pacer?

J.R.: "Well, despite all the controversy and problems it seems the Pacer light is good. There's mixed emotions among the drivers. Personally I think today as leader you hate to give up all the hard earned ground behind between second. On the same token if it's gonna be a problem and everyone screams about somebody cheating or whatever, then do away with it and put the Pace Car out and pack up."

QUESTION: And make a new race for the fans?

J.R.: "It would make a new race each time. The speedway in their thinking always felt this way; they hate to have the leader give up ground he's earned. I think that's good but hard to police."

QUESTION: Is cheating a real problem?

J.R.: "There has been a lot of squabbling among the racing fraternity about what really happens."

Fourth Turn T & T Society Populated by Avid Fans

By DAVE PARKER

It is an accepted fact that auto race fans are among the most loyal group of sporting event followers around. Recently, we have seen the formation of the Goodyear Motorsports Club, a nation-wide chain of enthusiasts bound together by their mutual interest in the sport.

While the Goodyear club is a welcome addition to the racing scene, it's a rookie in terms of tenure. There's a group known as the Fourth Turn T and T Society that's been around the Indianapolis Motor Speedway for decades.

J.D. Gould, president of his own solenoid valve company and unofficial president of the society translated the group's title.

"T and T stands for timing and tipping, glasses if you like, or anything you care to. We sit in our area in the fourth turn on qualifying weekends, root for race cars, and have a good time," Gould says.

He is quick to tell the Society's history. "We have been here since the 30's although we didn't name ourselves until 1961. We just wanted to stay away from the crowds so we rope off an area and people leave us alone," he added.

Gould explained that the group began sitting in the third turn and then moved into turn four when it was still reserved parking. "Turn three began to get crowded so we moved into four where we are today." He said.

In 1961 the Society named itself and the Speedway responded with its recognition.

"They erected a flag pole for us and Mari Hulman gave us our first flag. It lasted until the 1973 storms blew it away but we have replaced it with the one that flies today," Gould added.

The Society spans the generations including Gould's look alike friend E.C. "Attie" Atkins and his family. Atkins mother, Mrs. Watson Atkins is in her 70's and is the Society's senior

Society president J. D. Gould, second from right, and other members display their banner.

member while Atkins' youngest daughter Elizabeth, 13 years old, makes it a three generation group.

Mrs. Atkins, known as Aunt Katy to the group, has been attending races since the 20's. She still sports a smile and commented, "the cars go so much faster than they used to."

While Mrs. Atkins is the group's senior member, the youngest is little Jamie Myers, daughter of Mrs. James Myers. Jamie at the tender age of 11 months seemed interested in the cars but didn't comment.

The T and T members argued about their prediction for the race winner. There were cries of Ruby!, Vukovich!, Bobby Unser!, McCluskey!, and of course A.J. Foyt!! But the final vote tally gave Gordon Johncock the edge with Foyt and Johnny Rutherford tied for second.

Gould endorsed the choice without reservation, "If that's what they want I will go along with it," he replied.

The Society meets only on qualifying days and race day the members sit in seats all around the track. The second Sunday and last qualifying day means the end of the Society's of-ficial business for another year.

"It's kind of sad on the second qualifying Sunday." says Gould. "We have a ceremony and lower the flag then wait for race day and next year."

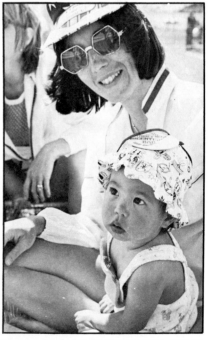

Her mother's lap is the favorite seat of Jamie Myers, the society's youngest member.

THE CITY

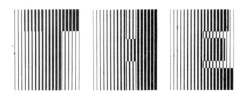

by Jerry Miller

Think of it as a city, a microcosm of American life that compresses the entire life cycle of modern civilization into three weeks in May.

It trades in the reckless fun and desperation of any city of 300,000 that knows its days are numbered. For 23 days every May, its streets are paved with dreams and frustrations, sex and violence, crime and punishment, and the security induced by a sense of community and high fences.

It is a city with its own police force, its own hospital, its own air force, its own civic identity, its own caste system, its own language, and its own auto race running through its front yard.

It is the city called Indy, never to be confused with Indianapolis, the rather ordinary Midwestern city that encircles it without threatening its sovereignty.

Indy is founded, the claims staked, at the dawn of its recorded history, the second weekend in May. The trailblazers tramp in, planting their flags on the 539-acre tract that squats like a space-age Fort Dodge along West 16th Street.

They are a hearty breed, indirect descendants of Daniel Boone and Zeb Pike, and their hands fit the business ends of monkey wrenches and steering

Link

wheels. They are the missing link between the Spanish explorers and the astronauts, professional risk-takers here to prove their theory that it is possible

Marsha Harney and Phyllis Reynolds of Lexington, Ky. showed their support this way.

to fly along the surface of the earth.

As soon as the news of their arrival leaks out, settlers start trickling in. They homestead just short of the frontier, keeping safety in their numbers and the strong fences between themselves and the paved trail that runs a 2½-mile circle around them.

These are the old hands, the migrants who have made the trek in the previous incarnations of this once-a-year city. They amuse one another with stories of the men who conquered the wilderness in years past-the Wilbur Shaws, the Mauri Roses, the Bill Vukovichs—and those who died trying.

The city swells like a town nearest a new gold strike. In only a week's time, it is a thriving metropolis, two-thirds grown.

This is the dress rehearsal, what is referred to in Indy language as Pole Day. The city has beer on its breath and the rasping sound of racing cars in its ear. The men who fly on the ground hold out a promise of what

Parker

T-shirts make great souvenirs of your 500 experience and this stand sold a bunch!

is to come, like those ads for retirement communities in the Arizona desert.

The citizens come and go for a week to get the lay of the land and wait for the carpenters to put on the finishing touches.

Then they go on holiday for a week. They wait impatiently, repressing the instinct that tries to drive them back like a bull elephant to the dying ground. To ease the anticipation, they organize a parade through the streets of Indianapolis as a gesture of diplomacy.

Then, with history accelerating faster than A.J. Foyt, the city comes of age. It begins in darkness, like all life, as the residents of the one-day Rome spill onto the highways leading into the city from all directions.

They seem to arrive in their new city at the same instant. 300,000 strong, their cars jammed nose-to-tail like an army of grunion surging for the same stretch of beach. Dawn breaks over the city on the last day of its

When the traffic begins to pile up some people prefer to peddle their way around.

life, and the city wakes to the sounds of car horns and opening beer cans.

The settling of the territory inside Indy's borders takes most of the morning. By the time everyone is here, it has become a study in overpopulation, 575 men, women, and children to the acre.

The city is alive and ready for demographers. The citizens have all chosen up sides and repealed the open housing ordinances.

The unsavory element is neatly

"Hello Mom, we got kind of dirty today out at the Speedway. It got a little muddy."

Wet and tired race fans endured the traffic but they didn't have to clean up this mess.

Johnny Parsons Jr. is the favorite here.

Young Kristin Koch of Pittsburgh is a Speedway veteran at age nine months. Wonder who is her favorite driver?

segregated in one corner of the infield, the one facing the first turn of the Indy municipal race track. In other cities, it is known as the Other Side of the Tracks. Here it is called the Snake Pit or the Zoo.

It is a ghetto of the young and restless. They are here as much because they want their own territory as because the townsfolk insist they have it. Their reaction is that of an occupied nation. They do everything they can to defy the rules set down by the absentee landlords of their conduct.

They shock the upstanding citizens by brawling, flipping out, taking off their clothes, copulating, and evacuating whenever and wherever it suits them. Young bodies fly 30 feet up from a blanket turned into a trampoline. The bodies don't necessarily land back in the blanket. Unsavory slogans are shouted or printed in crude letters on cardboard. The scent of burnt rope drifts uptown insistently.

The management sends in its heavy guns, imported from Indianapolis and the State. Police helmets and heavy nightsticks swagger through the smoke and taunts. Blue uniforms ride through

Whitlow

Outside turn two stand the suites. For five figures a year you can watch the race from your own private veranda far from the madding crowd. More champagne?

on horseback, sitting stiff and proud like Pershing or Mussolini, depending on your side of the fence.

It is a skirmish that lasts all day, as each side tries to have its way. An occasional epithet or amber bottle is hurled at a uniform, and the police

charge after the offender in the fashion of the defensive unit of the Pittsburgh Steelers. It is bigger sport here than the auto racing going on behind them.

In another corner of the world's largest picnicground is the home base of the city's founding families. Though not the monied class of this society, they survive on their pride. They were here before there were such unseemly colloquialisms as Turbocharger and Snake Pit.

They have drawn together in a fraternity they call the Fourth Turn Society. Unlike the Snake Pit, they do not make their homes on the green earth, but on the back steps of campers and on lawn chairs. They drink their beer from glasses.

The aristocrats can be found, but not reached, sipping Scotch on the top level of the main grandstands, overseeing the entire city as they do their conglomerates, and in the plush line of suites which sit austerely just beyond the second-turn wall. They have impressive stories to tell at the Tuesday board meeting of how Bobby Unser stopped by after the race.

The rest of the mass of humanity filling in the grandstands and infield vacancies are the breed of people who splashed out of a melting pot into a land where their sons supposedly could become president someday but never did. They are barbers and secretaries and factory workers and Little League third basemen. They are heavy drinkers and teetotalers. They are racing fans and good-time Charlies.

If all these people have something in common, it is the belief that,

Whitlow photos

This cooperative young lady obliges for a hustling photographer.

Fox

"Going up?" sounds ridiculous here but this is an old first turn custom. Grab a blanket, ten friends, and one volunteer.

since you can't go home again, you can at least go to Indy. It is what makes this city work better than the everyday variety.

To the last man, woman, or child, they believe that this is something worth being a part of, this auto race, that is never just that. It is a motorized Mardi Gras, a four-on-the-floor fertility rite that takes the other 11 months of the year, out there in the world of long-term cities and people who don't understand the differences of their shoulders for awhile.

Each inhabitant does his part to keep the city of Indy functioning. They watch the race, or don't. They press forward to see the movie stars wave and tip their cowboy hats from passing convertibles, or they wonder who all those people are milling around among the racing cars before the race starts, not knowing that newspapers and television stations from around the world have sent people to report on this phenomenon.

They eat, drink, and have good times—or don't—to the rhythms of 33 screaming engines and their silent pilots, those gaunt throwbacks to Ponce de Leon.

If they eat too much, drink too much, overtax their hearts, soak in too much sun, or accidentally run into the path of a nightstick, they go to Indy's hospital. If necessary, and none of the racing drivers has fallen off his personal mountain, he can be airlifted out by helicopter.

Other choppers beat the air, bringing in newspapers from the outside world.

The restless can take their wallets and wander through the makeshift Indy shopping mall, a string of mobile concession stands along the west bank, and buy anything from instant pizza to an invisible dog for three times its worth. It is a Miracle Mile gone tacky, but it is the best a gypsy city can do on such short notice.

It is a day in the life of a city that wills itself into existence. By the middle of the afternoon, all its will is gone, exhausted in one last shout of enthusiasm or a bellyfull of beer, The men in the high-sounding cars have taken on another final frontier, and one of them can now be saluted for giving his name to the historians on the Fourth Turn Society.

The city begins to die then. The populace gives it a last fond glance, its hero accepting their tributes and a fat check, and wishes it well in its next

Some prefer to watch. These are the fifty-yard line seats along Georgetown Road.

Practically anything is available outside the Speedway, even a little brotherly love.

life. They file out, the classes melting back into a homogenized mass of empty picnic baskets and peeling sunburns.

They find their way to their cars, if they're lucky, and re-enact the traffic panic of the morning. A few, reluctant to give in to the returning darkness, hang back and watch the exodus.

The pathfinders are already packing up their gear and turning their thoughts to a new frontier called Milwaukee.

By dusk, the citizens of Indy are taking the trains back to streets paved only with asphalt. They are leaving their one-time home in ruin, its every inch spoiled with trash. They are running out on her as if she had the plague.

By morning, the city of Indy is a scene from On The Beach. The sea of papers, beer cans, and carcasses of sandwiches lay like dead birds, the wind ruffling their usless wings. Gray

garbage trucks snuffle along through the tons of debris like carrion beetles.

With Indy, it is as it is with most human civilizations. In the end, the scavengers have their way.

No, this is not a rocket sled destined for the Hall of Fame. It's another joker on Georgetown Road doing his thing.

PRESENTING

The Field

2—1975 McLaren Drake Offy - Driver Johnny Rutherford - Chief Mechanic Denis Daviss 1975 Lloyd Ruby Started 6th Finished 32nd. 1976 Started 1st Finished 1st.

14—1975 Coyote Foyt - Driver A.J. Foyt Jr. - Chief Mechanic A.J. Foyt Sr. 1975 Started 1st Finished 3rd, 1976 Started 5th Finished 2nd.

20—1976 Wildcat II Drake Goosen Sparks - Driver Gordon Johncock - Chief Mechanic George Bignotti. Started 2nd Finished 3rd.

40—1976 Wildcat II Drake Goosen Sparks - Driver Wally Dallenbach - Chief Mechanic George Bignotti. 1976 Started 7th Finished 4th.

48—1974 Eagle Drake Offy - Driver Duane Carter Jr. - Mechanic Jerry Eisert. 1974 Bobby Unser Started 7th Finished 2nd; 1975 Unser Started 3rd Finished 1st, 1976 Started 6th Finished 5th.

68—1974 McLaren Drake Offy - Driver Tom Sneva - Chief Mechanic Jim McGee. 1975 Entered but didn't run; 1976 Started 3rd Finished 6th.

21—1975 Parnelli Cosworth - Driver Al Unser - Chief Mechanic Hywel Absalom. 1975 Al Unser and Mario Andretti Practice Only, 1976 Started 4th Finished 7th.

6 — 1974 McLaren Drake Offy·Driver Mario Andretti - Chief Mechanic Jim McGee. 1974 Mike Hiss Started 3rd Finished 14th; 1975 Bobby Allison Started 13th Finished 25th, 1976 Started 19th Finished 8th.

77—McLaren Offy - Driver Salt Walther - Chief Mechanic George Walther Jr. 1974 David Hobbs Started 9th finished 5th; 1975 Salt Walther Started 9th Finished 33rd, 1976 Started 22nd Finished 9th.

3—1974 Eagle Drake Offy redesigned as a 1976 Fletcher Cobra - Driver Bobby Unser - Chief Mechanic Wayne Leary. 1974 Jerry Grant started 17th Finished 10th; 1975 Bill Vukovich Started 8th Finished 6th, 1976 Started 12th Finished 10th.

51—1974 Eagle Drake Offy - Driver Lloyd Ruby - Mechanic Mike Devin - 1974 Ruby crashed in practice; 1975 Sam Sessions Started 25th Finished 17th; 1976 Started 30th Finished 11th.

93—Eagle Drake Offy - Driver Johnny Parsons - Chief Mechanic Bill Finley. This is a spare tub not raced until the 1976 season. Started 14th Finished 12th.

23—1974 Eagle Drake Offy - Driver George Snider - Chief Mechanic A.J. Watson. 1974 Wally Dallenbach Started 2nd Finished 30th; 1975 Backup, 1976 Started 27th Finished 13th.

24—1973 Eagle Offy - Driver Tom Bigelow - Chief Mechanic A.J. Watson. 1973 Mike Mosley Started 21st Finished 10th; 1974 no attempt to qualify; 1975 George Snider Started 24th Finished 8th, 1976 Started 32nd Finished 14th.

12—1974 Eagle Drake Offy - Driver Mike Mosley - Chief Mechanic Jud Phillips. 1974 Bill Vukovich blew engine on 1st qualifying day; 1975 Mike Mosley Started 5th Finished 26th, 1976 Started 11th Finished 15th.

8—1974 Eagle Drake Offy rebuilt from Trenton April, 1976 crash with tub from 1975 Andretti car. Driver Jan Opperman - Mechanic Todd Gibson. 1974 Gordon Johncock Started 4th Finished 4th; 1975 not entered, 1976 Started 33rd Finished 16th.

69—1973 Eagle Offy - Driver Larry Cannon - Mechanic Glen Hall. 1973 David Hobbs Started 22nd Finished 11th; 1974 John Mahler failed to qualify; 1975 Not Entered, 1976 Started 10th Finished 17th.

9—1974 Eagle Drake Offy - Driver Vern Schuppan - Chief Mechanic Jack McCormack. 1974 Bobby Unser's Backup machine; 1975 Bobby Unser's Backup car, 1976 Started 17th Finished 18th.

97—1976 Dragon Drake Offy - Driver Sheldon Kinser - Chief Mechanic Grant King. New for 1976 this car Started 29th Finished 19th.

96—1973 Kingfish Drake Offy - Driver Bob Harkey - Mechanic Grant King. 1973 Greg Weld did not qualify; 1974 Bentley Warren no qualification attempt; 1975 Sheldon Kinser Started 26th Finished 12th, 1976 Started 28th Finished 20th.

98—1976 Dragon Drake Offy - Driver John Martin - Chief Mechanic Grant King. Twin to the No. 97 and new for 1976 this car Started 15th Finished 21st.

83—1974 Eagle Drake Offy - Driver Bill Puterbaugh - Chief Mechanic Danny Jones. 1974 Gordon Johncock short track car; 1975 Puterbaugh Started 15th Finished 7th, 1976 Started 18th Finished 22nd.

28—1973 Eagle Drake Offy - Driver Billy Scott - Mechanic Jim Wright. 1973 Graham McRae Started 13th Finished 16th; 1974 Bill Simpson Started 20th Finished 13th; 1975 Follmer and Opperman Practice, 1976 Started 21st Finished 23rd.

92—1973 Eagle Drake Offy - Driver Steve Krisiloff - Mechanic Bill Finley. 1973 Lloyd Ruby Started 15th Finished 27th; 1974 Ruby Started 18th Finished 9th; 1975 Johnny Parsons Started 12th Finished 19th, 1976 Started 23rd Finished 24th.

86—1971 McLaren Drake Offy - Driver Al Loquasto - Mechanic Clint Brawner. 1971 not entered; 1972 not entered; 1973 not run; 1974 Mahler left in qualifying line; 1975 Al Loquasto bumped by Eldon Rasmussen, 1976 Started 24th Finished 25th.

63—1974 Ras-Car Offy - Driver Larry McCoy Jr. - Chief Mechanic Shorty Mosley. 1974 passed Driver's Test; 1975 Started 28th Finished 30th, 1976 Started 26th Finished 26th.

73—1974 Eagle AMC Stock Block - Driver Jerry Grant - Chief Mechanic Dave Klym. 1974 Steve Krisiloff Started 15th Finished 22nd; 1975 Grant Started 14th Finished 20th, 1976 Started 20th finished 27th.

45—1973 Eagle Drake Offy - Driver Gary Bettenhausen - Mechanic Phil Casey. 1973 Mike Hiss Started 26th Finished 17th; 1974 Jim McElreath Started 30th Finished 6th; 1975 Rick Muther first alternate, 1976 Started 8th Finished 28th.

33—1973 McLaren Drake Offy - Driver David Hobbs - Mechanic Tom Smith. 1973 Pete Revson drove at Pocono and Ontario; 1974 Salt Walther Started 14th Finished 17th; 1975 Bob Harkey Started 23rd Walther relieved Finished 10th, 1976 Started 31st Finished 29th.

7—1976 Hopkins Drake Offy - Driver Roger McCluskey - Chief Mechanic Chuck Looper built this new machine designed by Eagle creator Roman Slobodynskyj. Started 13th Finished 30th.

5—1975 Eagle Offy - Driver Bill Vukovich - Chief Mechanic Johnny Capels. 1975 Didn't run at Indianapolis, Andretti drove at Pocono, 1976 Started 9th Finished 31st.

17—1973 Vollstedt Drake Offy tub redesigned for 1976 - Driver Dick Simon - Mechanic Hal Sperb. 1973 Bill Simpson did not qualify; 1974 Tom Bigelow Started 23rd Finished 12th; 1975 Bigelow Started 33rd Finished 18th, 1976 Started 16th Finished 32nd.

19—1971 McLaren Drake Offy - Driver Spike Gehlhausen - Mechanic Ed Baue. 1971 Peter Revson started Pole Finished 2nd; 1972 Revson Backup; 1973 Roger McCluskey Started 14th Finished 3rd; 1974 McCluskey practice only; 1975 Graham McRae didn't qualify, 1976 Started 25th Finished 33rd.

Multi-Million Dollar Facility
Hall of Fame

From its inception, the Indianapolis Motor Speedway has been considered more of an institution than a race track. No other facility in the world has received more publicity as a mecca of speed. And no other race track has done more to publicize and perpetuate the sport which made it famous. With the completion of the track's Hall of Fame in 1976, historic racing and passenger vehicles shall forever have a facility befitting their heritage.

Simply, the automotive world should be forever indebted to Speedway owner Anton (Tony) Hulman for his pride of preservation and uncompromising dedication to making the famed track the capitol of auto racing.

If the above paragraph sounds as though it were meant to be etched in a bronze plaque and presented to Tony himself, then consider it so. Hulman and company have erected what amounts to racing's Taj Mahal They didn't just build a new museum out of some steel and concrete, they handformed a monument that contains 96,960 square feet of marble, terrazo, glass and other finery usually reserved for visiting dignitaries.

While the Indianapolis 500 Yearbook has followed construction of the new museum since its inception, even we did not anticipate the quality of the finished product. When describing it over the phone we've found ourselves saying, "You oughta see it . . . . looks like the FBI building." Now we've never seen the FBI building, but the new museum certainly reminds you of a Washington monument.

It is located inside the track in the area commonly referred to as the south short chute, that short straight-a-way between turns one and two. In order to make access easy, Hulman and company first dug a four lane tunnel with 14 foot clearance under the race track that leads directly to 16th Street. Greyhound buses pass through the new tunnel with ease.

Surrounded on all sides by smooth blacktop, the pre-cast, white cement structure has been erected on a small rise that makes its overall appearance even more awesome. In total, they put one hundred and forty-four cement panels along with Wyoming quartz around the perimeter of the building.

Once inside, you are greeted by the ticket department on the right, headed by Fran Derr, a lovely lady who has spent over 30 years working at the track. Across the wide entrance hall the new gift shop offers a pot-pourri of Speedway memorabilia. Gift shop manager Kay Eddleman blushes the sentiments of her crew when she says, "Gosh, this place is so beautiful we really have to pinch ourselves just to see if we aren't dreaming about it."

As you head on back toward the car displays, you're greeted by a pair of 26-foot oval fountains located under a transparent dome in the roof that has been designed to give as much natural light as possible. On your left you find a portion of Tony's antique automobile collection (which includes several makes that were once manufactured in Indiana. . those are his favorites) and dozens of race cars are displayed on your right.

When the new facility opened in May there were 18 cars included which have accounted for some 22 Indianapolis 500 victories. It was just twenty years ago that the first Speedway Museum opened, a 4,800 square foot building that in itself had been a dream among Hulman, former driver Wilbur Shaw and Karl Kizer, museum curator.

Shaw is credited with actually saving the Indianapolis Motor Speedway from becoming a housing subdivision just after WW II. The track's previous owner, Capt. Eddie Rickenbacker, the famed flying ace of the first war, racing driver, auto manufacturer and later president of Eastern Air Lines, had operated the plant on a not very profitable basis for 18 years through the Depression. Years of inactivity during the second war (1942-45) had seen the track deteriorate.

"It looked like a jungle in Africa out there," Kizer commented about the condition of the track in 1945.

Wilbur Shaw not only held the distinction of being a three-time winner of the "500", he was also known throughout the racing world as a statesman. After the War he learned that Rickenbacker would rather sell the track than undertake the expensive restoration process. Wilbur began looking for a buyer, or group of buyers who would perpetuate the famed 500 after Capt. Eddie told him that the plant could be purchased for $750,000. He solicited several firms for a minimum of $25,000 investment and received many encouraging replies. However, most wanted to alter current operating procedures and utilize the track for promotion of a particular product. Shaw's idea was to carry on with a business as usual policy and continue the 500 mile race as not only the greatest sports spectacle in the world but as an automotive proving grounds as well.

As has been written many times over, it is now history that Shaw found Hulman, the civic-minded Terre Haute, Ind. businessman who believed in the tradition of the "500" as being a part of Indiana. Tony wasn't particularly interested in auto racing at that time and he installed Shaw as general manager and president, a position he held until his death in a plane crash in 1954.

Automobile racing was fortunate to have Wilbur Shaw as one of its spokesmen. The other man to whom credit must be given is curator Karl Kizer. Kizer has also devoted his lifetime to the sport of speed and is today considered one of the grand old men of another era who knows how to keep pace with the changing times.

Kizer operated a machine shop from 1930-55 in Indianapolis that catered to the professional racer and worked on many of the museum's cars back when they were in actual competition. Karl sees more than most in the cars that are now stilled from the rigors of competition. His seventy-plus year old eyes twinkle when he looks at the number 8 four-cylinder Stutz that one Earl

Your first trip to the new Speedway Hall of Fame will probably overwhelm you. This palace houses the new museum, Speedway offices, and a gift shop. The building at left combines snack bar facilities with another gift shop with ample parking.

Cooper drove in the 1915 race. The gentle Kizer was Cooper's riding mechanic in this very car on the rough and tumble dirt circuit in 1916.

Karl likes to tell the stories of first finding important old Speedway car and its accompanying restoration.

"The Eddie Rickenbacker car, the Duesie he drove in the 1914 race was really a sight," he says. "We found it in a barn in Farmland, Ind. and was a home for everything from chickens to termites."

Many new body panels along with several vital engine pieces had to be hand fabricated before the Rickenbacker Duesenberg reached its present restored state. Although Kizer lived through the eras that many of the cars were actually competing, he cannot be expected to remember every mechanical detail of the varied makes.

The "we" that Mr. Kizer refers to, belongs mostly to craftsmen Barney Wimmer and Bill Spoerle, the Speedway's two full-time restoration men. They turn out an average of two cars per year and have a waiting list that should guarantee their employment for the next several years. Barney has been a racer all his life and still attends many Sprint and Midget car programs throughout the Midwest. Bill Spoerle is of German descent and learned his mechanical trade through the motorcycle industry.

One day we asked Karl Kizer about the famous Parnelli Jones winning roadster, the number 98 that was entered by J.C. Agajanian. "Will it run," I inquired after admiring the recent restoration.

"Pour a little liquid in 'er and we'll give you a couple of quick laps in it," was the reply.

Every car in the facility is capable of running and one or more of them usually does on race morning with one of

yesterday's drivers taking a parade lap in pre-race ceremonies.

While it may appear the new museum is literally chock full of valuable old cars, enough to satisfy even the most avid fan's imagination, the search for particular Speedway machinery goes on. They've been looking for a Frontenac racer for years and Karl Kizer sees little, if any hope they'll ever obtain one.

"Back in 1922," he says, "I sold a pair of Fronty's for driver-builder Louis Chevrolet. Today I'd give anything to get one of them back."

Although they haven't obtained a complete car yet, the men of the museum recently finalized a purchase of an original Frontenac engine. And that's the way it goes in their continuing search; sometimes you settle for one piece at a time.

"The Old-Timers club is really a big help in locating some of the things we're looking for," says Speedway employee John Fugate. "After all, they're the real experts when it comes to authenticity."

The Old Timers Club that Fugate refers to is an organization numbering nearly 350. Requirements for membership state that one must have twenty years or more tenure as a Speedway driver, owner, mechanic official, etc.

Upon occasion an Old Timer will bequeath his life-long auto racing memorabilia collection to the Speedway, and up till now there really hasn't been a suitable place for display.

"There has been an enormous amount of collectible material published about the Speedway," says Director of Publicity Al Bloemker, "but it is very difficult to handle. You have to seal everything in plastic and almost nail it

 (Continued on page 202)

THE INDIANAPOLIS 500 YEARBOOK

PRESENTING

The Rookies

THE ROOKIES

by Jerry Miller

Whyalla, South Australia.
San Bernardino, California.
Jasper, Indiana
Easton, Pennsylvania.

Unlikely as it might seem, those four far-flung cities had something in common in 1976. They each had a hometown boy making his debut in the Indianapolis 500.

Vern Schuppan, Billy Scott, Spike Gehlhausen and Al Loquasto did their bits for civic pride in May of '76, and did even more for their own personal pride as the four graduating rookies of the year's class of hopeful newcomers to the May 30 lineup. And their racing backgrounds were as diversified as their geographical roots, with Schuppan coming over from international road racing, Scott from beginnings in drag racing, Gehlhausen from the midgets and Loquasto from a history in hillclimbing.

Oddly enough, it was none of those four backgrounds that got the bulk of the attention when the gates opened up for the 60th round of pre-500 activities at the big speedway on 16th Street, U.S.A. On May 8, it was Lakewood California, and New York City that had the rookie watchers occupied.

Lakewood sent Bob Olivero onto the Indy scene with all the credentials necessary for annexation of Rookie of the Year honors. And Olivero, champion of the California Racing Association sprint car circuit in '75 and a frequent winner in the USAC midget ranks, quickly flaunted them, taking care of his 40-lap rookie test in one fell swoop on the first day of practice. That made him the first freshman ever to get his orientation over in one day's time, as he looked smooth and ready for action in the number 78 Eagle

Although he was bumped from the race, rookie Bobby Olivero breezed through his test and impressed the veterans. He has, however, been driving for quite some time. Above is a 1954 photo.

owned by California's Morales brothers, Gil and Alex.

The greatest attention, however, was being paid to Janet Guthrie, the pride of New York City and the ERA. But the first female entrant at Indy wasn't having things go as smoothly for her as they were for Olivero.

First, her luggage was lost somewhere between the Big Apple and the big speedway, so she had to borrow a racing uniform and crash helmet from Billy Vukovich. Even then, it was three days before she actually needed such items, and hers had arrived by then.

A variety of mechanical quirks kept Guthrie from getting into the car entered for her by Rolla Vollstedt until Monday. And it was only the beginning of a much-publicized two-

The whole Gehlhausen family helped Spike make the show and he responded favorably.

[119]

week struggle to race through the Indy sex barrier.

The other newcomers, meanwhile, were having their own troubles. Gehlhausen, not far from his home in Jasper, broke a piston in his father's "Spirit of Indiana" McLaren opening day. Scott, a long way from San Bernardino, was struggling with an uncooperative "Spirit of Public Enterprise" Eagle.

And Schuppan, who was somewhere between Whyalla and the next F5000 race, wasn't even a glimmer in the Stark & Wetzel Rookie of the Year trophy's eye yet.

Then there was Denver, Colorado's brief visit to the flatlands. Eddie Miller, Super Vee champion, found the flat Indy speedway even rockier than the mountains back home when he made a very large and expensive mistake in turn one on Tuesday.

Miller's Thermo-King Eagle made a short slide after entering number one a bit high, then shot off the inside of the track surface. It cleared the drainage ditch, its snout digging in on the opposite bank, and began flipping end-for-end toward the tunnel that runs under the short chute.

The tumbling car cleared two fences and landed just short of the traffic tunnel. Miller was pried out of the wreckage, shaken and hurting from four cracked vertebrae in his neck.

"The problem was that I went in too high," he would later explain. "The track had changed quite a bit that day from when I took the first part of my rookie test. There were shadows from the grandstands across the track which hadn't been there earlier."

So much for Denver's chances and a $32,000 insurance policy on the Thermo-King chassis from Lloyd's of London that had been part of young Miller's deal with the Gerhardt operation.

While fast Eddie was leaving on a stretcher, other would-be rookie Indy drivers were getting around on foot. On the familiar Gasoline Alley beat, the one that runs from garage door to garage door in search of a ride, were people like Bill Engelhart, Ralph Liguori and Jerry Sneva.

It is a frustrating routine, since car owners usually want more collateral than a good record on the half-mile tracks and a winning smile. It was especially disheartening for Sneva, who impressed everyone by getting good speed out of a less-than-competitive

Polite Vern Schuppan was chosen for one of the Speedway's best rides, a Jorgensen Eagle, which he handled very well. With him is Pete Biro, ace racing photographer and accomplished magician.

It was a long road from Madison, Wisc. to the Speedway for Billy Engelhart. He's shown here prepping for his rookie test. Lack of practice kept him out of the show.

car the previous May.

"Everybody told me that what I did last year would help me get a ride this year," reported Tom Sneva's younger brother. "But it hasn't worked out that way so far. Maybe it'll be better next week." It wasn't.

Midway through the first week, a new rookie entry arrived, completely unannounced. It was Schuppan, who is Dan Gurney's F5000 driver, and, if there was any doubt about the Australian's ability to adapt to turning left all the time, it was removed when he tripped through his rookie test with the same dispatch as Olivero. He put the second Gurney Eagle through its paces and, almost as quickly as he arrived on the scene, the soft-spoken young road racer had become a serious

threat to outdo the other first-year men and woman.

By the Friday before time trials, five of them were fully certified to take their shots on Saturday and Sunday. Olivero, Scott, Gehlhausen, Loquasto and Schuppan had their testing in and could go racing, if they had the speed to do it for four laps.

Guthrie, on the other hand, could only sit on her hands. The mechanical problems had lasted most of the week and she failed to get her 40 laps in by Friday. With the traffic on the Speedway getting as frantic as I-465 at five o'clock, Speedway officials barred all untested rookies from the track Friday.

Saturday didn't prove to be a great day for the rookies, either. The warm-

Billy Scott obtained usage of the former American Kids Racer and had problems early in the month. With the help of mechanic Jimmy Wright he qualified for his first 500.

Ed Crombie can say he made it to the Indianapolis Motor Speedway as a driver, but a fourth turn spin and crash cost him his chances of making the 1976 starting field.

up period set back three of them. Loquasto had to be towed in when his Frostie's Root Beer McLaren quit cold on him. Then Gehlhausen put his orange number 19 into the wall in turn one, and Scott had to spin number 28 to miss one of Spike's wheels as it bounced across the track.

Nothing improved very much once the time trialing got started. Olivero, Scott and Loquasto all moved away from the starting line amid the cheering and anticipation, but none had their acts together enough to call for the green flag.

Sunday was a better day, or so it seemed. Olivero clocked in with four laps at 180.288 mph, a speed everybody kept trying to tell Bob was absolutely safe. But the bespectacled Californian had his misgivings.

"I'll feel a lot better about it when I see it in the papers after next weekend," he advised, more far-sighted than those who were offering assurances.

Scott took his shot, too, but three laps at 178 mph brought him back to the pits unqualified. Schuppan did much the same, as a last-minute wing adjustment upset the handling of the powder-blue number 9 Eagle.

Finally, later in the afternoon, the Gurney crew got their wings flying right and Vern took his four laps at 182.022 mph, guaranteeing himself the best starting position of any rookie to make the race.

"When we went out on the earlier run, the rear wing position had changed, and we had to guess at it," Schuppan related. "The car acted unstable and was difficult to drive at the right speed. We got it corrected for the second run."

That was it for the rookie class on the first weekend, but they were going go make more of the headlines during the second seven days in May.

Guthrie did it big on Monday, finally getting the Vollstedt car to hold together long enough for her to get her rookie test in. It was a run that was smooth and, of course, long overdue. "I can't believe that we finally got through it," said the only woman ever to clear that particular hurdle.

Engelhart got his break, too, landing a ride in Dick Simon's Eagle. Bill worked his way through the rookie test over the first two days of the week and was ready to search for qualifying speeds.

Ed Crombie never got that far. Williams Lake, British Columbia, wouldn't have any hometown pride going for it on May 30, because Crombie crashed his near-antique coming out of turn four on Tuesday as he worked on lap eight of his rookie test and put himself out of the running.

Loquasto, who had been threatening to become the new Ralph Liguori with six unsuccessful tries at Indy, dented up the yellow-and-white number 86 on Wednesday, but crew chief Clint Brawner had the car back out on Thursday.

Saturday came, as it always does, and time was running short for our new lads. Loquasto quickly left the legends to Liguori, going out early and doing 182.002 mph. It was cause for much joy and reflection by the dark-haired Pennsylvanian who had been bumped from the lineup the year before.

"These things don't come easy,"

said loquacious Al, during the celebrating.

If anything, the celebrations were even more energetic for the next two freshmen to discard their beanies. Scott, after two weeks of struggle and strife which sometimes reached the shouting level back in garage 23, put the pedal to the metal and did four laps at 183.383 mph, fastest of all the rookies of '76.

He left no doubt how he felt about it, throwing up a jubilant fist as he pulled to a stop for the post-qualifying photos. "This is the happiest day of my life," said the mustachioed ex-drag racing champion. "I thought it was going to be the unhappiest, but we sat down and just decided we were going to get it on, and we did."

The field was full when Gehlhausen went out in the repaired McLaren, but it didn't stop him from making his first Indy field at the tender age of 21. Spike made it with a run of 181.717 mph, bumping the venerable Jim McElreath in the process.

"I don't know what happened," he said, in something of a joyous daze. "We just went out and picked up three miles an hour. I guess I just got my head on straight after the crash and got my speed back up there."

There was no celebrating for the rest. Guthrie was getting nowhere with her car. Teammate Dick Simon could get only 174 out of it, and Guthrie stayed with him at 173.5, but that was as fast as either of them could get the balky car to go.

[121]

So, on Sunday morning, one of the most incredible sequences in speedway history unfolded. None other than A.J. Foyt rolled out his gleaming backup car, taped over the gauges, and assisted Janet Guthrie into the driver's seat.

With a slightly astounded audience looking on, Guthrie showed what she could do, working the Foyt car up comfortably to 177 in less than a dozen laps. A few adjustments by the Foyt gang and she ticked off a 181.6, fast enough at the time to make the show.

Then, as suddenly as it had unfolded, the drama was over. Foyt moved the number one car back to his garage for keeps, but Guthrie had established that she could cut it at the 500 speedway, if she was driving a car that could do the same.

"I'm quite disappointed, of course, that A.J. did not decide to let me run the car, but it was understandable," she reported. "At least we gave it a good shot, I think."

The rest of Sunday, the rookies were getting shot down. Olivero's name was tossed out of the Monday galleys when veteran Lloyd Ruby came along to bump him at mid-afternoon.

Engelhart, short on practice time, made a last-ditch bid late Sunday, but could come up with no more than 177.6 and had to wave off.

So, the final rundown on the rookies who made the grade at Indy '76 showed four first-year men in the line-up, two of them "pure" rookies who had never run a 500-mile champ-car race before or made a shot at Indy before -- Schuppan and Gehlhausen.

Their two colleagues lost their purity, so to speak, at Pocono, where Loquasto had run the last two 500's, and Ontario, where Loquasto had done two 500's and Scott one.

Race Day didn't do great things for our foursome of first-timers, although three of them at least got half-a-race worth of experience. Gehlhausen didn't get anything near that, however. He only got a pace lap's worth.

"I was checking all the gauges carefully because I knew, once the race started, I was going to be too busy to notice them for awhile," related a dejected Spike. "All of a sudden, the oil temperature started rising and the oil pressure was gone completely, so I knew there was nothing I could do."

Gehlhausen pulled into the pits on the pace lap, his race over before it began. "I guess now I'll have to wait until next year to show what I can do," he said later.

The other three made it to the flag but, with the race pulling up at 255 miles, they had little chance to iron out any of their problems. All three encountered handling difficulties of one type or another and were running in the back half of the field when the rains came.

Loquasto was 25th among the 27 cars still running. Scott was 23rd and able to look at the experience philosophically. "Well, 250 miles is 250 miles," said the 27-year-old ex-rookie, as the rain showers swept through Gasoline Alley.

Schuppan fared somewhat better. Set back by a blistered tire that required an extra stop at the Dan Gurney service station, the road racer worked his way back up to 18th, the highest placing among the first-year drivers and good enough to earn the 33-year-old Aussie a place on the Rookie of the Year trophy.

The more experienced drivers may have made most of the headlines in this Indy 500, but our four rookies still were the talk of the town -- at least back in Whyalla, San Bernardino, Jasper and Easton.

ROOKIES -- '76

Spike Gehlhausen, only 21 years old, wrecked, then qualified only to see his hopes end when oil pressure dropped on the pace lap.

Billy Engelhart in Dick Simon's car couldn't find enough speed.   Al Loquasto Sr., Jr., and Clint Brawner finally celebrated success.

Billy Scott put Warner Hogdon's No. 28 solidly in the field and raced to 23rd position.

Janet Guthrie did well in Foyt's backup, but he decided not to race the car. Bobby Olivero and mechanic John Capels looked good.

Rookie of the Year
Vern Schuppan

Almost no one imagined that Vern Schuppan would be racing in the 1976 Indianapolis 500.

He wasn't entered when the gates opened in early May. His regular boss, Dan Gurney, had only one driver of record, Pancho Carter. And the only time he'd ever driven an oval track was in a pace car, not a race car.

So how come Vernon John Schuppan of Whyalla, South Australia, is Indy's Rookie of the Year?

Here's how it happened for the boyish 33-year-old with the winning smile and soft Aussie accent. Basically, it happened because there was one person who wanted Vern Schuppan to drive at Indy, and that was Vern Schuppan.

"This is something I have wanted to achieve ever since I took up auto racing," Schuppan revealed after he qualified Gurney's second Bird's-egg blue Eagle for the '76 Indy race. "I'd been dropping a few hints to Dan all along."

The hints apparently sank in with Gurney. Midway through the first week of practice, with Carter's car successfully worked up to speed, the Gurney crew rolled out Eagle number nine and the fair-haired Australian road racer strapped himself in.

Schuppan, who campaigns Gurney's F5000 Eagle, quickly ran through his rookie's test like a kangaroo bounding through the outback. And, when the second day of time trials came along, he was as ready to go Indy racing as anyone whose name had been on the entry list in April.

It took two tries, as it turned out. Schuppan took the green flag for a qualifying run, only to find his lap speeds had dropped to 178 and 179 mph when he had been running 182 earlier. He came in, the Gurney crew did some expert fiddling with the car, and later that Sunday he put himself solidly into the Indy lineup with a four-lap average of 182.011 mph. Vern Schuppan had managed to convert from a road-racer to a so-called "roundy-rounder" in less than a week's time.

"I treated it like going to any new
(Continued on page 204)

Link

Torres

A. J. Foyt's Coyote Foyt V-8

Gordon Johncock's Wildcat II Drake-Goosen-Sparks

Mike Mosley's Eagle Offenhauser

Mario Andretti's McLaren Offenhauser

New Cars At Indy
DESIGN '76

by Ted West

As it does every year, this year's Indianapolis 500 brought together the best technical minds in all of the world of auto racing. And great minds produce great racing cars. While on the surface of it the entry for 1976 seemed to have a fair number of older cars, no competitive Indy car is really "old"—they all go through constant modification in order simply to remain competitive. And there are always those three or four really new machines each year that point the way to the future at the Speedway.

One reason for the number of older cars at this year's race is that the United States Auto Club had not finalized the rules for the 1976 season until late winter. In an important move, USAC changed the maximum allowable turbocharger boost from eighty-inches down to seventy-five inches. This move was made to control the speed of the cars and, as much as it seemed like a penalty to the venerable four-cylinder Offy (because only turbocharging had allowed the four-cylinder to remain competitive with V8s), the reward in this rule would remain unchanged for five years. Since the amount of boost allowed has a great deal to do with the amount of engine cooling needed (less boost means less engine heat), the boost rule affects how much radiator will be needed. The amount of radiator needed can seriously influence the overall de-sign and size of a Champ Car, so most car builders waited till the boost rule had been agreed upon before starting design work for a new car. By the time the decision was made official, it was too late to build new cars for this year's race, and most teams went about simply modifying their old cars while the new cars could be designed for 1977. Now that the rule is locked in, you can expect many new designs for 1977.

Which isn't to say that there was no equipment in the pits in 1976. Besides the totally new Roman Slobodynskyj-designed Hopkins car built for Roger McCluskey, the Team McLaren Hy-Gain Ml6CD and Dan Gurney's Jorg-gensen Eagles had both received maj-

(Continued on Page 205)

Wick photos

Bobby Unser's redesigned Eagle featured a narrower nose, more streamlined cowling and relocated radiators. The Sinmast Wildcats are no higher than the wheel hubs except where the driver and engine are tucked in the middle. The most obvious change on the Parnelli-Cosworth (21) is the reshaping of the nose and rear wing.

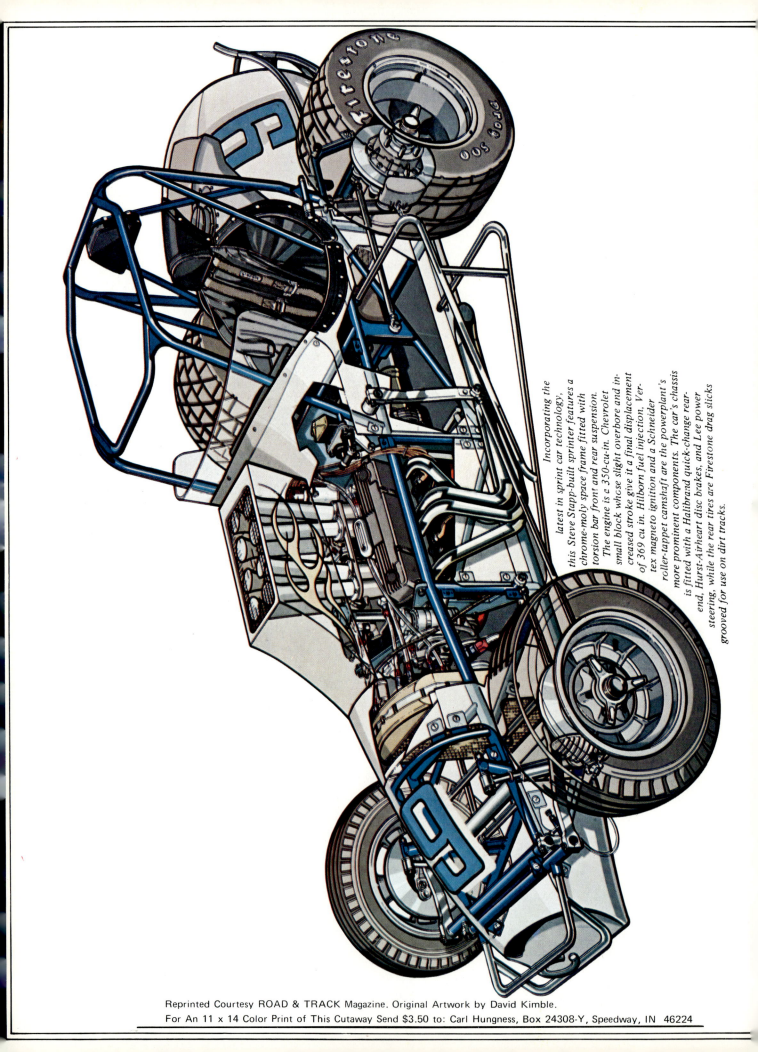

Incorporating the latest in sprint car technology, this Steve Stapp-built sprinter features a chrome-moly space frame fitted with torsion bar front and rear suspension. The engine is a 350-cu-in. Chevrolet small block whose slight overbore and increased stroke give it a final displacement of 369 cu in. Hilborn fuel injection, Vertex magneto ignition and a Schneider roller-tappet camshaft are the powerplant's more prominent components. The car's chassis is fitted with a Halibrand quick-change rear end, Hurst-Airheart disc brakes, and Lee power steering, while the rear tires are Firestone drag slicks grooved for use on dirt tracks.

Introduction To
SPRINT
CAR
RACING

In The Midwest They Call Them

THUNDER & LIGHTNING
Machines

Once we were in the press booth next to Formula 1 World Champion Denis Hulme at a Sprint car auto race and we half-heartedly asked him: "Think you're ready for these things yet?" to which he replied,

"Mate, I don't think I'll ever be ready for those bloody monsters."

Bloody monsters, he had called them. Sprint car champion Pancho Carter once likened driving a Sprint car to wrestling a starving alligator. Another driver we know named Gordy Lee, aptly described Sprinters as "over-powered brutes that are drunk with horsepower."

Hulme didn't ever want any part of Sprint car racing; Carter is a second generation Sprint car driver which makes him one of the rarest breeds around; Gordy Lee never has conquered Sprint racing to his own satisfaction and even though he's nearly been killed in the process, he continues to challenge them some 30 weekends a year.

Auto racing history hasn't ever told us the exact date that Sprint cars appeared in America. One thing is certain though, they are strictly an

Jackie Howerton takes a wild ride at the Terre Haute "Action Track" after his Sprint car hooked a rut. Fellow driver George Snider watches.

Mahoney

Jungle Park was a famous old Indiana Sprint racing track. Note the lack of driver protection. Styling hasn't changed much either.

Johnny Gerber drove this bob-tailed Sprint to numerous wins.

Doc Williams in another early-day Sprint car. Brake on left.

The legendary Rex Mays shown at Indiana State Fair in 1941.

Indy winner Bill Holland leads the great Tommy Hinnershitz.

Ira Hall was one of the greatest Sprint drivers.

Ray Meyers was lucky enough to tell about this crash at Winchester.

[131]

Ted Horn in a famed car he called "Baby". It was built in 1938 and ran its last race in 1962 and compiled over 75 track records along the way.

This is none other than Mario Andretti in his first open-cockpit Sprint ride. Same car is pictured above. Place is West Lebanon, N.Y. 1961.

Roger McCluskey leads Bobby Unser at Terre Haute in 1966.

Gary Bettenhausen, 2, and Larry Dickson, 5, are probably two of the best Sprint drivers ever to appear on the racing scene. Below, Gary's father, Tony, is shown challenging Elbert "Grandpappy" Booker in a pre-war race at Dayton, Ohio.

George Snider qualifying at Terre Haute.

[132]

Cy Fairchild takes a direct hit from Tom Bigelow on the banks at Winchester. Over the years Sprint fans have expected the unusual to happen.

American phenomenon. No other country in the world can claim responsibility for the introduction and sustainment of the most devastating racing vehicle devised. To a man, such famed names as A.J. Foyt, Mario Andretti, Bobby Unser, all agree that Sprint car racing is the single, most competitive and dangerous form of the sport.

Historian Jack Fox believes that racing promoter J.C. Agajanian popularized the name "Sprint" in his West Coast races just after the second World War. Aggie was promoting races on half-mile tracks and the short distances run (usually 20 laps) coupled with the close competition dawned the description Sprint.

Prior to the War, the same vehicles had been termed "Big Cars". The name became especially popular from the years 1933-42 to help the public differentiate between a new form of racing that had its beginnings in 1933, Midget auto racing. The astute, and and sometimes shoddy promoter, would many times bypass the name Big Car in favor of the term "Speedway Car". For advertising purposes the Big Car was in fact the same vehicle that they raced at the Indianapolis Motor Speedway. Telephone pole posters and newspaper ads often times married the local race track to the famed two-and-one-

half mile oval that made Indianapolis famous. After all, the cars they raced at Indy were sometimes the same ones they ran on the dirt tracks and promoters have been known to use every ploy available to hype their gate receipts.

Whether called Big Cars or Sprints, they have always been the ones that have separated the serious racer from the amateur. When you strap on a Sprint car, you're at the top of the mountain with no safety wires to hold you should you fall. You're about to prove that you are equal to the men before you who have challenged the legendary beast. Beast, or half-crazed maniac is not too light a description. You have to see one of of these graceful appearing machines trip in its path around an oval before you can feel the full impact of its wickedness. Something seemingly as insignificant as a small rut can send a smooth powersliding Sprinter into an epileptic gyration that will make a man wish he had never been introduced to the sport of speed. It's not uncommon to see a driver carried from a crashed Sprint car with the whites of his eyes bloodied. Sprint cars break blood vessels, bones and spirits on a regular basis.

The Sprint car is characterized by functional design. It's a single seat, open-cockpit and open-wheeled vehicle with virtually no frills. The

open-wheel aspect is probably the most important ingredient for providing excitement. It is possible for two Sprinters to run side by side and rub wheels without incident, but, should a trailing driver run over the tire of the car in front, he may be sent into an upward spiral that makes it look like a mammoth fish gasping for its last breath.

Yesterday, woe was the Sprint driver who wound up wearing his car. For decades, all the way up to 1970, Sprint drivers were afforded absolutely no protection in case of a roll-over. During the Sixties a single-roll bar was mounted over the tail of the car and was supposed to protrude above the driver's head and ultimately save him from a broken neck. Throughout the history of Sprint racing in general, it is fortunate that the human body flexes and bends as much as it does, because the token roll bar that was once popular served virtually no purpose whatsoever. Often as not, it would snap like the proverbial toothpick. Some local racing associations demanded more protection for their drivers and a vehicle known as the Supermodified evolved from jalopy racing. The Supermodified was simply a Sprint car with a full roll-cage assembly installed above and around the driver.

Old-time purists dreaded the day that the roll-cage would infiltrate true

Sprint car racing with cries of, "It makes it look like a modified," and "Real race cars don't have all that garbage sticking up on top." Finally, the nation's leading open-cockpit sanctioning organization, the United States Auto Club (USAC), made roll-cages mandatory in their Sprint and Midget racing divisions. Today, all Sprint cars run with cages and there is really no longer a difference between Sprints and Supermodifieds.

Over the years a multitude of engines have been bolted into a Sprint car. For the past 15 years however, the small block Chevrolet V-8 has dominated. It's reliable, affordable, and provides more horsepower than is usually necessary, an ingredient that has always characterized Sprint racing.

The tracks that stage Sprint races have become more famous than the men who have raced on them. While both coasts have created memorable Sprint facilities, it has been the Midwest where Sprint drivers come to prove themselves. The half-mile located in Winchester, Ind. and named after that town is the second oldest operating track in the country. First track in longevity is the Indianapolis Motor Speedway which of course opened its doors in 1909 and ran the first 500 in 1911. Winchester began as a near flat facility in 1919. Over the years, its banking was gradually raised to the present height of 25 feet an an angle of 34 degrees.

Racing promoter Frank Funk saw the advantages of advertising the world's fastest half-mile, and for years staged a running battle with a similar track located in Salem, Ind. Of course Funk ran Salem also, and the two speedways annually headlined their advertising with, "See if The World's Half Mile Record Will Be Broken... $500 Goes To The Man Who Sets A New World Mark." On one grisly day in 1951 a talented Cecil Green took his best shot at the record and made it no further than the apex of the first turn before plowing through the guardrail and plummeting to the green pasture and death below.

Bill Mackey followed Green's tracks and he too became a Sprint car statistic in the same spot that Green died. Pancho Carter's father Duane, known as one of the smoothest men to ever drive a race car, followed Green in the qualifying line and set the fastest time-trial of the day.

Even today, Winchester remains as a proving ground for the Sprint driver seeking recognition. A good showing in a USAC Sprint race at most any track can put a man's name in headlines, but even more so if he's made his bones on the "hills" as Winchester, Salem and a similar track at Dayton, Ohio are known. Quiet Tom Sneva, once a school principal treked to the Midwest, won several USAC Sprint races in rapid succession and was offered a Speedway ride. Today he drives for Roger Penske, one of the best rides available in Championship racing.

Parnelli Jones said, "Any guy who runs Sprinters that much and wins as often as he Indy," after reading of Jan Opperman's exploits in the early Seventies. Opperman was an "outlaw" Sprint driver, outlaw referring to any sanctioning body that isn't USAC. Jan was winning with alarming regularity and as he puts it, "putting my head on the chopping block some 65-70 times per year.

To try and chronicle the great and memorable Sprint drivers, cars and races of the past here would be a futile attempt. Consequently, the publisher of the 500 Yearbook is compiling one volume now that is tentatively titled, "The Illustrated History of Sprint Car Auto Racing." This article however, is not to serve as a commercial for our own publications. Rather, if you've never seen a Sprint car auto race, do so, for it should be an experience you'll never forget. In no other sport will you witness a man trying to tame a machine that has a personality all its own, one that surfaces when its powerplant is switched to the on position. And take a good look at the man who throws the switch for he is truly an individual who does not know the meaning of defeat. If he did, he would be one notch below the world's bravest racing drivers.

The Sprint car races are probably the most photographed races in the Midwest. Usually, the drivers are the ones who receive all the publicity, so here we present the photographers themselves, many of them contributors to the "500" Yearbook. Top row, left to right: Marvin Scattergood, Randy Christie, C.P. Davis, Lloyd Masing, C.W. Wallace, Don Carmichael, Randy Lowe, Pat Taylor, Steve Ellis, Armin Krueger, Trotty Heck, Gene Crucean, Rick Lane. Bottom row, Harry Goode, Vern Plotts, Dennis Torres, Tom Dick, Steve Lingenfelter, John Mahoney. Photo taken by writer/racer Robin Miller.

THE LITTLE 500

Dick

A Quarter Mile Race Track. . .

33 Sprint Cars. . .

500 Laps. . .

It's No Place For The Timid

by John Sawyer

Interstate 69 sweeps out of Indianapolis and heads on across the heartland of Indiana like a giant snake. Swiftly this marvel of asphalt engineering knifes through the placid countryside as it heads for Fort Wayne, The Michigan Line, and all points north. A thousand destinations can be reached along that paved pathway, but to some of us only one of them matters. Lurking within the very shadows of Indianapolis, only thirty-six miles away, is the thriving, industrial city of Anderson. To the casual observer there is nothing unusual about Anderson, Indiana. In fact, it is a fairly typical Midwestern town with numerous factories, an abundance of farm implement stores, and a seldom used railway station. However, don't let all of this Corn Belt conformity mislead you. There is something incredibly different about the place; a uniqueness that is awesome, to say the least.

You see, Anderson, Indiana is the home of Sun Valley Speedway; a tiny ¼ mile speed bowl whose scarred crash walls reflect the sinister aspect of its cantankerous personality. Surrounded by sprawling grandstands, the rugged little "bull ring" might well have shared the anonymity of so many of its relatives, but for one fact.

In the final days of May, these last twenty-eight years, Sun Valley Speedway has been the site of the worlds' most flagrant example of auto racing audacity - The Little 500.

The Little 500, the race that some people once believed to be an impossibility. The race that exhausts the most extensive vocabulary in the search for adjectives to describe its brazen displays of human courage and mechanical fortitude. To those of us who are captivated by the mere thought of sprint cars and the valiant few who dare to race them; Anderson, Indiana has come to represent a legion of epoch making legends. The Little 500 is that kind of happening - a brawling, roaring extravaganza that has been cussed at, cried over, and cheered for through more seasons than many of its current challengers have been alive. There never has been and never will be anything like it. Not, at least, to those of us in the dusty brigades that roam up and down this spacious land following our beloved sprint cars.

Now, just what is so special about this one of a kind study in mechanized madness? Well, let us begin with a full field of thirty-three untamed, snarling, widow-making, flame-belching sprint cars. Fill each of their cramped cockpits with an arrogant, defiant individual who thinks that he is the almighty best throttle stomper in captivity. Send them all off - three abreast - in a hell raising, flying start that threatens to vibrate the old track into a total structural collapse. Continue this wild behavior for 500 grinding laps, 2,000 muscle tearing turns, and 125 heart pounding miles. Unbelievably, all of this takes place in an arena which is barely big enough to house a good sized moving van.

Somehow, it seems a bit sinful to refer to such an event as one of a kind. Definitely, stronger language is needed. More appropriately, The Little 500 might be described as a totally unprecedented collage of unrivaled bravery, flashing colors, deafening noise, and unrestrained emotionalism. Categorize it as one of those tantalizing spectacles

"All of this takes place in an arena barely big enough to house a good size moving van."

that you are afraid to watch but wouldn't miss for anything. No matter what - to answer the above question - The Little 500 absolutely is special. If it isn't, then the Cardinal is no longer The State Bird of Indiana and sprint cars don't run on alcohol.

Certainly there is an endless line of race drivers who would agree with this thesis. All of these many years, they have trudged into Anderson carrying their battered helmets in one hand and a satchel full of nerve in the other. Armed only with inherent self-confidence, these rugged characters seem to blow in from anywhere and everywhere - all for the privilege of pounding themselves and their machines into oblivion around Sun Valley's merciless pavement.

Floyd's Knob, Indiana; Garden Grove, California; White Bear Lake, Minnesota - these are typical of the names that ring of hard-core American racing tradition. The kind of tradition that breeds and nurtures sprint car racers. From such places, The Little 500's supreme challenge has lured the best of a breed of fierce people. Grizzled veterans, boy wonders, unknowns, and well established heroes - they have all answered the call. Their determination and courage have provided cornerstones for one of the more durable foundations in auto racing's heritage: The Little 500.

Motivation for such a dedication to speed is difficult to determine. Who knows for sure the identity of that fact which motivates a race car chauffeur. Fame, glory, or money; no one can say positively - not even those who

actually do the driving. Particularly mysterious are the reasons for coming to Anderson's yearly May carnival, as it is easily one of the most demanding and physically punishing of all motor races. For some, competing at The Little 500 is an end in itself. For others, that same competition is a means to an end.

In the case of the latter group, its membership peers through oil smeared goggles at a dream which lies thirty-six miles away. Amidst the impenetrable maze of alcohol fumes and flickering exhausts that dream is always there. Even the most wearied set of eyes, staring blankly through the narrow slit of a Bell Star Helmet, can see it. After all, it isn't that far away; just a scant thirty-six miles down Interstate 69 to Indianapolis and the corner of 16th Street and Georgetown Road. That spot, of course, marks the home of the hollowed ground, the big casino, The Racer's Mecca - THE INDIANAPOLIS MOTOR SPEEDWAY.

With all due respect to the view held by a few skeptics, the evidence obtained by careful statistical examination firmly proves that a strong link does exist between "The Anderson Classic" and The Indianapolis 500. Obviously, not every Sun Valley warrior has managed to ascend the rocky path to Tony Hulman's stage that annually features the ultimate in automotive drama. For many of them, the bridge spanning the distance between 1,320 feet of Anderson asphalt and 2½ miles of similar, rubber-coated pavement at Indy has been far too wide. Also, keep in mind another fact. Each of those individuals who has confronted the grimness of The Little 500 has been, first of all, a sprint car driver. As was said earlier, to some, this could easily serve as an end in itself. It has been enough to say - I am a sprint car racer and I drove The Little 500.

Still, there are those who have continually emerged as the super-talented, ambitious types - the kind of men once referred to by T. E. Lawrence as "the dangerous daylight dreamers". To such intense personalities - sprint cars, The Little 500, and everything else, for that matter, only exist as rungs on the ladder to glory. At the top of that ladder dwells the vision of championship cars, giant tracks, and The Speedway. To date, twenty-five men have actually arisen from Sun Valley's bruising battlefield to qualify and run at Indianapolis. Two others, Bill Holland and Larry Dickson, having already known the glory of Indy, still felt the need to try The Little 500.

Amidst that total of twenty-seven travelers in both worlds, one can readily spot the sheen of some real gold plated players of the most dangerous game. For example: two graduates of The Little 500, Parnelli Jones and Johnny Rutherford have been winners at The Indianapolis Motor Speedway. Likewise, four members of various Sun Valley graduating classes have claimed the pole for the world's most famous auto race. They are Dick Rathmann, Pat O'Connor, and again - Parnelli Jones and Johnny Rutherford. Rutherford's image is especially glossy, as he has twice occupied that coveted number one starting position. Larry Crockett, Jim McElreath, John White, Bill Puterbaugh and the legendary Jones comprise a group that also shares some common ground. All of them blasted out of the brutal world of sprint cars and The Little 500 to be named as Indianapolis Rookies of The Year.

Perhaps the most amazing story of all, in this relation-

ship between two shrines of speed, is that of Bill Holland. For those too young to remember, Bill Holland once rode "the bricks of Indy" with an unsurpassed perfection. Back in the long ago days of "the true big cars", he drove one of Lou Moore's Blue Crown Spark Plug Specials and helped establish the mystique of that illustrious name. From 1947 to 1950, Holland piloted the elegant beast around the deadly, concrete-lined corridors of Indianapolis with incredible results - three second place finishes and a victory in 1949. But for a tragic breakdown in communications between driver and pit crew, he could probably have nailed down another victory.

Ironically, Holland's triumph in 1949 came at nearly the same time as the inaugural running of The Little 500. In the jubilation of that moment, Bill could probably have cared less. However, it wouldn't always be that way. Ten years later, long after the stately Blue Crowns were but

LITTLE 500 DRIVERS
WHO MADE IT TO INDY

1. Dick Rathmann
2. Red Amick
3. Larry "Crash" Crockett
4. Elmer George
5. Jim Rigsby
6. Bob Scott
7. Jim McWithey
8. Al Miller
9. John White
10. Ron Duman
11. Arnie Knepper
12. Bob Mathouser
13. Bud Tinglestad
14. Bill Holland *
15. Parnelli Jones
16. A.J. Shepherd
17. Jim McElreath
18. John Rutherford
19. Greg Weld
20. Gary Congdon
21. Sam Sessions
22. Tom Bigelow
23. Bill Puterbaugh
24. Larry Cannon
25. Lee Kunzman
26. Sheldon Kinser
27. Larry Dickson *

* Had already seen action at Indianapolis Speedway when Little 500 participation occured.

memories in dusty photo albums, an aging Bill Holland did a surprising thing. He qualified for and drove in The 1959 Little 500. At its conclusion, exhausted and sweat-soaked, Holland crawled from his grimy car to find he had survived the experience to finish seventh. Relieved to have it all over with, Bill wouldn't deny that Anderson's tiny track had been tougher than he had expected. Whatever the reason for it, Bill Holland's mysterious presence had lent considerable luster to Sun Valley Speedway's greatest claim to fame.

Along with this very positive influence on Indy, The Little 500 has skyrocketed many of its more formidable participants to everlasting sprint car racing fame. Within the ranks of USAC alone, the amazing record speaks for itself. Since 1956, no less than eight men have emerged from Sun Valley's howling traffic jam to become champions of that organization's sprint division. Reflect for just a moment on the quality of the following names: Pat O'Connor, Elmer George, Parnelli Jones, John Rutherford, Greg Weld, Larry Dickson, Sam Sessions and Rollie Beale Together, this worthy group has produced a total of twelve USAC Sprint Titles and a composite of 167 feature race

thrill bloodthirsty fans - this challenge is offered. Show me, if you can, any continuing tradition in sprint racing that has provided more leverage in the building of great racing careers. However, before any large amount of effort is devoted to such a project, listen to what Johnny White has to say about The Little 500. Yes, that same Johnny White who has to rank as one of the most fearless and talented race drivers ever.

"My great dream was to get to The Speedway. It always had been. To me, "The Little 500" was a quick way to convince the big champion-ship car owners of my ability. I went to And-erson with that idea in mind and raced my guts out in the process. Apparently it paid off. Running The Little 500, all of those times, was a real education. It taught me how to handle the traffic, fatigue and constant pressure of long distance racing."

In my opinion, this statement is proof enough of the dramatic contributions of Anderson's Little 500.

Almost as intriguing as the race itself, is the fascinating tale of how the zany, Hoosier spectacle came into being in

Anderson's Sun Valley Speedway prepares for another Little 500. The quarter-mile bowl is some drivers' big step to Indianapolis.

victories.

Not to be ignored is the enviable achievement of some of IMCA's more solid citizenry. Pete Folse, John White, Jerry Richert, Gordon Wooley, Karl Busson, Darl Harri-son and Jerry Blundy all saw heavy action at The Little 500. By the same token, each of them eventually became champion of the historic Midwestern Club. At age thirty-eight, Harrison is still a regular competitor at Sun Valley Speedway's big day in May and is always a favorite to appear in the winner's circle.

To those individuals who have doubted any useful pur-pose for the existence of The Little 500; to that same rank and file of critics who say it serves only to crush lives and

the first place. One day Joe Helpling, an Anderson filling operator, decided to build a race track. Now it obviously takes an audacious individual to entertain such a notion, but then Joe Helpling has long been known for his irre-pressible audacity. In 1947, without benefit of professional planning or consultation, Helpling's tenacity prevailed and Sun Valley Speedway inhaled its first breath of life. It has been breathing the acrid, alcohol-infested air ever since.

Yet undaunted, Joe Helpling still wasn't satisfied. How could he be an ordinary race promoter, staging ordinary races? No way, he just had to resort to the path of least resistance. In his case, that was to do something spec-tacular, something unbelievably wild.

Thus it was that in September of 1948 Helpling called a special meeting at The Anderson Hotel. Invited to attend were the various officials of the Mutual Racing Association, one of three national outfits then featuring "the red hot roasters" as automotive competition. When everyone was seated, "Crazy Like a Fox" Joe announced his plans to stage a 500 lap production, utilizing those same roasters and the wild and wooly men who drove them. He went on to describe a regular miniature Indy with eleven rows of three and the traditional flying start.

Aghast, those "hard bitten" racers sat there, stunned into silence. Finally their voices erupted in loud protest. Comments like impossible, it can't be done, and some others - more or less unprintable - shot around the room. The general consensus of the opinion was that neither men nor machines could stand such punishment. As usual, Joe Helpling stubbornly clung to his view. "We are going to have this race and I don't care if it takes 'till daylight we will have one car run 500 laps." So stated Joe Helpling and again, as usual, he got his way. The following spring, in 1949, the very first Little 500 field roared away to its unknown destiny. Contrary to the universal pessimism directed toward it, the race was a resounding success. Twenty-four cars were somehow running at the conclusion and the impossible had been overcome.

**"I don't care if it takes 'till daylight. . .
One car is gonna finish 500 laps."**

1953 was a terribly significant year for The Little 500, as the first sprint cars appeared in the starting field at that time. By 1955, the entire lineup was comprised of sprinters and The Mutual Racing Association's sanction had been replaced by that of Tom Cherry's own All American Racing Club. The die was cast, The Little 500 was forever to be a sprint car race.

By 1961, Helpling's show had become world famous. Tom Cherry was phasing himself out of racing and so the sanction was turned over to IMCA, an organization blessed with an unlimited supply of sprint cars and entire regiments of people brash enough to drive them. IMCA stayed on in its sanctioning capacity through the 1970 event and then, for reasons unknown to me, the happy home broke up. The leaders of IMCA went their way and Joe Helpling went his. An era had ended at Sun Valley Speedway.

The American Speed Association was the next agency to provide machines and official direction to The Little 500 and it continued to do so until 1975. In that year a local group was formed appropriately entitled The Rocket Racing Association and its purpose was to direct and perpetuate the running of America's longest sprint car race. To date, it has succeeded in both of these endeavors.

1949, being the first year for The Little 500, presents one of the most amazing accounts of all. Bob Flock, of southern racing fame, came to that premier event without ever having seen an asphalt track, let alone a high banked one. Through the locked gate, his eyes tried to penetrate the darkness of night to get a glimpse of Sun Valley Speedway. He couldn't see much, but he saw enough to satisfy his curiosity. Quickly he told his car owner that under no circumstance did he, Bob Flock, intend to drive at such a place. Shocked, the car owner eyed Flock with dismay and then he announced that he had no intention of pulling out,

Elmer George in 1956, before becoming an IMS vice president.

Rollie Beale raced home ahead of the 1966 Anderson 500 field.

Pat O'Conner was killed at the start of his fifth Indy race.

not yet anyway. They had come too many miles to surrender without, at least, trying. At that point, while Flock stared glumly at the Indiana sky, a coin was crammed into a pay phone and Joe Helpling's telephone began ringing off the hook. Helpling, dazed by his rapid exodus from a deep sleep, could faintly hear a pleading voice requesting his immediate presence at the track. Still a bit groggy, he complied and was quickly confronted by a nervous car owner and a slightly disgruntled driver. As soon as he was aware of the problem, Helpling provided a possible solution to it. "I'll turn on the lights and you can try out my track," he is reported to have said. At 4 a.m., the lights came on and Flock took to the oval. Lap after lap he ran around the slick pavement, until his confidence began to build. Shortly after daylight, a happier Bob Flock agreed, at last, to race that evening. He did exactly that and finished second after nearly being the winner.

Interestingly enough, one of Flock's rivals in that particular race was a twenty-three year old "hot rodder", Dick Rathmann, who was driving for a Chicago speed parts merchant by the name of Andy Granatelli. In just a few years, both names would become familiar fixtures on press releases issued by The Indianapolis Speedway.

When "The Fabulous Fifties" roared on to the American scene, auto racing was injected with much of the vitality of an era blessed with boundless energy. The Little 500 was not to be slighted in all of this glorious activity and many of its greatest moments are found in the record of that long ago decade.

1950 saw the first real national attention directed toward Joe Helpling's race. Jim Rigsby - a part time lobster fisherman and full time racer - apparently thought The Little 500 to be of considerable importance. He had his Coast Grain Special flown in from California by air cargo, something that was unheard of in that time. Soon Rigsby would make it to Indy and soon he would die in a hideous sprint car crash at Dayton, Ohio. Jimmy was gone but his bizarre method of car transportation had served its purpose. Racing people everywhere knew about The Little 500.

"Jones twisted himself into a pretzel and became sick from exhaustion while trying to defeat the intrepid Ron Duman."

Then, in 1952, there is the case of two buddies, also from California. Labeled "The Cabbage Kings of Salinas", these two rugged dudes - Elmer George and Johnnie Key - towed a car to Anderson that they had paid for by growing a host of those nickname producing vegetables.

Two men were to win The Little 500 in most unusual fashion during that ten year span (1950-1960). One of them, Bob Cleberg drove his wife's GMC powered sprinter into the 1956 field via the alternate route. When a qualified machine failed to start, Cleberg - the first alternate - was allowed to start in last position. He simply charged to the front and won going away. The other young man, Johnny White also drove a GMC engined car to victory in 1957. His effort manufactured the most lopsided race ever run at Anderson when he finished twelve laps ahead of his nearest rival.

Bob Byrne, noted racing historian and Sun Valley official, loves to recall the debacle that occured at The Little 500 in 1953. It seems that in that particular time a car which had been bumped from the field, during qualification, could requalify when a change of ownership resulted. Otherwise, if a bill of sale could be presented to the officials, the bumped car had to be granted a new timing opportunity. On and on the time trials went. Finally at 3 a.m., with the field still in question, "the powers to be" called a meeting and instituted a reformed policy. It was later realized that some cars had qualified dozens of times and one persistent individual had purchased the same machine on six different occasions.

With the appearance of 1960 on the calender that hung in Joe Helpling's speedway office, a new generation of racing and racers invaded tiny Sun Valley Speedway. Especially it was the racers, themselves, who set the tone for what was to come. "Gents" like Parnelli Jones who was determined to win The Little 500. Driving the Fike Plumbing

Bob Scott ran only 63 laps in two Indianapolis races.

Chevy, Jones twisted himself into a pretzel and became sick from exhaustion while trying to defeat the intrepid Ron Duman. Duman won the race with Parnelli coming in second. One year later, that same Parnelli Jones would be named Rookie of the Year at Indianapolis.

Prowling the pit area during the 1964 race was a scrawny kid from Michigan, whose face was constructed along the physiological principles of a razor blade's edge. Desperate for a ride, he jumped into a car, parked by its original driver because of a distinct lack of brakes. Not at all intimidated by such a hazardous condition, the gutsy guy stormed on to the track and raced in a creditable fashion for 207 laps. His name was Sam Sessions and fame was soon to come his way.

However, by far the most unique story emanating from "The Sixties" has to do with F.M. "Dizz" Wilson and his mystery driver of 1961. Long disillusioned with the unkind treatment shown most of his Little 500 cars, Wilson sought out Bob Byrne - public relations director for Joe Helpling's race. "Bob, I have finally found a driver who will not wreck my car and he definitely is going to win this year's event," said Wilson. "Great," replied Byrne. "Who is he?"

"His name is Jim McElreath and he is from Texas," proclaimed "Dizz" Wilson.

"Fine," commented Byrne, "but I don't know anything about him."

"You don't have to, just build him up, because he is going to win," the positive Wilson concluded. Mr. Byrne acted on that advice and sang the praises of the unknown McElreath. It was well that he did - Jim McElreath won The Little 500 just as his jubilant owner had predicted. It was the first victory for both a Wilson car and an Offenhauser engine in "The Sun Valley Classic". For Jim McElreath, the man of few words, his triumph served as a catapault to stardom.

While glancing through the recent pages in The Little 500 chronicle of courage it is quickly realized that the quality of legend making material has not diminished. Proof of this can be found in the form of Larry Dickson - the most successful driver in USAC sprint car history. When "Lightning Larry" walked through Sun Valley's pit gate in 1974, his career seemed to be over - reduced to a pale shadow of its former greatness. Most everyone had written off "The Buckeye Flyer". On that night, Larry strapped himself into Ernie Ensign's sprinter and took stock of his situation - dreary as it was. This had to be it; he must get the job done. Like a rocket he ripped his way through the tangled mass of snarling machinery and won the race.

Johnny White in his 1957 winner. He won again in 1963. In 1964 he ran 200 laps to finish fourth at Indianapolis in his only appearance.

Utilizing the most impressive kind of bravery, Larry Dickson had thrust himself back into prosperity. In his case, Sun Valley Speedway had provided a renaissance, a second chance. Obviously, it has not been wasted.

In conclusion, there are two extremely young men who are worthy of mention. Both of them have the same last name and together the sum total of their years wouldn't equal the ages of many Little 500 regulars. First there is Danny Smith of Indianapolis who in 1975 received his high school diploma in a special pre-race ceremony and then went out to earn third place in the final standings of the grueling test. Then we come to Robert Smith, a resident of Gibsonton, Florida and Bull Frog Creek. 1976 saw him qualify second fastest in the field of thirty-three on a virtually flat tire. Who knows, maybe these quiet youngsters will be the next successful travelers on that crowded highway to glory.

On May 29, 1976, thirty-three gleaming sprint cars were

LITTLE 500 FACT SHEET

Race Winners

Year	Winner	City
1949	Sam Skinner	Muncie, IN
1950	Tom Cherry	Muncie, IN
1951	Red Renner	Woodburn, IN
1952	Tom Cherry	Muncie, IN
1953	Bob King	Muncie, IN
1954	Tom Cherry	Muncie, IN
1955	Tom Cherry	Muncie, IN
1956	Bob Cleberg	Rio, WI
1957	Johnny White	Warren, MI
1958	Wayne Alspaugh	Anderson, IN
1959	Ron Duman	Dearborn, MI
1960	Ron Duman	Dearborn, MI
1961	Jim Mc Elreath	Arlington, TX
1962	Arnie Knepper	Belleville, IL
1963	Johnny White	Warren, MI
	Bob Coulter	Torrance, CA
1964	Dick Good	Mishawaka, IN
1965	Chuck Taylor	East Alton, IL
	Bob King	Muncie, IN
1966	Rollie Beale	Toledo, OH
1967	Darl Harrison	Tiffin, OH
	Cy Fairchild	Saginaw, MI
1968	Karl Busson	Toledo, OH
1969	Buzz Gregory	Speedway, IN
1970	Darl Harrison	Tiffin, OH
1971	Herman Wise	Taccoa, GA
1972	Jeff Bloom	Kalamazoo, MI
1973	Dick Gaines	Floyd's Knob, IN
1974	Larry Dickson	Marietta, OH
1975	Darl Harrison	Tiffin, OH
1976	Dick Gaines	Floyd's Knob, IN

The Most Successful Driver:

Tom Cherry easily claims that distinction. He competed in six races with a record of four wins, a second, and a third. Of a possible 3,000 laps that he could have run, 2,991 were actually completed. Obviously this is a record of incredible proportion.

[141]

Johnny Rutherford couldn't win at Sun Valley but placed one, two, one in the last three of his 13 races at Tony Hulman's course.

Mahoney

Greg Weld had several Indy rides but made the show only once, finishing 32nd in 1970.

Dick

1974 win boosted Larry Dickson's career.

pushed on to the main straightaway at Sun Valley Speedway in preparation for the 28th running of The Little 500. Bold lettering on their heavily waxed hoods spelled out the very essence of sprint car racing. "Down home", earthy names that have always indicated the grass roots image of the sport - "Indiana Limestone Sprinter", "Benny's Country Lounge", "Crawfordsville Liquor Special", and perhaps the most appropriate title of all simply read "DESPERADO".

Tension hung thickly in the air. Like a dense fog, it covered everything and everyone with its jittery gloom. Around each of those precious machines hovered a small group of men. Some polished chrome, some adjusted injectors, others just tried to look busy - anything to steady down their nerves. Even the drivers, men always capable of a brave appearance, fidgeted with their helmets or sat quietly contemplating the possibilities of the next two hours.

One veteran driver stared blankly off toward an empty corner of a grandstand. Possibly he imagined the ghosts of Frank Toth, Harry Kern and Billy Tennill were sitting up there. Once upon a time, each of them had waited - in just this way - for a Little 500 to start. Once upon a time, each of them had taken his last ride on Sun Valley's weatherbeaten asphalt. Somewhere, amidst all of this heavy atmosphere, they must be waiting again - just like those mortals down on the track.

At last the call went out to mount up. Trembling hands pulled on Nomex gloves and accordingly tied scarlet bandannas across taut faces. Perspiring bodies were wedged into the cockpits to sit rigidly in anticipation of the jolt of the push truck that would set them in motion. One by one, the gaudy cars and their heroic riders were shoved away; until the entire field was rumbling along on the slow parade laps. As the eleven rows of fire-spitting machines passed the grandstand for one last leisurely circuit, each driver raised his hand in salute to the crowd and even more to the tradition of The Little 500. At precisely this moment you had to give some thought to Joe Helpling, now aged and sick, and to his race that was once laughingly referred to as a total impossibility.

With the unfurling of the green flag, a gigantic explosion of noise and color burst upon us all. Down through the first corner, the pack of thirty-three banged and shoved its way. Thirty-three, unlimited in size, engines roared their collective challenge and thirty-three desperate drivers wrestled with hand blistering steering wheels. Lap after lap, the battle raged and from the vantage point of this writer, just inside turn one, the ground seemed to be shaking with the

Jim McWithey went the distance in the first of two Indy races.

WHAT SOME OF THE WINNERS THINK ABOUT THE LITTLE 500

Rollie Beale (1966)
"The Little 500 is absolutely the toughest race that I ever ran. I thought my neck would never quit hurting after it was over. My strategy was simple - pace myself in the beginning; but, at the same time not fall too far behind. When the congestion eased a bit around 125 laps, I put the move on. It takes supreme concentration and a car that handles perfectly to win the race."

Larry Dickson (1974)
"All my life I wanted to run that race, but none of my car owners would go along with it. I even offered to buy the tires. When I did get the chance, I wanted to make the most of it. Particularly since my career was at low ebb then. In my opinion, it is something every race driver should experience. I will never forget it, but neither will I ever go back. Once was enough."

Karl Busson (1968)
"It is an incredibly tough race, but I got a break. Rain forced the running of the event over two days and I was spared that horrible fatigue. I guess I wasn't sure we could finish, so I ran flat out to win the lap money. Most important of all factors is to have a good handling car."

Jim McElreath (1961)
"I had been running the IMCA fairs for "Dizz" Wilson in 1960 and he suggested we try The Little 500 in '61. I couldn't think of any reason not to, so I agreed. It gave me my first real look at pavement and you can learn a lot in 500 laps around that place. Positively it helped me get to The Speedway in 1962."

Darl Harrison (1967, 1970, 1975)
"People say that I am crazy to keep running this race, but it is just in my blood. The challenge - that is what drags me back year after year. All of those cars, the terrible traffic, the confusion - the whole thing simply provides the best in racing for me."

Johnny White (1957, 1963)
"When I first went there to race, I decided only one man could teach me enough to become a winner. That was Tom Cherry. One winter I spent two weeks at his shop in Muncie. I pumped him with questions and memorized every detail of his cars. Eventually I became that winner - twice I won and should have won a third time. Of course, I got a break when the chance came to drive for Hoy Stevens. He was a great owner and his little GMC really worked on that track. My pal Duman did pretty well with it after I left the car. As far as the race was concerned, it just about wore out my aching neck every time I ran it."

Parnelli Jones raced seven times at Indianapolis, winning in 1963 and nearly repeating in 1967. Joe Pittman views his 1962 sprinter.

Mahoney

In the writing of this article, I am forever indebted to Mr. Bob Byrne of Chesterfield, Indiana. Long known for both his knowledge of and devotion to The Little 500, he was kind enough to share with me some of his memories, experiences and thoughts concerning his favorite race. Without that help, my efforts would have been futile - at best.

A padded head rest helps relieve neck strain during the 500 laps.

Dick
Scott

violence of it all.

Standing there, locked within that crescendo of deafening noise, several lines from a recent hit song by "The Eagles" somehow crept into my thought process. Right there, blended in with the screech of sliding tires and the loud snapping of exhausts, those words repeated themselves time and again.

"So put me on a highway,

show me a sign

and take it to the limit, one more time."

"TAKE IT TO THE LIMIT" - such a musical composition as this, could well serve as the anthem for sprint car racers. Especially to those scores of men who have been favored with enough raw courage to confront the awesome challenge of The Little 500.

Red Amick was eleventh in his second and last Indy 500 in 1960.

HOOSIER SPRINTS

There's A Race Track In Indianapolis Called The Fairgrounds Mile...

It Proves How Good Indy Drivers Are

by Carl Hungness

Editor's note: It is generally agreed among current stars such as A. J. Foyt, Bobby Unser, Mario Andretti that Sprint car racing is the single most demanding and competitive form of automobile racing ever invented. Most of the drivers in the Indianapolis 500 have spent time racing Sprint Cars. They're the acid test of a man's ability. It's been said that Sprint cars are wild-mechanical machines, drunk with horsepower, you never know what they're going to do.

Take a walk with us now to one of the nation's most anticipated Sprint races: The Hoosier Sprints on the Indianapolis Fairgrounds mile track. Throughout the summer months you can watch these same cars and drivers on such famed tracks in the Midwest as Winchester, Dayton Salem, Eldora, Terre Haute. No matter what type of auto racing fan you consider yourself, you would be remiss if you don't attend at least one Sprint car event sometime to judge them for yourself. We think you'll like what you see.

It's only natural that the world-famous Indianapolis 500 should draw some secondary events to the city of Indianapolis during the month of May. Parades, banquets, press parties and general recognition gatherings notwithstanding, there is another automobile race here that will make you wonder why they don't hold one just like it every week.

The race is titled "Hoosier Sprints" and is more than a single Sprint car race : It's a pair of them, 50 laps each around the Indiana State Fairgrounds one mile dirt track It's even more than two exciting Sprint car races. It's a gathering of the clan; a place to see some of the Indianapolis 500 drivers show their versatility through a form of automobile racing that dates back to the inception of the car itself.

Traditionally held on the Friday night before the 500 itself, this year's event was postponed until after the race because of rain. Last year, the king himself, A. J. Foyt decided to, "play in the dirt," awhile and wound up winning both 50 lappers. When asked about his high-riding pitch-it-sideways style of driving after the first event was over, 'ol A. J. commented, "Shucks, I was just clownin'. Haven't been in a Sprinter in quite some time and really missed it."

The Hoosier Sprints are the races to run in if you want to be noticed. Old pro Sprint driver Bobby Grim once said, "Sprint cars are for young men in a hurry to get there..... and old men with no place to go." Both statements held true during the l976 event.

Duane "Pancho" Carter continued to uphold the name his father put before racing fans for over two decades by winning the first 50 lap event after staging a memorable duel with another of the second generation racers, Gary Bettenhausen. Just a few short years ago Gary was the anxious youngster seething for Sprint car victories and now he's considered one of the division's elder statesman. He's only 34 years old, but life on the Sprint Car circuit has a strange way of aging a man.

Bettenhausen arrived at the track with his left hand swollen nearly twice size. He said he was bitten by a horsefly while mowing the grass at his Monrovia, Ind. home. It didn't make any difference though, Gary's entire left arm just sort of dangles as he walks, although he does an Academy award performance job of trying to look natural. The arm doesn't work but he keeps telling himself and those around him that they're really going to have to race with him soon because it's getting better. And it is getting better, ever so slowly. He wracked up all sorts of nerves in the limb two years ago at Syracuse, N.Y. and it hasn't been the same since. But now he can at least raise it. We think he's driving one-handed and uses the limp limb for balance. We also think that Gary Bettenhausen is the single, most determined individual we've ever met. Day in and day out, he has to be considered one of the foremost Sprint car drivers ever to appear on the American racing scene.

So Bettenhausen goes out to qualify at the Hoosier Sprints, a rich-enough Sprint car race alright, but a risky one too, especially in view of the fact that he could easily bang himself up just enough to miss the 500 and a real pay-day.

"Put that thing back like it was before we qualified", he says to his long-time Sprint mechanic-owner Willie Davis. "I made a mistake— — —there ain't nothin' but marbles out there now." He's referring to the chassis setting on his Sprinter.

Gary would ultimately wind up with fourth fastest time of the evening, not bad for an old warrior against some 47 other cars. Soon after he pulled into the pits his close friend and constant needler, Billy Vukovich showed up and started his usual philosophizing. Vukovich doesn't drive Sprint cars much and likes to tell Bettenhausen that he's crazy for driving in a race that's so close to the 500.

"Bettenhausen, you're really dumb, you know that don't you?" the lanky Vukovich asserts. "They're having a million dollar race on Sunday and here you are beating your brains out for. . . .how much? A grand? Two Grand? You really ain't too smart. I just wanted you to know that."

And Gary's lovin' every minute of it. His hand hurts like hell, but his pal Vuky is helping to relieve the pain with his verbal needle.

"You'll never learn," Vukuvich continues. "You know that nothin's ever gonna change, leastwise you. Why, what's changed around here in the last 50 years?" he says referring to the sport in general.

"They still got the women (referring to the wives) in the nickel bleachers. They oughta give 'em hundred dollar seats. . . .if they had hundred dollar seats."

Vukovich continues to lecture Gary B. on the unsavory aspects of Sprint car racing and challenges him with, "Now you tell me, how do these things look any differently than they did thirty years ago." He points in the air when he really wants you to understand what he's saying. Vukovich doesn't go to many Sprint car races, but neither does he miss the Hoosier Sprints. He won't admit it, but he wants to watch and encourage Gary. They're friends.

"Whaddya mean?" Gary finally answers. "Why now we've got wider tires, bigger torsion bars," Gary smiles as he tries to counter Vukovich's assertion that the car he's driving belongs to another era of automobile racing. Gary is a tinkerer, a mechanical genius when it comes to making innovations that will give him an edge in racing. He is always thinking ahead: of a way to beat the competition, but grins as he runs out of things to say when he's trying to tell Vukovich about the progress of the Sprint car. He glanced the Davis machine over from front to back, and mentally admitted that yes, the damn thing did probably look just like the one his dad had driven back in 1940.

"The only smart thing that the Sprint car drivers have ever done is put these things on," Vukovich says as he pounds on the roll-cage that is currently serving as his seat of judgement. Billy hops down and walks off without another word. It's seldom that he says good bye. He just leaves. You're supposed to sit there and think about his last statement.

Down pit row Vukovich struts, up to another California Kid, Bruce Walkup. You'd never know it by looking or talking to him, but Bruce is a grizzled veteran of Sprint car racing. He's been blasting around the toughest half-mile tracks in the country for a decade now, but he's still

Gary Bettenhausen and Billy Vukovich while away the time before Gary readies for the feature event. They're the best of friends.

Mr. Suede Shoe, the young fella they always ask to be master of ceremonies at all the Midwest auto racing functions because no one else in racing can match his keen-witted personality. Bruce has just come in from qualifying his Sprint car third fastest and doesn't have to worry about running in the 500. Bruce doesn't have a ride for the 500, he hasn't had one in a few years now, but it doesn't bother him outwardly.

He says that automobile racing is a great hobby for him. A few years ago he was one of California's babies who was really going to make it big at Indianapolis. Bruce and Indy veteran Mike Mosley both used to blow their doors off back at California's Ascot Park in their quest for recognition. Now, Mosley says he wouldn't drive a Sprint car unless he absolutely had to, and Bruce considers it fun. Bruce made it to the Speedway all right, even made the show in good shape. This writer has always wondered exactly why he wasn't chosen as a regular along the Championship Trail with his contemporaries. No matter now though, Bruce has a Chevrolet dealership and seems to be enjoying himself.

"Hey Tommy," Walkup says to Tommy Astone, who is Vukovich's former brother-in-law and near twin in actions, words, and complete personality. The similarities are so close they're frightening. They walk, talk and act the same. Astone is bumping his way up the racing ladder just as Vukovich and Bettenhausen did a few years back. Tommy has a good Sprint car ride tonight but it didn't look like the car was handling very well during hot-laps.

Would you buy a used car from this man? Whether racing or just idling around the pits, Bruce Walkup is full of enthusiasm.

Walkup and Vukovich are sitting on the guard rail and Walkup asks Astone seriously,

"Tommy, do you want to go to the big race track in the sky?"

Vukovich falls forward in a thunderous roar of laughter. He looks up and keeps laughing. Astone has to wait until one of his heroes stops laughing at him before he can answer.

"Do you want to go to the big race track in the sky?" Vukovich says out loud and laughs some more. Astone just stands there with his head down. Walkup is waiting for an answer.

"No, I don't." Tommy says like a little boy who's just been caught doing something wrong.

"Then just why in the hell are you running that god-aw-ful tire on the back of you lil racer, Tommy?" Walkup asks in his best fatherly tone.

That got Vukovich's attention. Without letting 'Stone (as he's known in the pits) say a word, Vukovich demands an explanation from Walkup. Bruce complies and tells Vuky what the tire will do to the car's handling and how it should be coped with.

"You wait here," he tells Astone and marches, up back toward Bettenhausen, Gary'll know. Gary'll know precisely what that "drag race" tire is supposed to do. All kinds of guys have been walking up to Gary these past ten minutes and asking him advice. The race track looks a little slick and most of 'em are wondering how to cope with the situation. What would Bettenhausen do? Gary explains that the car Astone is driving has extremely good brakes and maybe Tommy isn't used to them and tells Billy how the car will react with the drag tire on it. No jokes, no wisecracks. Vukovich the interrogator is like the old sergeant commanding some answers and his witness is telling him everything he wants to know. Vuky got it straight. Again he

doesn't say good-by, thanks, see ya later or anything. He leaves and stalks Astone's car owner, Paul Leffler. He doesn't say hello, how-are-you, how ya been. He simply starts explaining what Bettenhausen said. Leffler agrees. He says that if that's what Gary says it must be right. He'll tell Astone. No he won't, Vuky tells him. Vuky says he'll tell him himself. . . .sort of one driver to another. Besides, Tommy's liable to get upset. . . .he'd have more confidence in Vukovich.

Vuky takes Astone aside for a few minutes and relates the situation to him. Vukovich has been there before. He knows what it's like trying to impress a car owner. A Championship car owner, so you can get to the Speedway some day and not have to worry about making enough money just racing Sprint cars.

" 'Do you want to go to the big race track in the sky?" Vukovich says."

The Hoosier Sprints is a good place to impress a champ car owner: or maybe a championship mechanic, or a sponsor, lots of em show up. It is also a good place to get yourself in trouble plenty. Sprint cars don't normally run on a one mile race track and the extra length, as compared to most half-miles, can strain both drivers and their cars. When you crash on the mile, you and everyone else usually remember it for a long time to come. Some drivers say that the rookie Sprint drivers shouldn't be allowed on the mile. You can bust your butt awfully easy out there.

Astone listens to Vukovich's advice and promptly qualifies the Leffler car in tenth position. Not bad.

Qualifying finally ends and they call for the semi-feature, a 15 lap race that will allow the first 8 finishers a starting position in the twin features. Sheldon Kinser wins the race and the notorious Jan "The Preacher" Opperman comes in second. A young Englishman touring U.S. race tracks comments,

"I thought that Jan was going to lap the entire field. He only came in second. From what I've read of him I was sort of expecting him to pass them all like a great flying gladiator."

A great flying what? we asked. He had a heavy accent and we thought he said a great flying glad he's here. Anyway, I said that I was glad Opperman was here too because he's really a good Sprint driver. The Englishman was an amiable sort of chap although he was visibly disappointed that the reknown Opperman didn't lap the field. I guess he didn't know it's a damn rare case that one Sprint car gets much further ahead than a car length from its nearest competitor.

There's a mix-up on the last lap coming out of the fourth turn and Larry Rice's position is questionable. He's been inching his way through the pack all race long and it appeared as though he had qualified for a feature position. Rice comes up to the judge's stand and very quietly states his case. He says just enough and doesn't get excited. Everybody likes Rice and they've even tagged him with the ultimate compliment, a nickname of Rice-A-Roni. Used to be he was a young schoolteacher but he decided to change his driving style from that of a conservative to potential winner and now he's a full-time racer. His name comes up a lot when they talk about the guys "who oughta have a shot at the Speedway." Without telling him that he's right or wrong, the judges simply read him the the feature line-up. He's in.

They finally call the cars for the feature line-up and crews are all checking fuel level. It's possible to run out of fuel at the Hoosier Sprints if they have too many pace laps. Nobody likes that. This ain't the 500. You don't run out of fuel in a Sprint race: You don't worry about things like that.

The first six qualifiers are inverted for the start. Dana Carter, Pancho's younger brother is on the pole. Hot damn, couldn't be in a better place on a better night. They'll at least know that there's another Carter around for a little while. Dana is clawing for a champ ride too. Next to him in the front row is Johnny Parsons, his half-brother and by his own admission one of the photographer's favorites. J.P. can usually be counted on to do something out of the ordinary when he races a Sprint car.

Now, Parsons has an Indy ride. Going pretty well too. He's been back in the Midwest for nine years and no one thought he'd survive his first seven. He started his career driving Sprints in the late Sixties and did his level best to either make a good showing or annihilate himself. He came perilously close to the latter on several occasions. John doesn't race Sprinters too much nowadays, but he likes the Fairgrounds mile and has done well there.

His dad, Johnnie, the 1950 Indianapolis 500 winner is justifiably proud of his boy's starting position and talks to him just before the start of the race.

"He knows how to get around this place ok," the senior Parsons says.

The race gets underway without incident but just after a few laps are completed the red flag is being waved: stop immediately. Sleepy Tripp, Jackie Howerton, Bob Harkey, and Jack Hewitt were involved in an accident between the third and fourth turn. Tripp and Howerton flipped and tore their machinery to pieces. Only five laps had been completed.

Last year Sleepy Tripp was a new breath on the Midget circuit. He made a shambles out of the competition and won the division's championship going away. He knew that with another successful year he'd be in line for a champ ride pretty soon. He thought he'd try the Sprint cars and further his career even more rapidly.

Jackie Howerton ought to be doing Arrow shirt ads. Or even toothpaste. He's a little guy who's clothes fit perfectly, manicured. He used to be a hero back in Oklahoma against the local competition and yearned for a spot in the big-time. He's been running Sprint cars on the USAC circuit for five or six years now, even works for famed mechanic George Bignotti as a champ car builder and has had a hint that he just might get a shot at one of the team cars one of these days if he keeps his nose clean. Howerton and Tripp were just nearly killed but they'll both probably be back for next year's Hoosier Sprints.

Harkey is an old man when compared to a youngster like Tripp. It's probably been a good five years or so since he's even taken a ride in a Sprint car, but he couldn't pass up the opportunity. As usual, for these past few years now, someone gave him an old Indy car and a couple laps practice and told him to try his best to qualify. And Harkey has again complied without complaint. He put 'er in the show. He never has received enough credit for his accomplishments. It might be nice to win a Sprint program too, he might have thought. Bob Harkey has spent a lot of

Young Dana Carter, left, qualified second for the Hoosier Sprint race, a notch in his belt. Right, Vukovich judges the situation.

time flying and jumping out of airplanes in his day. He's 46 years old and can still make a Sprint car do what it's supposed to.

Nobody really knows who Jack Hewitt is, he hasn't made his mark in USAC style racing yet, so he's just another number flogging around back there somewhere. Then somebody says that he's the guy who just came from 19th to fifth in the semi-feature. With that kind of activity, they say he just might make a race car driver.

Bettenhausen stops on the front straight and Willie Davis looks the car over. Gary doesn't bother to pull the mask down anymore, too hard to get back up with just one hand. Gary tells a crew member to put some cold water on the fuel pump. Always thinking. The thing could have a hard time re-starting, from a vapor lock, if you don't cool it down. He waits. Then he looks up at Willie and says, "Guess that Sleepy's been reading his press releases too much."

Davis comes back with his patented laugh that goes, "Ha! (long pause) Ha! (second long pause) Ha! Three ha's and that's Willie's laugh. You can't miss it.

The race resumes for another ten laps when the red is shown again. Jack Hewitt managed to re-start after the tangle but is now flipping wildly in the third turn. You try to count 'em. One, two three . . . . . Jesus, he's never going to stop. Seven or eight flips at least. He lands on all four wheels. His bell has been rung. They'll have no trouble remembering Hewitt's name for the next couple days.

This time Gary comes in and gets out of the car as do many others. Brother Merle walks up and can see that Gary is reaching for his goggles with his one good hand. Merle reaches out with his left arm, his only arm, and grabs one side of the goggles. Gary reaches up with his right arm and grabs the other. In unison they stretch the goggles away from the helmet and upward. It was a smooth operation.

Merle Bettenhausen ran in the Hoosier Sprints three years ago with one arm also. The year before he'd had his right arm cut off in a championship car race at Michigan.

[148]

After putting on a fine driving performance earlier, Jack Hewitt suffered the above mishap in the feature. He wasn't injured.

Before that, when he too was looking for a champ ride he used to say, "I'd give my right arm for a shot in one of those things." He recuperated from the horrendous crash and became a better race car driver with one arm than he was with two. Now, Gary tells him that he understands what Merle was talking about when Merle was driving with one arm. It teaches you how to drive a race car smoothly, Merle would say. Gary didn't used to be smooth. He'd make the damn car go to the front even if he had to carry it. Then Gary crashed at Syracuse and Merle retired on the spot. At the time he had been running second in the Midget point standings, better than ever before. At his last Hoosier Sprint race everyone told him he looked good. Merle too wanted to win on the mile.

Pancho Carter leads the race on the restart and Gary is right behind, only a few feet away. The crowd loves it. On the 32nd lap Gary slides around Pancho and holds the lead for eight laps. Carter might have seen red, Gary's tires might have been giving him a little trouble. Neither one of them were worried about pit stops like at the 500, this is a Sprint car race, good old flat-out racin'. No excuses, just stand on the gas pedal. Pancho won and Gary was second.

When he came in the pits after the first race Gary asked who was third and Willie told him that it was Larry Dickson, Gary smiled. He'd beaten Dickson. His arch rival, Dickson is an absolute animal in a Sprint car Gary had said before. Back in the old days, from 1968 through 1971 they swapped the first and second place finishes in the division back and forth twice each. All the racing writers

started calling the USAC Sprint car division the "Larry &Gary Show".

Dickson was back at the Hoosier Sprints after a layoff. Everyone thought he was washed up as a Sprint driver two years ago and he went back to the outlaw tracks. He was 38 years old, had made the Speedway five times, but never starred as a championship driver. Some said he didn't like those rear engine cars. But boy could he drive a Sprinter. Too bad that he was over the hill. Those old Larry and Gary duels were memorable.

Dickson fed his ego enough to last a long time when he came back to USAC in 1975 and won the Sprint car title. He's sure he could do it again in '76 and needed the points at the Hoosier Sprints. He had just tried to make the 500 with Willie Davis as his chief mechanic, but they were relegated to marginal equipment and missed the program. He would have been running at the Fairgrounds even if he had made the 500.

Gary knows that Dickson will be close by for the second race and likes the idea of beating him although he doesn't say so. Anytime you beat Dickson fair and square you've driven a good race.

Pancho Carter is long gone in the second 50 lapper. He's going to win by half a mile. Then Johnny Parsons gives the photographers what they came for and spins on the 39th lap. Pancho nails him as he has nowhere to go. Gary inherits the lead and Dickson closes in on his old rival. The announcer is spewing something about "Larry and Gary!" as they run side by side through the turns. The fans are a mass of motion: you can see arms waving and bodies twisting. There's a lot more cars on the race track than Bettenhausen's and Dickson's, but right now you couldn't prove it by anyone in the pits or grandstand. Only three laps to go, the two journeymen fight for supremacy entering the first turn and Bettenhausen spins.

The starter waves the checker and red flag at the same time as the incident is taking place. Gary had it won for sure. Dickson nailed him. No. Bettenhausen just drove it in too deep and spun himself out of contention. Who knows? Gary comes in at the same time Dickson reaches the stage on the front chute where they award the trophies and arrives in time to hear the crowd boo Dickson. It is not a short booing session. It is a very long booing session that goes on and on. The announcer is drowned out. He stops talking for a moment. Bettenhausen complains to Willie that Dickson flat ran into him. He curses and a crowd forms around his pit. They are still booing. There is a possibility

The two men above don't drive race cars, but are responsible for staging some of the Midwest's best Sprint races. Don Smith, left, is Director of Racing at the Fairgrounds and Bill Hill is his PR man.

[149]

Seasoned Sprint car racing fans like nothing better than to see Gary Bettenhausen and Larry Dickson dueling for first.

that they could get violent, start throwing something maybe.

Finally announcer Bob Forbes says, "What do you think Larry, tell us what happened down there?"

"We never touched," the black-haired Dickson says, "What am I supposed to do, give him the race and forget about it?" he continues. Dickson used to have a whole lot of gray hair, and it's easy to understand why.

Bettenhausen is still cursing Dickson to no one in particular, but by this time has drawn a crowd of about 40 onlookers. Suddenly he jumps up from the cooler he has been sitting on and starts toward the stage.

"Bet he's gonna punch his lights out," someone in the crowd says.

The stage isn't even a hundred feet away from Gary's pit, but he looks like a vigilante leader with the crowd behind him. He jumps up on the stage, eyes squinted and jaw set tight. Then he turns around and flashes a full grin as the entire stadium cheers. He moves up next to Dickson and gives the fans a wave as Forbes carefully moves the microphone between the duo and says,

"What. . . .What do you think Gary?"

"I think this is just like old times. The Larry and Gary show. It was a helluva race."

Gary smiles again and says, "I think this is just like old times. The Larry and Gary show. It was a helluva race."

Dickson removes the winner's garland from around his own neck and places it around Gary's and the crowd roars again. Gary fumbles with his beer and tries to lift off the ring. He's smiling wider than ever, but can't lift the ring with just one hand that's already occupied. His other arm dangles. Dickson glances at the beer, and relieves Gary's hand of the burden. Bettenhausen lifts off the ring and places it around Forbes' neck. Everybody's happy.

Dickson, Bettenhausen and announcer Bob Forbes are all smiles in this photo. Moments before, however, the crowd was booing Dickson.

DENNIS TORRES
RACING PHOTOGRAPHY

For over a decade, racing teams, companies and advertisers have utilized Dennis Torres racing photos to show their involvement in the sport.

We annually travel nation-wide on a full time basis following the most professional racing circuits in the United States.

If your company, product or team requires color or black and white prints of your past, present or future activities in auto racing, we'll be happy to quote on your particular needs.

Dennis R. Torres
3501 Beeler Ave.
Indianapolis, IN 46224
(317) 297-0857

Ralph Ligouri

When They Write The Book About
All The World's Race Car Drivers,
They Can't Leave Out His Name

by Jerry Miller

Ralph Liguori is still the oldest rookie in the world.

Another month on the Gasoline Alley beat and $11,000 in hard cash could do nothing to alter that fact. Liguori, who began chasing his Indy dream back in 1959, was left behind again when the 1976 version of the world's biggest auto race rolled away from the starting line.

It wasn't for lack of trying. As anyone familiar with Liguori knows, he's no quitter. Otherwise, he could never have become Indy's most valiant failure since Ralph DePalma tried to push his disabled car across the finish line in 1912.

And he wouldn't be known as "Ralphie the Racer," either. The determination of the swarthy curmudgeon from the dirt tracks to make it at Indy, in the face of years of near misses, crashes, and blowups, earned him that affectionate nickname.

For awhile, it seemed it would all pay off in '76. Liguori, it turned out, was not the only one who was tiring of his being left out at the 500 speedway. In September of '75, ads started appearing in the racing papers, headlined "Let's Give Automobile Racing Back To The Racers!"

Beneath the headline was a photo of Liguori and a short explanation of how advertising dollars from large corporations had pushed the small independents out of modern auto racing. That was followed by another bold headline: "Now You Can Beat The System With Ralphie The Racer."

The ads concluded with a plea for donations from racing fans across the country, the purpose of which was to

Ralph Ligouri, right, along with fellow veteran Jim McElreath in front of a Speedway garage. McElreath has been a regular at Indianapolis for years, and Ralph is still hoping.

Dick

[152]

Back in '59 the Speedway had Roadsters, Mobil Oil. . . and Ligouri.

He made the transition to rear engine cars. Still, luck was bad.

put Ralph Liguori in a good car for the 1976 Indianapolis 500.

The ads were the brainchild of Bill Goldwasser, a 53-year-old aluminum distributor and admitted racing nut from Minneapolis. The idea jelled after Goldwasser discovered that another Minneapolis businessman he'd known for years, Frank Liguori, was the younger brother of "Ralphie the Racer."

Together, the two businessmen decided to do something about Ralph's status as the longest-standing rookie at Indy. "We knew that Ralph might hang up his spikes after this year, so we decided to do what we could to give him one last shot at Indianapolis," Goldwasser explained.

What they did was form the Back The Racers Association and set out on the fund-raising circuit. Accepting contributions of from $20 up, they tried to collect $40,000, which could then be taken to an Indy car owner and offered as sponsorship money. The only condition: Ralph Liguori would drive the car.

"It's been absolutely amazing," Goldwasser said in February. "People have contributed from one end of the country to the other. We have one guy down in North Carolina who sends us a dollar a week. I think he's up to seven dollars now. I know we said it would take twenty dollars to get your name on the car, but that guy's name is going to be there because he just has to be a real race fan."

That kind of response sparked great optimism from Goldwasser, who knew all he would have when he went to Indy was a certified check and a 49-year-old rookie. "It's looking pretty

In 1965 Ralph flipped his Demler Spl. coming out of the third turn but was ok.

good now," he said in February. "We're already getting inquiries from car owners.

"Now, we know we're not big-shots and may not be able to get with one of the big teams, like Pat Patrick's, or A. J. Watson's, or Roger Penske's. But there are 27 or 28 other cars in that race, and most of them could use this kind of sponsorship money. We just want a competitive car and a competitive crew."

The enthusiasm was not restricted to Goldwasser. Ralphie the Racer was starting to sound like a 49-year old war horse who thought he was a yearling. "Hey, this could be a whole new career for me," said Ralph, chuckling

at the prospects for the coming May. "Who knows, maybe I could run Indianapolis two or three more times after this year."

Such over-enthusiasm could be forgiven in a man who had pretty much resigned himself to going back to Tampa in the fall to settle down with his wife and family, turn 50 gracefully, teach his sons the tricks of racing (two of his four sons already race motorcycles professionally), run his trailer court, and occasionally raise hell with the city council over the water rates.

"To tell the truth, I had flat given up on going to Indianapolis," he admitted. "I figured I'd just run a few more sprint cars and dirt track races

The only veteran Indy chauffeur here is Steve Krisiloff, right. Tommy Astone is looking for his first chance, and so is Ralph.

this year and then quit. So, this came like a shot out of the blue."

He could also be forgiven for repeating what he has always said: If he could just make the race, he had as good a shot at winning it as a lot of people. "I'm going to take it one step at a time, but, sure, I think I can win it," he asserted before heading for Indy. "Anybody who gets in a race car should think he can win or he doesn't have any business in the car. You race to win, don't you?

"Maybe my chances are only a hundred to one, or a thousand to one, but I'm still going to try to win."

That approach to racing is how they came to call him "Ralphie the Racer" in the first place. After 27 years in the sprints, midgets, stocks, champ cars, and just about anything else with four wheels, Liguori was for it with the youthful abandon of a man half his age.

"Age isn't something on a calendar," Ralph commented, a boyish smile flashing across his dark face. "It's how you think and feel when you get up in the morning, and I feel young every morning."

"I'm definitely the oldest rookie at Indianapolis and will be until I make the race, but things like that don't bother me. I think I've proved that I'm not too old by racing against guys who aren't any older than my own sons."

But, before he could run at Indy,

he first had to walk, from one garage to the other, in search of someone who would put wheels under his own self-confidence. The going was tough in the first week of practice at Indy, as it had been for Liguori most of the 17 previous Mays, and he was still a pedestrain when the first weekend of time trials came along.

"I'm in a position where there are actually no cars available right now," he said, as he made his Gasoline Alley rounds. "But there are three or four backup cars I could possibly get in, once they get their first cars into the race this weekend.

"By next Monday, I hope to be out there running. After this weekend, somebody is going to need a little money and a lot of publicity, which is where I come in."

But nothing seemed to work out according to Liguori's plan. First, Eddie Miller destroyed one of the Thermo-King cars, planting some seeds of doubt about the idea of drivers "buying" their Indy rides. Then, some people who might have had reserve cars to offer up had their own problems in the first weekend of 500 qualifications.

Wednesday of the second week of practice was Liguori's deadline, since it was the last day he could go through his umpteenth rookie test. The day came and went, and it was official for the 18th time—Ralph Liguori wasn't going to lose his rookie

stripes at Indy.

Liguori, naturally, was crestfallen. He had been rejected by the race he wanted desperately to make at least once before he turned in his helmet. He had seen people turn down the $11,000 contributed by his loyal fans.

He had seen at least one car he had a shot at, the third in the A.J. Watson stable, held back because one team car qualified slower than expected and might (would) be bumped and the other didn't even get qualified on the first weekend.

All he could do was promise to send back everybody's money, which Goldwasser confirmed the organization would do, and try to keep his tireless hopes from collapsing.

"I want to run here, but I don't think there's much of a chance anymore," he said, after his time had run out for '76. "I'm afraid there is something of a stigmatism attached to me which I can't get rid of. I'm really disappointed."

Still, Liguori held out at least the thinnest whisper of that old unconquerable determination when asked if the saga of his Indy yearnings was now a closed book. "I'm not a quitter," he said, "but the only way I could possibly come back here is to have a ride going in or as a spectator."

When you are Ralphie the Racer and have held onto such things for 18 long years, your dreams die hard.

[154]

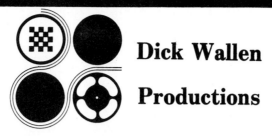

HERB PORTER

One Man Who Has Dedicated His Life To Speedway Racing

Ever hear the phrase, "Three turning and one burning?"

If you haven't, it means you're not an oldtime airplane buff, or you didn't see the movie, "The High and The Mighty." It also means you've never spent much time around Herb Porter. The phrase has a double meaning for Porter, now a scowling, tall fixture of the Indianapolis 500.

He first heard it back in World War II, when it was his job to keep all the aircraft engines turning instead of burning. Now it could as easily apply to his work as the man who tries to see to it that all four cylinders of a turbocharged Offenhauser racing engine keep turning.

It has been a long road from Parsons, Kansas, to Gasoline Alley. Along the way, Porter has been an inventive kid running an electric train in a house with no electricity, a Midget racing driver, a wartime guinea pig, a prime mover in the development of the Offy, and the man they've come to call "the father of the turbocharger."

The first recorded demonstration of Herb Porter's ingenuity probably was when, as a youngster, he figured out how to tap a neighbor's power lines to run the train he'd received for Christmas. It was a short jump from there to motorcycles, which he souped up and entertained himself by tearing up countless Kansas farm fields.

Once he became bored with motorcycles and saw that the wind-swept and Depression-starved flatlands of Kansas held out little for a mechanically inclined youth, Porter turned his eyes toward the skies.

Herb and five of his friends pooled their resources and formed something called "The Gypsy Flying Circus." In the best traditions of Waldo Pepper, the group barnstormed the Midwest, performing aerial stunts and giving the farm folks a taste of flying among the clouds--all for a fee, of course.

"The most memorable incident with the flying circus is the one that ended it, Herb recalls. "One of my partners was flying the plane across country and ran out of gas and tore the hell out of the plane when he crashed. He wasn't hurt himself but, with the Depression on, we had no money to fix it, so that ended the circus."

When the flying act came to a crashing halt, Porter headed West. He arrived in California just in time to get in on the beginnings of the Midget racing boom.

"I was looking for a way to make a dollar during the Depression, and auto racing looked like a good way to make money while doing something I liked," says Herb.

He hired on with Ronnie Householder, whose legendary Midget career was just getting into high gear. Porter maintained the cars in the Householder stable and, before long, was driving one of them himself.

The schedule was hectic, obviously, for the aspiring

Herb Porter driving a midget at San Diego's Balboa Stadium just 30 days before leaving to sign up with the Royal Canadian Air Force.

race driver/mechanic, with Midget races to go to--and prepare for--six or seven nights a week. But Porter and Householder still found time to participate in one of the more peculiar speed runs of the century.

That was the time the two auto racers were talked into assisting an enthusiastic Frenchman who wanted to set a new land speed record for bicycles. For their part, Porter and Householder built an air deflector, which they mounted to the rear of one of their Midgets.

Then, when the American Automobile Association

Herb at the wheel of a midget in the early forties.

set up a measured mile along the highway outside of Bakersfield, Cal., Householder drove along in front of the pedaling Frenchman, breaking the wind and "pulling" him along until he reached a record speed of 108 miles per hour. That record for bicycles stood for nearly 35 years.

The racing game came to a sudden halt for Porter, as it did for most Americans, when war was declared in 1941. Herb was looking to the skies again and had almost decided to join the Royal Canadian Air Force when he was notified that Uncle Sam wanted him more.

His aeronautic talents weren't wasted in the Army. He went through aircraft engine school and was eventually assigned to a Mobile Training unit as an engine trouble-shooter. He was put to work on the familiar B-29 and P-47 aircraft and, at Uncle Sam's expense, laid some of the groundowrk for his future career in automobile racing.

The B-29, you see, was equipped with something

Porter skids to a stop after losing the same wheel for the third time on the same night at Balboa Stadium to end a frustrating night.

called a turbocharger, a device that was designed to increase the horsepower of the aircraft engine. Unlike its predecessor, the supercharger, which was driven mechanically by the engine, the turbocharger was driven by the exhaust gases from the engine, which of course, meant it did not rob any initial power from the powerplant like the supercharger.

That information would come in handy when Porter returned to the racing wars. In the meantime, there was still the real war to deal with. And that meant Iwo Jima and one of the least attractive jobs a man could get.

Porter was put in charge of the "test flight" brigade, which meant he not only had to repair crippled aircraft, but he had to go up in them with the pilot to make sure the plane could at least limp back to Guam for more permanent repairs. Now that was a bad job.

"Listen," Herb exclaims, with a smile, "give me a race car engine to troubleshoot anytime. At least if it blows up, I don't blow up with it!"

Fortunately, none of them ever blew up Herb Porter. When the war ended, Porter flirted with the idea of a career as an Army officer, then toyed with the notion of becoming a commercial pilot. Finally, however, he came back to his first love, racing.

"When I first got out of the service, I applied for a job with TWA with the thought of being a flight engineer or becoming a pilot, but the pay was so low then for those jobs that I reconsidered," Porter advises.

"Ronnie Householder had just gotten out of the service, too, and we talked it over and, after spending the last five or six years in the service, we really weren't ready to rush into anything. We wanted to do something we were good at and something we could make money at.

"Auto racing seemed to be the answer and, besides being good at it and making more money than with the airlines, I knew by then that I loved racing."

Herb initially resumed double duty as racing driver and racing mechanic. But the driving aspect soon lost its appeal for the Kansan who'd always been partial to working

with wrenches in his hands rather than a steering wheel.

"I could be competitive driving," he recollects, "but I realized it would mean more to me to have a car I had mechaniched win Indy than to have one I drove run sixth or seventh, which is what I thought I'd be capable of running.

"The years I spent in the service working on engines had switched my desires and now what I wanted most was to make those machines run well."

Porter went to work with another auto racing pioneer, Stu Hilborn, whose name would become synonymous with racing fuel injection systems. The two began experimenting with superchargers on racing engines, successfully incorporating a blower on a 110-inch Offy.

Installed on a Midget that had been "stretched" into a Sprint car, the supercharged Offy held its own against the standard 220-inch Offys in the other Sprinters. Leroy Warriner, in fact, set a new world's record for a half-mile track at Salem, Ind. in the blue No. 22, which was known as the Peterkin Special.

The first endeavor justified Porter's faith in supercharging as viable alternative in racing. "In racing, you're always looking for power and, in those days, the supercharger looked like the way to go if you wanted to win," Herb says. "My interest in supercharging goes back to those days after the war when I was searching for more power in my engines."

The next project for Porter and Hilborn was an Indianapolis car. Equipped with Herb's supercharger and Stu's fuel injection, the familiar Miracle Power Special was qualified by Andy Linden for the middle of the front row in the 1952 Indy 500. The car lasted only two laps before a sump pump failed, but the pioneering pair knew they were headed in the right direction.

"There were a lot of bugs in the supercharger back then, but we knew we were on the right track," says Herb. "The big drawback of the gear-driven supercharger was that it took power from the engine to run the blower, which, in effect, meant you paid a price for the increase in power."

While he wrestled with that problem, Porter became involved in another significant racing enterprise. In 1952, Chrysler decided to go racing, and they came to Herb for help in developing their 331-inch hemi V-8 into a competitive racing powerplant.

Some 5,000 miles were logged in at the Indianapolis Motor Speedway that summer and, by the time Porter had worked out the bugs, driver George Conner had the test car lapping at 142 miles per hour, three mph faster than the existing record. That should have promised big things for the project the following May.

But, over the winter, the AAA Board of Directors cut back the maximum displacement allowable for such engines from 335 inches to 274. Porter and the Chrysler engineers complied, but the cutback in horsepower was just too great. Connor managed only 135 mph in the car in May and missed the 1953 Indianapolis race.

The Chrysler project was dead, but Porter's quest for

A frenchman set the land speed record for bicycles in 1940 with the help of Ronnie Householder and Porter.

Jimmy Daywalt driving Herb's stretched midget-sprinter, the blue number 22 Peterkin Special, powered by a 110 cubic inch supercharged midget Offy, is shown at Salem, Indiana passing Troy Ruttman and his famous 220 cubic inch Offy powered Black Deuce sprinter. Daywalt lead until near the finish but lost his position moments before crossing the finish line.

a better racing engine wasn't. He became chief mechanic for the Indy cars owned by Roger Wolcott and turned his attention back to the supercharger.

"At that time, you could count on one hand the people who believed in the supercharger and thought it would work," he recalls. "With no one believing in my project, I got very little help, no money other than my own and some of Hilborn's to work with and little encouragement from my fellow racers.

"Roger Wolcott also helped by letting me use his cars to test it on. Drivers who drove the car when the supercharger was working also believed. Paul Russo was one of those drivers and the one who believed the most. He drove it when it was running good and got very excited and knew someday it would be the way to fly."

Porter's midget was on rollers as he and Clark Gable posed for this picture during the making of the racing movie, "To Please a Lady".

The driver who finally put the supercharged car into the winner's circle, of course, was Rodger Ward. "He did the best job for us," notes Porter. "We won races with Ward. As I recall, some of the ones we won were Trenton (N.J.), Springfield (Ill.), and we won Milwaukee (Wis.) two or three times with Ward."

The death of Wolcott in 1959, however, cut short the success of the team. Porter moved on to form a new team in 1960 with a car owner and driver who remains one of his closest and dearest friends, J.E. Rose, better known to speedway fans as "Ebb".

Known as Racing Associates, the team put competitive cars under such drivers as Paul Goldsmith, Don Davis, Roger McCluskey, Bob Veith, and Lloyd Ruby during the early 1960's. It also started something of a revolution in the world of Championship Dirt cars and Sprinters.

Porter brought out a Chevrolet-powered dirt car for the 1962 season and, with Davis driving, turned heads at dirt and paved tracks alike. With the car still unpainted and showing rust in places, Davis set down the Offy-powered roadsters at Trenton, putting a new qualifying record on the books.

Then, at Milwaukee, the car went straight from seventh to first in the first 16 laps, passing the roadsters of A.J. Foyt and Don Branson in one fell swoop of the first turn. Davis later blew a tire and, after one of the more frantic pit stops in Milwaukee history, came back to finish eighth.

That started a lot of people thinking about switching to Chevy power, which today is accepted as the way to go in Sprint cars and most Championship Dirt cars.

"Rocky Phillips did most of the chassis work on that car, and I tried to build the Chevy engine to run like I thought it should run," Porter reports. "We built our own parts here and there for it and made the car and engine run like we thought it should. We worked out of Traco's shop in California.

"When the car did so well at Milwaukee, people came up and wanted me to build a Chevy for their cars. I wanted to race and not go into the engine building business, so I sent them to Traco to get their engines built. As I recall, Traco got orders for six or seven Chevy engines right after Milwaukee.

"I still have a sore spot in my heart when I think of that car," Herb goes on. "It was a car that should have won and never did. It always ran up front and then Lady Luck always stepped in, like shredding a tire at Milwaukee when it was leading.

"At Phoenix that year, Ruby was driving the car and

Johnny Rutherford leads the field at Sacramento in 1964 in the same Chevy powered Sprint car Donnie Davis beat the Offys with at Milwaukee.

it really looked like he was coming up strong and ready to pass the leaders, when Elmer George got upside-down in his car and they called the race and stopped it with Ruby running third. That car was a real winner that never won."

It didn't win in the USAC Board meetings, either. Over the next winter, the Board trimmed the maximum on stock block engines from 335 inches to 305. Like he had with the Chrysler project, Herb Porter found one of his better ideas legislated out of existence.

"We did go ahead and cut it back to 305, but the smaller engine just didn't have enough power to run in front then and stay together," he says. "So, I just put it all down to more education as one must do when the rules rule you out."

It wasn't long before Porter came upon an innovation that no one could legislate away. This time, it was a driver, not an engine trick.

When Davis was killed in a racing crash, Porter and Rose were in the market for a new, hot, young driver. They came across a relatively unknown kid from Texas, whose father had crossed paths with Porter back in the days when they were flying barnstormers in the Midwest.

The young driver was Johnny Rutherford and it was under the wing of Herb Porter that he put in the apprenticeship that would eventually make him a two-time winner of the Indianapolis 500.

"I guess you could say I hired John on a hunch," Porter recalls, "I had never really watched him drive, but I had read about him and heard people talk about him.

"I could see then that he had a lot of talent. What I liked most about him is he had extremely quick reflexes.

He ran hard--sometimes, too hard!

"And he was a good student. He seemed to understand most of what I wanted him to learn. You can teach a guy how to do something, but first he has to have the talent to be able to do it. John had that talent in him to be a good driver."

The student remembers the teacher with equal clarity. "Herb gave me the best ride I had had up to that point," says Rutherford, "I drove his car at Springfield that year and sat in the front row right next to A.J. Foyt himself. It was quite a thrill.

"In my opinion," Johnny continues, "Herb is a very good teacher. He knows this business of auto racing and he knows how to teach it to others. I'm very glad I have been and can continue to be a student of his. He's almost like a race track father to me."

That was 1963 and the teacher-student relationship continued on a full-time basis until 1966. (It continues on a part-time basis even today.)

For 1966, Porter had his hands on something that was going to change the face of Indy-style racing. Harking back to his war days, he had found a way to put a turbocharger to work on a racing engine.

Working with Air Research Corp. in the early 1960's, Herb developed a turbocharger unit for the racing Offy. It was quite a shock to the racing community, especially to those drivers who first tasted the kick of power from the turbos.

Foyt was the first, testing the new engine in a roadster at Phoenix in the spring of '66. The first time the boost came on from the turbocharger, A.J. thought it had exploded. "Man, I think that engine blew up. Something sure went wrong," exclaimed Foyt, only to find that it was only the nature of this new beast called a turbocharger.

"Hell, I didn't know what happened to it, either," confides Porter. "It was the first time in a race car and when you are the first to do something there is no one to go ask for help, so we just rolled it out, took another look at it, and ran it again."

Undaunted, Porter took his experiment to Indianapolis. He had no driver, and the prospects of finding one for an old roadster with some new-fangled powerplant weren't exactly the greatest.

"When I got to the Speedway, Bobby Grim didn't have a ride and I asked him to drive," Herb relates. "I told him if later he got a better offer to take it.

"I can't say enough about Grim. He was really cool and an excellent driver to work with. He took everything as it went. He was an awful lot of help in getting the bugs worked out of the turbocharger.

"He'd go out and run it, something would happen, and we'd try and fix it, and then he'd give it a go again. He was offered better rides that month and I told him to take them, but he'd say, 'Hell, no, let's get this car in the race. I want to see this project go.'

"Before qualifying, we got the car up to 160 miles an hour and it tickled the hell out of all of us. On qualifying day, the car wasn't working quite right, so we only qualified at around 158. But that was still the fastest a roadster had ever gone."

The "Stagecoach"--as the roadster came to be known among the crew--never got to show its stuff in the race, being one of 11 cars wiped out in a first-lap crash on the Indy frontstretch. But people were at least aware that Herb Porter's turbocharger had potential.

And no one spoke more enthusiastically about it than Bobby Grim. "That thing was wild," Bobby still recalls. "It would cheep, twitter, bark, and then, blam, it would take off like crazy! It was really ragged then. When you took your foot off the throttle the boost dropped and when you put your foot back on the throttle you played a real guessing game as to when the boost would come in.

"The turbo was a lot more complicated then than it is now. The boost came nowhere near to coming in as smooth as it does now, but it was a real challenge and I loved it.!"

Perhaps most aware of the potentialities of a turbo-

Porter in his special chair during filming of the movie "Winning." Porter served as racing consultant for the movie.

charged engine were the people at Goodyear. They made that clear in 1967.

"That was when Goodyear asked me to take over the development of the turbocharged engines they wanted to use for tire tests," Porter notes. "They had three engines for tire testing and we got to run a lot of miles that wouldn't have been possible otherwise. We could run until something broke and then we'd fix it and make it stronger."

It was strong enough in 1968 to become a winner at Indianapolis. At a time when people were beginning to write off the Offy as a has-been, the turbocharged version of the reliable four-cylinder blunted the onslaught of the V-8 Ford racing mills that had started winning Indy in 1965.

Bobby Unser drove a turbocharged-Offy car into Victory Lane in 1968, and the next year all but three of the Indy starters had the turbos bolted into the engine compartment. Since then, turbocharging, whether on an Offy or Ford, has been the only way to get in on the glory of Indy.

Such was the success story of Herb Porter's idea, and it has given him more satisfaction than most men ever find in racing. "It was a big thrill for me to see the turbocharger come into its own," says Herb. "I was really pleased when Bobby Unser won for Jud Phillips with it in '68.

"Another personal satisfaction I got was when engines out of our shop sat in the front row for the "500" for four straight years, 1971 thru 1974. We had loaned those tire-test engines to people who had engine trouble at the last minute and needed an engine to qualify on.

"Peter Revson used our shop engines in 1971 and 1972, Mark Donohue in 1973, and Mike Hiss in 1974. Peter sitting on the pole in 1971 was really a big personal thrill for me. I got a lot of self-satisfaction that day.

"With our engines in front that many years, I felt they could compete with anyone," he adds. "We have helped these teams along now to such a point that, in the past two years, they have had few engine problems qualifying and we haven't needed to loan them our engines.

"Last year, we didn't need to bail anyone out. This makes me feel we have done our job in helping them and they have done a good job in using our help."

But, as Herb Porter himself says so often, "Development is something that never stops." Of late, the engine pioneer has worked with Drake Manufacturing Co. in the revising of the Offy powerplant.

The new Offy features a lower valve angle, redesigned combustion chambers, and revised intake and exhaust ports. Like any new engines, the early models had their share of bugs, but the new powerplant still sat on the pole at Indy in 1976 and was driven to victory by that same Johnny Rutherford who went to school with Mr. Porter a few years before.

And it won't stop there. Herb is already looking at the newest thing to come along lately, the turbocharged Cosworth. "It has all of the things in it it needs to be a good running engine," Porter observes. "It needs some more development work, which I intend to be a part of.

"The fact, however, that it can perform well on a race car has already been proven. There are some areas which still need work. You never know when you'll land on the right square.

"There are, of course, others besides myself working on it and I think, between us all, we'll get it running well. And then like everything else, you will have all kinds of people eager to claim it after the fact."

If one is going to delineate the contributions of Herb Porter to American racing, he can't overlook the crop of young mechanical wizards who have matriculated in the Porter shop. Names like Dave Laycock, Don Brown, and Davey Crockett are but a few of those who have served

Porter and the late Bruce McLaren talk racing in Gasoline Alley in May, 1970. Porter still is a valued engine consultant for the team.

Porter and Bobby Unser at the Speedway in 1976.

their apprenticeships at "Porter Tech," conveniently located in the garage at the northeast corner of Indy's Gasoline Alley.

His former students tell you this about Herb, the teacher: He's tough and he knows his business.

The first part is summed up on the unofficial motto of the Porter shop, which hangs on one wall: "Rule One: The Boss is always right. Rule Two: If the Boss is wrong, see Rule One."

Addressing himself to the other half of the Porter experience, Don Brown sums it up this way: "I worked for Herb around 15 years ago and his never-ending quest for knowledge rubbed off on me then and has become a part of my life."

Porter has also found time to do a few less-monumental things in his career, it should be noted. He has been technical consultant for two racing movies, "To Please A Lady" and "Winning."

He even made some mistakes along the way. "I made a lot of mistakes in my career and probably will continue to do so," he admits. "You can't try to be the first in doing something new and different without making mistakes along the way.

"If you're smart, you learn from all your mistakes. I tried to learn from most of mine and can't really single out any one certain one that stands out in my mind right now."

He even has found time to be either the worst hunter in the world or the best, depending upon who you talk to. Says Lloyd Ruby, "Herb has been my good friend for many years and he's far ahead of anyone around in his knowledge of turbocharged engines. But he sure can't do anything but talk when it comes to hunting.

"I have been hunting with him between Christmas and New Year's every year now for the past 12 years and he's killed a sum total of one antelope and one deer."

Ebb Rose is quick to come to his friend's defense, however. "Now that's not just so," contends this Texan. "Herb's a good hunter. Rube just likes to ride him. You should have seen the big black buck antelope Herb got, not to mention the big horned sheep he killed this year."

Through it all, the one thing Herb Porter, father of the turbocharger, has never done is sour on the sport of racing. "I feel the sport has really been good to me and, no, I don't feel bitterness about any of it," he says.

"Each experience, whether good or bad, I have benefited from by learning something from it. The sport has been my life for most of my life. It gave me an opportunity to earn a living doing something I like and that's what life is all about, isn't it?

"It hasn't been easy by any standards, but it has been rewarding."

Editor's Note: Our sincere thanks to Jan Cindric for the compilation of facts, quotes, etc. for the above article. Jan's husband, Carl, is an engine builder who works for Porter and she is reluctant to accept credit for her efforts but we couldn't have produced the work without her.

Bobby Grim in Porter's 1966 roadster.

Lloyd Ruby, Herb Porter and friends display the results of a hunting trip. How good a hunter Porter is depends on who is telling the story.

WALLY MESKOWSKI

If a race driver can be classified as a super-star of auto racing, his name probably has appeared on the side of a Wally Meskowski race car somewhere along the line.

Mechanic, car builder, machinist, and car owner, Meskowski has, through his nearly 40 years in racing, also been one of the sport's best talent scouts. The slightly-built, balding racing innovator has uncovered or developed some of the most famous race drivers who ever strapped themselves into a sprint car or Indy-car.

A quick glance at the list of nearly 100 drivers who have driven for Meskowski tells you such interesting things as this:

A total of nine different Indianapolis 500 winners have driven Meskowski cars at some time in their early careers.

The first five finishers in the 1976 Indy race were all former Meskowski

IMS

Johnny Rutherford and Wally Meskowski posed with their No. 1 sprinter at the Indianapolis Motor Speedway in 1966. Their teamwork had led to the championship in 1965.

drivers.

One-time Meskowski drivers have won 17 USAC national Indy-car championships (and 4 AAA).

Meskowski drivers have gone on to win eight USAC sprint titles, three dirt-championship crowns, and two midget championships.

Clearly, Wally Meskowski has had an extraordinary eye for spotting raw talent and helping polish it into championship form. There was the time in 1965, for example, when he hired a boyish young driver for the cockpit of his sprint car.

The young racer had only shown the rest of the world his penchant for crashing. But Meskowski saw something the rest of the world didn't. "Steve Stapp had fired him at Raceway Park and I hired him to drive my car," recalls Wally. "I thought he had some potential, and the first time he drove my car, at Eldora, he had the race won going away until a rear tire went flat."

The young, unproven driver was Johnny Rutherford, winner of two of the last three Indianapolis 500s. He went on to win the '65 sprint car championship in Meskowski's car to prove Wally knew what he was doing when he hired him.

"After we won the championship, Steve Stapp's father told him, 'Of all the dumb things you could do, you fire a guy who goes out and wins the

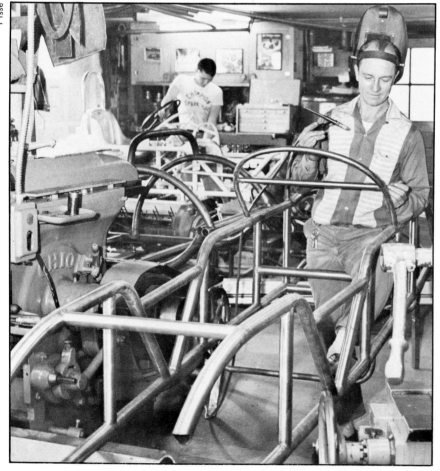

Fisse

Meskowski at work on the instrument panel support of A.J. Foyt's first Speedway ride.

championship!" Wally relates, with a good-natured laugh.

There are countless other stories of Meskowski's talent for uncovering diamonds in the racing rough. "That's about the same way I hired Mario Andretti, too," he says. "He had been crashing about every week or so. He was a nobody then, too, but he won the first two races he ran for me, in '66.

"The only scratch he ever put on my car was the last race he ran for me, at Manzanita, which he won. He just bent the rear bumper a little bit."

In some cases, Meskowski didn't even have to see a driver perform to come up with a spectacular find. Sometimes, he had only heard of his next driver and decided to take a chance, often with remarkable success.

Meskowski and Mario Andretti were hot in 1966. Here they collect the hardware at Cumberland, Maryland.

Wally sneaked in a quick nap in the cockpit of Bob Veith's mount during 1960 practice.

"I gave A.J. Foyt his first ride," Wally notes. "I didn't know the guy; I just hired him from what I had heard about him. He finished fourth at Salem in his first race for me.

"He also ran one of my dirt cars; we were running two of them at that time. I remember he bought a brand new Edsel to tow one of the cars, and it broke down the first time we went to a race."

Then there was the smiling, crew-cut youngster Meskowski hired "sight unseen" to drive for him at Langhorne. His name was Bobby Marshman.

"He came walking into the pits with his helmet bag and said, 'Hi,'" recalls Wally. "The car was looking real nice and shiny then and he looked at it and said, 'You mean you're gonna let me drive this thing. Boy, are you brave!'"

Marshman, of course, went on to drive for Meskowski and eventually became one of the top stars of American oval racing.

Meskowski's phenomenal good for-tune in hiring unknown drivers is demonstrated even further by his selection of Bobby Marvin after seeing him race a supermodified at a backwoods track and his choice of Scratch Daniels to drive his sprint car strictly on the basis of a telephone conversation with him.

Meskowski can even take credit for discovering the driving talents of actor Paul Newman, now known as P.L. Newman to road-racing aficionados. Wally was the first to spot Newman's ability when he drove Meskowski's Indy car for the movie "Winning" at the 500 track.

"Hey, that guy was good," Wally says. "He drove everyday; he'd do about 180 on the straightaways and coast through the corners.

"I remember Rodger Ward, who was the technical advisor for the film, kept telling me not to let him run it. But I told Rodger, 'Hell, the way he's going, I might just have to hire him to drive it all the time.'"

Unfortunately, not all of Meskowski's finds provided storybook endings. There was young Dick Atkins, who was well on his way to becoming a racing super-star when he was killed in a sprint car crash in Wally's car at Ascot.

"He was a natural," Wally relates. "He would have been a winner, for sure. Of course, he should have been a movie actor; he really was a good-looking kid."

Even his association with Johnny Rutherford ended in near-tragedy. It was Meskowski's car that Rutherford was driving in 1966 when he became the star, unwillingly, of the most publicized sprint car crash in history.

Life magazine carried a full-page picture of the number one sprinter sailing over the outer railing at Eldora, Johnny's arms straight up in the air like someone was holding a machine-gun on him. The crash broke both of Rutherford's arms and delayed his rise to racing super-stardom.

"I had two cars running that day; Mario was driving one and John the other," Wally recalls. "Mario was running sixth and John was fifth. I saw some of the guys run up high on the track, so I signaled John to move up on the race track.

"He went up high into the first turn, but he wasn't really ready to go up there and Mario dove underneath him and went by. I think that made him leary of the outside, so he went back down to the inside.

"When he came by the next time, he gave me the finger, in fact. That lap, coming off two, he hooked a rut and got hit in the eye with a rock, which is what sent him sailing out of there."

When Rutherford's injuries healed, he and Meskowski teamed up again,

[163]

but the magic was gone. "Close to the end of '66, after his arms had healed up, he was having trouble getting going again and kept finding fault with the car," Wally says. "I think I finally did fire him. But John and I always got along very well, and still do."

To underscore Wally's uncanny ability at picking drivers, he is hard-pressed to remember any driver who surprised him, either by making it in racing when Wally thought he wouldn't, or vice versa.

"The only thing I can remember is that I did hire a driver once and then fired him after one race," Wally reports. "That was Earl Motter. And I don't know of anybody I said wouldn't make it and then did."

There was at least one promising driver who got away, however. "I had a chance to hire Mike Mosley at one time," he recollects. "He asked me to drive the car at Altamont. In fact, I half-promised him he could. I told him we'd have to wait and see what A.J. was going to do, because A.J. had asked to drive it if his regular car broke down or something.

"Well, Mosley stayed in the pits all night. A.J.'s car broke down in hot laps, and Mike just kind of wandered off. I never did get to put him in the car."

Ironically, the spotting of raw driving talent has really been but a sideline for Meskowski, who has actually been one of the most successful car builders and mechanical innovators in oval-track racing. To his credit are such achievements as building the first cross-torsion bar sprint and dirt-championship cars, using heliarc welding on sprint and dirt cars for the first time, building dirt cars with such efficiency and reliability that 16 of them started in the 18-car Hoosier Hundred field one year, and preparing the first turbocharged Offy Indy-car to complete the 500.

Born in Cleveland, Ohio, Meskowski had no racing interests to speak of until the early '40s. He was working as a machinist at Cleveland Pneumatic Tool Co., building landing gears for military aircraft. At the end of the war, IMCA sprint car champion Deb Snyder happened to take a steering gear to Frank Spillar of Midwest Racing Equipment.

Spillar knew of a young machinist who he thought could do the work for Snyder, so he referred him to Wally Meskowski. That was how Wally's racing career got started.

In 1946, he went to work for Snyder and even once had a chance to drive one of Snyder's cars.

"He was getting ready to take two cars to the Florida State Fair and he asked me to drive one of them," Wally recalls. "I was thinking about it, but we had some kind of falling out and I ended up quitting.

"Later, Deb came over to my house and asked me to drive it again, but I said nope."

Meskowski went on to work on the midgets driven by Neal Carter, a star of the Midwest midget boom of the late '40s. Racing seven nights a week, the two-car team put in a lot of miles. But it paid off with victories and prize money.

"In '48, Neal Carter won 28 AAA features and Ralph Pratt won 56 in the other car," Wally says. "We made pretty good money, for back then. There were so many race cars and so many races that you could take your pick and run one of three or four places.

"We'd run seven nights a week, and I could make about $100 a night. I remember one year, at the end of the year, we had $120,000 in the bank, clear, for the car owner."

In 1949, Meskowski made his first trip to the big speedway in Indianapolis, as mechanic on the Lutes Truck Parts Special driven by Paul Russo. The car missed the race when the engine expired on Russo's final qualifying lap.

Over the following winter, he went to California to take a look at the various racing shops flourishing there. After seeing the operations of men like Luigi Lesovsky and Frank Kurtis, Meskowski decided he might try his hand at building race cars.

"I looked over their operations and said, 'Hell, I can do that myself'," "It didn't look very hard to me."

While he geared up for a career as car builder, he joined up with the well-known racing team run by Ernie Ruiz. The Travelon Trailer Specials fell under Wally's care, which meant sprint cars and a brand-new Kurtis roadster for the Indy 500 in 1953, the year Meskowski took up residence in the Indiana Capital.

The speedway car had originally been slated for '52 race winner Troy Ruttman to drive, but arm injuries suddenly put Ruttman out of the picture. The Travelon sprint car driver, Andy Linden, shook down the new car, but he was already assigned to another Indy ride, so the team found

themselves searching for a driver.

Of course, Wally Meskowski's scouting talents came into play. "Across the alley from us, Jim Rathmann was driving for Lou Moore, who had a super-lightweight car and Jim didn't like it at all," Wally notes. "He'd come over and look at our car, and pretty soon he asked to take a ride in it.

"I let him take a ride in it and he quit Lou Moore to drive our car."

Rathmann started 25th in the car and worked his way up through the field to take the lead during the first half of the race. But, this was '53, the year of the killing heat, and after 300 miles Rathmann pulled in, exhausted and asking for a relief driver.

"We didn't have a driver lined up to drive relief," Wally says. "But Eddie Johnson was standing around back of the pits so we put him in. He couldn't even see out of the car because he was quite a bit smaller than Jim. He couldn't go very fast that way, but we still finished seventh. I'm sure if Jim could have stayed in it, he could have won the race."

After that race came another of the incidents prominent in Meskowski's collection of interesting racing episodes. The Travelon team went to Terre Haute for a sprint car race, with Linden slated to drive. But, during his heat race, Linden suddenly pulled off the track complaining about the car's handling and telling Wally and Ernie Ruiz to get somebody else to drive it.

They got the legendary Jimmy Bryan. "Jimmy came over and asked me what gear I had in it and walked around and picked up the wheels to see how the weight was," Wally relates. "He had to start last in the consy and I think only the first two spots got in the main then, so I said, 'Jim, you gotta win this thing'. And he said, "Aww, we'll win 'er.'

"So they dropped the flag and he was leading it coming off of two. So he won that and that started him on the last row for the main. The third lap, he was leading that and won that hands-down. I never touched the car! And he gets out and says, 'God, I never drove a car like this before.' "

Over the next few seasons, Meskowski continued to put competitive cars under such drivers as Frank Armi, Ed Elisian, Bill Homeier, Jack Turner, Bob Scott, and Elmer George. In 1957, he began his car-building career, creating the first cross-bar, heliarced dirt car, which Don Branson debuted at

Nehamkin

Ted Halibrand and Sam Hanks were pleased with the 1964 Shrike Meksowski was working on.

Springfield.

Branson posted fourth quick time that day and led the race going into the first turn. He led the first 50 laps, but a flat tire and the ensuing makeshift pit stop dropped him to seventh at the finish.

A second Hoover Motor Express Special was soon built for Foyt and his Edsel tow truck.

Meskowski's race car "factory" kept turning out sprinters and championship machines, reaching its peak in 1960, when six dirt cars and two Indy roadsters rolled out fresh from the Indianapolis shop where Wally and associate George Morris plied their trade. One of the roadsters quickly caught the eye of one of the day's top 500 drivers.

"Eddie Sachs, who was driving for Pete Schmidt at the time, wanted to drive this car in the worst way," says Wally. "So, he called Schmidt in St. Louis and asked if he could make a deal using his engines. Schmidt came to Indianapolis to make a trade with me. He ended up giving me his Kuzma dirt car and two engines and an old sprint car for the new champ car. Sachs won three races with it that season."

Along the way, Meskowski developed a long-standing association and friendship with a man he had first met on that early journey to California, Ted Halibrand. Working with Ted at Halibrand Engineering, Wally became involved with some of the more innovative projects to come along, and not always restricted to to the world of auto racing.

The pair unveiled the first American-built monocoque rear-engine Indy-car chassis ever built, named the Shrike, in 1964. The car enjoyed great success at the hands of Lloyd Ruby, and later models were driven by Parnelli Jones and Dick Atkins.

A half-dozen years later, Halibrand and Meskowski were also involved in a project so unusual that it deserves mention, even though it was not racing related. They built a train engine, but not your ordinary, run-of-the-mill locomotive.

"It was a government project," Wally explains. "Air Research was the prime contractor and Halibrand was the subcontractor. We built the whole chassis and the fabricators there at California Metal Shapers shaped the aluminum.

"They're still testing it. What they were really after was a new concept of power. This thing ran on tracks, but that didn't mean it was always going to. The concept was power, and this was linear induction.

"There's a turbine engine that drives a generator. The generator creates power and the train runs on two tracks, with a third track in the middle that had two magnetic fields on each side of it, which is what propelled the the train.

"I never got to ride on it. It left the shop on a flatcar. It was around 45 feet long, but that's just the motor to pull the cars."

Still, the main thrust of Meskowski's existence was auto racing during those years. He was chief mechanic on the car Sachs drove at Indy in 1964, the year he died in a fourth-corner accident.

He was also the man who prepared the Vita-Fresh Special that Bobby Unser drove to eighth place in the 1966 500-miler, the first turbo-Offy to finish an Indianapolis race.

Even as Meskowski began to slack off on his car owning and building activities in the early '70s, his cars carried his reputation onward. The 20 or so dirt cars and his sprint cars continued to be raced by others, and his designs often formed the basis for the cars built by people like George Bignotti and Grant King. Today, a Meskowski chassis can be found in the lineup of any dirt-championship race.

"The first car I built and the last one started side-by-side in the third row of the Hoosier Hundred a couple of years ago," he notes. "One was the Windmill Truckers car and the other the Pizza Hut car."

His sprint cars are a little harder to track down--" they are all gone and scattered everywhere"--but his design

Meskowski and Halibrand Engineering did much of the work on this special power plant.

[165]

concepts can still be seen in the cars turned out by builders like King and Paul Leffler.

In 1973, Meskowski retired as an active car owner, as well. For the record, the last race he entered was the twin-50s at the Indiana State Fairgrounds, with Sam Sessions in the cockpit.

"It was just getting too expensive with no return," he advises. "And it was getting to be more work than I cared to do."

Meskowski now works as a machinist in the race shop of Bignotti, but remains a familiar figure along the racing trail, dressed in the blue-and red uniform of the Bignotti crew at Indy-car stops or simply in civilian clothes at the sprint car circuits.

He'll be seen back on the dirt-championship trail, too. Meskowski plans to work on a new Leffler-built dirt car owned by Bob Walford, powered by a four-cam Ford, and piloted by Billy Vukovich. "I'm just going to do it in my spare time," says Wally, who vows he won't get involved in running his own racing stable anymore.

"Not unless somebody hired me and footed the bills," he reports. "I do miss it, in a way, but I find myself enjoying watching the other guys working instead of me."

Of course, not even that kind of semi-retirement can keep Meskowski from exercising his celebrated talent for spotting new driving stars on the rise. He still has the keen eye that has made him the the Ted Mack of racing.

"The guy I think is going terrific right now is Dana Carter," observes Wally Meskowski. "He'd already have won a couple more races if he hadn't run into a little bad luck. And, of course, guys like Tommy Astone need a break, too. Or Bubby Jones, or Chuck Gurney, or Roger Rager. I think they've all got what it takes."

Following is a list of drivers who have driven for Meskowski. It's quite a list of all-stars!

Mario Andretti
Donnie Allison
Bobby Adamson
Dick Atkins
Frank Armi
Dale Breedlove

Jimmy Bryan
Don Branson
Ronnie Bucknum
Norm Brown
Tony Bettenhausen, Sr.
Merle Bettenhausen

Rollie Beale
Steve Cannon
Gary Condon
Neil Carter
Pancho Carter
Danny Caruthers
Leon Clum
Ronnie Duman
Scratch Daniels
Wally Dallenbach
Ed Elisian
Edgar Elder
Rex Easton
A. J. Foyt
Elmer George
Todd Gibson
Bobby Grim
Bob Gregg
Bill Homeier
Jim Hurtubise
Bobby Hogle
Jackie Howerton
Bob Harkey
Parnelli Jones
Paul Jones
Eddie Johnson
Gordon Johncock
Harold Leep
Jud Larson
Ralph Ligouri

Andy Linden
Bobby Marshman
Jim McElreath
Bobby Marvin
Earl Motter

Al Miller
Roger McCluskey
Bob Mathouser
Paul Newman
Lee Osborne
Johnny Parsons, Jr.
Larry Rice
Jim Rathman
Johnny Rutherford
Jack Rounds
Paul Russo
Eldon Rasmussen
Chuck Rodee
Jimmy Reese
Bob Scott

Eddie Sachs
Sam Sessions
A.J. Sheppard
Chuck Stevenson
George Snider
Bob Sweikert
Mickey Shaw
Al Smith
Bob Slater
Dick Sutcliff
Deb Snyder
Bud Tinglestad
Jack Turner
Bobby Unser
Bob Veith
Bill Vukovich Jr.
Rodger Ward
Johnny White
Bruce Walkup
Carl Williams

A. J. Foyt talks racing and draws a crowd at a GMSC meeting.

Aurora slot racers provide race fans with a test of their skills.

Goodyear Bringing Fans, Racing Closer
Motor Sports Club

Those blue and white tents seem to be popping up everywhere lately.

Where was it you last saw them? Daytona in February, Sebring in March, Darlington in April, Indy in May?

The tents mark the nomadic home of the Goodyear Motor Sports Club which has 26 stops this year across the width and breadth of the country.

In Indianapolis the night before the first day of qualifications at the Goodyear Warehouse Park located next to the Speedway grounds, more than 2,000 members enjoyed the benefits of the club and met driver after driver after driver.

The open house and hospitality areas at various tracks is just one of the benefits members obtain when they join the club, and it's one of the most visible.

Race drivers and other personalities drop by to sign autographs and talk with members. A race winning steering wheel is given away during a drawing. This past May evening it was Mike Mosley's winning wheel from a race at Milwaukee the year before. Free Coca-Cola was available for the thirsty ones and even an Aurora slot car set was in racing order for all.

When the club isn't at a track, it's still going 24 hours a day, seven days a week. Those people under the GMSC tents saved a few bucks in admission prices through the discount available to all members. More than 100 racing events around the U.S. and Canada have discounts for GMSC members. A newsletter is published twice a month for members, bringing them up to date on what's happening in all phases of racing plus race results and discounts on upcoming events. Five times a year, members receive CHALLENGE magazine, containing stories and photos by the best racing writers and photographers in the country.

Members also receive discounts on Hertz Rent-A-Cars, the famous Auto World catalog, and the club's own merchandise catalog has offered prices no other racing apparel outfit can match. Then there is the membership card and certificate, driver prints, racing portfolios and a host of other little extras all designed to bring the fan closer to racing.

That's what the club is about. If you're interested come on over and sign up. If you can't right now, write us at P.O. Box 66, Akron, Ohio 44316. Or just wait until you see the blue and white tents again at a major racing event.

Former driver turned car builder Dan Gurney always draws a crowd.

Racing discussions can parch throats, but Coke has the answer.

Chris Economaki
Racing's Premiere Editor, Announcer
& Best Gossip Columnist

By Bob Cutter

He has been the expert voice of the American Broadcasting Company's wide World of Sports for better than 15 years. Over that span probably 2 billion — not million — billion people have seen and heard him.

He has announced and conducted interviews over public address systems at race courses literally thousands of times. Probably 10 million people have seen and heard him this way in the past 28 years.

He has been a byline writer on racing for better than 40 years, and he has been editor and publisher of "National Speed Sport News"—the bible of the racing fraternity—for better than a quarter of a century. Two million readers a year these days, perhaps 15 million readers over the life of the newspaper, which was small when he came and is big now.

He is a man whose name is known, and respected, by just about everyone in auto racing, famous or unknown, here, and abroad, active and inactive.

Yet, most people don't know much about Chris Economaki, and what they think they know often is wrong. This is an attempt to correct the record and take the true measure of the man and broadcaster who is such an integral part of the Indianapolis scene each May.

1. Despite the fact that Chris Economaki has been in New Jersey for better than 50 years and has always been closely identified with racing and public life in that state, he was born, of all places, in Brooklyn.

"I was born at 133 Gates Avenue, Brooklyn, N.Y., in the front room. I didn't go to New Jersey until the first grade - about age five or six--but I've lived there ever since, really in a very small area in and around Ridgewood."

Chris's father was born in Volos, Greece, his mother in New York, of Irish and Scotch parentage. "Toomeys of South Carolina, on her mother's side, Burts of Edinburgh, Scotland, on her fathers' side."

Like that of another famed Greek, Telly Savalas, Economaki's father was a well-to-do man who lost his businesses in the 1929 Depression. He had a big candy store on Broadway and his own custom shirt business, Econel, as well as other lucrative businesses.

After the crash, he became a butter and egg salesman, but he managed to keep the family--including Chris's brother, George, six years younger--together and living in the friendly town of Ridgewood.

2. Chris Economaki first became involved in racing in 1932, and with a few interruptions like World War II, has been involved ever since.

"I was about 11 and trying to find reasons, as an 11-year-old would, for getting out of the house. Often, I'd hear this roar off in the distance, which I discovered was the sound of racing engines at Hohokus Speedway, about two

Chris Economaki, one of the hardest working men the sport of auto racing has ever seen. Even though he travels nearly every weekend, he still comes home to Ridgewood, N.J. to put out his weekly newspaper, the National Speed Sport News.

and one half miles away.

"Sometimes I'd go up and look through the fence, but I needed an adult to get me in. It was then I discovered the man who cut my hair, the local barber, had pictures of racing cars and drivers on the shop wall. He was the father of one of that day's leading drivers, Bob Sall, Eastern champion, an Indianapolis 500 runner in 1935, and even later a NASCAR official.

"Once father Sall saw my interest, he offered to take me to the races if I could persuade my parents, which I did. He was a very responsible man, and so they let me get up at 5 a.m. to meet Mr. Sall and go off to the tracks.

"Here I was, just turning 12 and making the circuit--Woodbridge, Reading, Allentown, Langhorne, Altamont, places like that."

3. The first "By Chris Economaki" byline story appeared

when he was age 15, and his first full-time newspaper job was right at the top--editor and publisher.

"There was a full-size general interest weekly in what then was East Paterson, now is Elmwood Park, Chris was approached by a man named Dick Vieldhouse, who just died a few months ago, about running auto racing results. They told him to sell some ads and they'd run the stories. He did, and that's how the back page became National Auto Racing News.

"It was so popular that it became the back two pages, then three, then four, and by the beginning of 1935, it was half the paper. Then they divorced it and made NARN a tabloid and started to print it over at the Ridgewood News, where National Speed Sport News is located today.

"In those days the presses were down in the building's basement, with a window that you could look through and see the presses running. I used to go there from age 15 or so each Wednesday night to get one of the first papers off the presses--we called it 'the racing sheet'-- right up until the war.

"One reason I did it was to see our ad, Another fellow and I had a little business in racing driver pictures. We'd take a driver's picture in uniform or out of it, sell it back to him, and also offer fans copies through the mail. We made $3 to $5 a week, which doesn't sound like much until you realize that men were traveling by train into Manhattan to earn $12 a week."

Because Chris was at so many races, the editor asked occasionally to write a story, and that first byline came from a Flemington Fairgrounds race later that same year.

"Paid for these stories? Not then, and not now," Economaki laughs.

Years later, Economaki did get paid, in a different way. After the war and more years of contributing "freebies" to what now was called NSSN, he worked parttime on the paper when its fulltime editor became ill, then took over as editor and publisher in April, 1950.

"I started as an employee, but right at the top," Chris chuckles in recollection. "After about ten years, and a rise in circulation from 3,000 to 30,000, they felt rather magnanimous about the paper, and through a complicated stock thing, I ended up as a part owner." The circulation of NSSN today is above 60,000.

Clean living, and hard work, and all that sort of thing. Meanwhile, though, there had been those other phases of the Economaki life.

4. He was a racing mechanic, and even a racing driver, long before he became a familiar byline in racing or ever thought of TV.

"I graduated from high school in 1938, and among the things I had was an automotive course. Kids in those days had it better. You used to buy an old car for $5 or $7 long before you were old enough to drive and run it around the fields. By the time you were 17 and able to get a license, you were an expert driver and shade-tree mechanic--you had to be to make those old jalopies work.

"I went to work for Duane Carter--not today's Pancho, now, but his father--at $15 a week as his mechanic. Got paid maybe one week out of four, but we were racing, and that's what mattered to me.

"It was an outboard midget--a car powered by an motor boat engine--and Duane was just getting known. He was to go to the speedway, or course, starting in 1947, when he didn't qualify, all the way to 1964. He

THIS YEAR'S "500" MOST SPECTACULAR IN HISTORY

The front page of this 1935 edition of "National Auto Racing News" was semi-sensational. Since after the war it has been called National Speed Sport News and is still going strong.

had better mechanics then.

"We'd go to some races in Duane's 1935 Chevrolet Coupe with his wife and him in front, and me in the rumble-seat, or on some occasions sitting in the race car back on the trailer. Or I'd hitchhike to the next Gasoline Alley.

"Monday at Yellow Jacket in Philadelphia, Tuesday at Hinchcliffe in Paterson, Wednesday at the Nutley boards, Thursday at Cedarhurst or all the way to Savin Rock in Haven, Friday at Paterson again or at Hensley, Saturday maybe Freeport, Sunday at Nutley again. Seven nights a week, at those tracks, or others just like them."

And every mechanic in those days knew he could drive as well as, or better than, the guy for whom he was working.

"I raced once in my life and proved to myself I was a worse race driver than a race mechanic, and that was saying something. It was early March or April, 1939, after our car had been sold to Eddie Cox, and I had gone along with it. At Ashley, Pa., I got my chance in a cycle midget, which they called 'the shakers' in those days.

"I found out why. The car shook so much I could hardly see in my borrowed crash helmet, which was substantially too large for me. It was traumatic going around that fifth of a mile. The purse that night--for everyone-- was about $300. I didn't see any of it. I did worse than poorly. Finish? I felt lucky to be alive after that race."

He had gone to Indianapolis for the first time in 1938, and no one knew him back then, of course, even if some people say they remember him from those days. He was up to his armpits in racing, but "there was no money in race cars in those days for most people," and in 1939, after seeing most of the Northeast on the racing circuit, he decided to find a "real" job. There was a little thing called World War II that came along, though.

5. Chris Economaki was a frustrated fighter pilot who became a member of the Second Armored, after a stint as a radiographic technician.

"Late in 1939 I became a parts clerk in the Jersey City factory branch of the Divco Corporation, or Detroit Industrial Vehicle Company, and next I went with Curtiss Propeller Company in Caldwell, N.J., in defense work in 1941.

"I was an X-ray inspector, or to give it its official title, a radiographic technician. It consisted of looking at a black sheet of paper for any white spots, or weld defects, but it was necessary for the hollow steel propeller blades we made there."

Economaki recalls that his first paycheck was $125 for a week's work, and he was flabbergasted since that was more than he previously had made in a month. "I worked 10 hours a day, seven days a week, and the overtime really mounted up.

"Maybe it was that job, or the fact that many racing people were getting involved in aviation, just like in World War I, but whatever it was, I trotted on down late in 1941 and tried to enlist in the Army Air Corps. I wanted to to be a pilot, or course--everyone did in those days."

As usual, Economaki had the thing well planned. His eyes already were slightly off (later he was to start wearing glasses most of the time), but with the aid of everyone else in the line, he rigged a way of passing most eye tests.

"Each man would say the lines of the chart very loudly, and I'd be memorizing them. By the time it was my turn I had most of the eye-chart lines down pat, forwards and backwards, "Chris recalls.

"Then I got patriotic or something and decided not to cheat, and I surprised myself by passing the test anyway. I passed most of it, but eventually they spotted my eye weakness and pilot training was out. I went back to the defense plant until war broke out and then I went into the foot soldier's Army.

"September 25, 1942, through February 4, 1946, or as we used to put it, 'born in the U.S. and reared in the ETO.'"

We marveled at the way Economaki always had the exact date, place or person in mind as he told the story. Chris laughed: "Sam Posey told me he describes me to his friends as the man who remembers everything. It isn't so, but having a good memory is useful for a writer or a broadcaster and I've tried to cultivate it."

Another date Economaki has down cold is March 1, 1944. "That's the day I met Tommye."

In case you didn't know, Tommye is Mrs. Chris Economaki, the former Alvera Tomljanovic of Woodward, Iowa, who happened to be in the Bamboo Club, described by Chris as the "in" place in Des Moines in those days, when a certain soldier and his buddy stopped in for a libation.

"The Bamboo Club was upstairs over Babe's at 6th Street, between Grand and Locust. The proprietor was Babe Bisignano, whose sons later included John, the race car driver. We went in and there were eight to 10 girls who had come there after a sorority party.

"I was immediately taken with this one girl, whom I met when my friend introduced me to the table when he saw one or two girls he knew. She left, but I didn't want to lose the connection, so I asked one of the girls who stayed

for a date and asked her to bring this other girl for my friend.

"That was Tommye, of course, and when we all showed up in a couple of days, I got in the car next to Tommye and my friend got in next to the other girl, just as I had planned, and things went as I planned from the first time I saw her."

On May 29, 1946, the Croatian-descended girl and the Scotch-Irish-Greek-descended boy, now a grizzled veteran of the Army at age 25, were married in Des Moines's St. Ambrose Cathedral. Two daughters were to follow, now both married.

From basic to replacement in the Second Armored to platoon sargeant to Sargeant Major. Landing at LeHarve, France, across Central Europe to the Elbe. Fourth American into Berlin. Economaki dismisses his war experiences, but he has lots of stories about postwar Europe, the Russians and his brief fling at high finance.

6. He once parlayed a $15 watch into $86,000 in less than a week.

Part of his G3 duties--headquarters company--with the Second Armored required him to accompany the Colonel every time they met with the Russians. One day Chris was standing outside such a meeting place at a German town when his Russian counterpart indicated he'd like to buy his watch.

"I indicated to him it was too expensive for him--we heard that the Russians didn't pay their combat troops anything, mainly because there just wasn't any place to spend the money--but he indicated he had lots of money.

"What we didn't know then was that once the Russians had gotten to Germany, they now gave their troops all their backpay and then some in the invasion script that the American Bank Note Company had printed for us and our allies.

"He offered me $1200 for the watch, and since it cost me just $15, I sold it to him on the spot. He seemed very happy, and I found out that good American and German watches were worth a lot to these guys.

"When I got back to camp I sought out a GI I knew with a shoebox full of watches that he had won at craps or 'liberated,'" and he was overjoyed to sell them to me for $15 each.

"Within three days I had sold the entire load one at a time for $1,000 to $1,500 each, and I had $86,000 in invasion marks in the shoebox. I spent a little of it and sent $20,000 home when an order came through stopping the sending of money back. Here I was with $65,000 or so and no place to unload it."

The war was over and the Army was being quite liberal with travel for restless troops who wanted to go home, but who had to stay put because transport wasn't available. Economaki evolved a plan and took "compassionate leave" to visit his dying grandmother in Greece. Grandma was a pure invention, of course.

"I hitchhiked on Army planes from Frankfurt to Athens, but the money situation was no better there. Across the field was a British air transport outfit, so I hitched with one of their planes to Cairo, and an Arab moneychanger who didn't know about the latest Army orders yet swapped me Egyptian pounds for some marks."

"I had a month, so I kept going, all the way to Karachi, India, and then came back to Frankfurt."

Eventually he came home with the shoebox still bulging with invasion money and he headed for the Pentagon. He almost had a Colonel ready to sign a check for $60,000 in exchange for the marks when the officer thought better of it, and Chris had an expensive souvenir of his European tour.

"I had the shoebox for years, but it got lost somewhere in moving. It really represented about 30 watches, two cartons of cigarettes and a couple of motorbikes. Did I tell the time I bought a cycle from a German for $300 and sold it to a Russian officer for $3,000 within two hours. those were the days."

Chris came back to his own business, a gasoline station that didn't pan out, and a stint back with Divco, this time as a stellar salesman, but when the National Speed Sport News opportunity presented itself in 1950, he opted for that, and he hasn't regretted it. Nor his broadcasting.

7. He announced his first race for a mere $40 in 1947 and hasn't stopped since.

"A driver named Buster Keller promoted a sprint car race at Selinsgrove, Pa., on the Susquehanna River, and he asked me to announce it. I said I had never done it before, but he said who cares. You know racing, so just say what comes into your head.

"I paid the sound man $2 for a record of the performance. It's a huge record--like three feet across," Economaki laughs. "I was incredible. I screamed into the mike. I had everyone in third place. But the crowd loved it.

"He had me back the next week, and pretty soon I was the 'official' announcer for the Penn-Jersey Auto Racing Club. It just kept growing and it was good for the paper.

"Sam Nunis gave me the first big break. I did my first National Championship race in 1952, July 4th, as a matter of fact, at Raleigh, N.C., the only major race at that speedway, 250 miles and a race to remember.

"Troy Ruttman pitted for gas on the last lap and still won the race."

"Everyone wanted to do the race, but Sam said no, I'll use my regular guy. That was me, and it was a real break. Bill France gave me a big break, too, in 1961, a break that led to ABC-TV."

Economaki and another announcer shared broadcasting duties at all of France's Daytona events in NASCAR. It happened that each was connected to a racing paper, and by splitting the duties between them, each gave France's races big play in their respective papers. The beach races attracted everyone, and Economaki got a growing list of clients to announce from his early days with France.

The biggest client was ABC, and it happened because CBS 'fouled up" in France's words his 1959 speedway extravaganza. "Bill thought Walter Cronkite and Art Peck did badly, and he viewed the telecast as a debacle," Chris recalls.

"When ABC showed up in April, 1961 with an offer to televise the July 4th Firecracker 250, he practically threw them out. But they wanted to do his race, and they asked what would satisfy him. 'Let me put a pro in the booth, and I'll go along,' he told him. I was the man he recommended."

Reluctantly, ABC hired Chris Economaki for $500, or 10 times what he was used to getting to announce a race.

"I heard them say, 'what will we have this guy do? We've got to keep France happy.' And they asked me to say what was on the paper. I read it and said, no, I didn't want to read that.

"Hugh Beech, the producer, looked at me and said, 'Christ, don't be difficult. What do you want to do?' I told him, and he said, 'Say that sounds OK, Go ahead.'"

He's known them all since the Thirties: Above, Chris talks with Midget racing great Dutch Schaefer in a late Forties photo.

It was OK. Economaki was brought back again and again. That was 15 seasons ago and he's still at it in almost every ABC auto racing broadcast. "I'd like to be in the booth, and they like it when I am, but they say they can't get anyone to do the job in the pits that I do," Chris laments.

8. He has never said 'What's It Like Out There?' to Mario Andretti or anyone else.

"I said it once, earlier this year, at Indianapolis as a matter of fact, and as a joke to Jackie Stewart after he finished taking the rookie test for our feature on it. I really did it as a joke, and I didn't even realize it would go on the air."

"Now everyone is reconvinced I have said it before."

But like "Come with me to the Casbah," "Quick Watson, the needle," "Play it again, Sam," and "I want to be alone," it was never really said.

"Bob Collins used it as a title for that book he did with Mario. I've never, never said it seriously, but I suppose it's the sum, the essence of all my questions, so I'm not going to sue anyone."

We asked if Chris thinks of himself as brash. Many people do.

"Brash? I don't think I'm brash in any way. Nobody should talk to a winner or a loser after he's washed his face and combed his hair. You want a sincere response, one at the moment it is being felt, not a contrived answer, so I try to get a man as soon as I can.

"I'll let a doctor reach him first, otherwise I want to be first, before he has a chance to cover up what he's thinking, and usually what's the truth."

Economaki says the hardest races to announce or broadcast are the dull ones. "And road races. Nobody passes anybody, and in my view passing is racing. But I've gotten some of my best reviews for road races, probably because I have to work harder on them.

"I've been turned down for an interview only once, by Fireball Roberts of all people. 'Look, 'he said, 'don't come near me with any microphones. We (Ford) are beaten before we are starting. Chryslers are winning everything."

"The best interviews I've done? Well, Wally Dallenbach is a great one. He always sounds like he's baring his soul. I'll never forget the 1975 Indy broadcast in which he answered 'I'll not rest 'til this race is mine.' Now that's a response.

"Peter Revson was a great interview. Precise, explicit answers, and in the language the average viewer could follow even on technical subjects.

"One of the best interviews I did never got on the air. The day A.J. Foyt split with George Bignotti. Some producer who was new on the block didn't think it was significant.

"People wonder about A.J. and me. They have seen him glower at me. But he's never mad at me, he's just plain mad at times. He's a good guy, and I think we both think of each other as real friends.

"You've got to be careful. The automobile has a tendency to go bad at times, and you might be attributing something to the driver because of it. There was a race in which Joe Leonard was weaving all over the track, and I said he probably was getting tired--arm-weary--and as soon as the race was over, Joe and Vel Miletich descended on me. The car was at fault, and Joe had to handle a bucking broncho through the whole last half of the race.

"You've got to be iffy once in awhile, much as announcers like to pontificate. It's true in every sport, baseball or auto racing, football or frisbee throwing. They are trying to overcome that with 'jocks' as announcers, in our case ex-drivers, or inactive drivers, but ego is such a part of a race driver's makeup that he has to guard against his personal feelings even more than the non-driver."

The most thrilling race Chris ever announced or telecast, he says, was not an Indy 500, or a stock car battle, or a Grand Prix. It was a mid-1950's sprint car race at the half-mile Raleigh track known as North Carolina State Fairgrounds.

"Tommy Hinnershnitz vs. Wally Campbell. Two drivers who hated each other. They passed and repassed the entire 20 laps. Tommy was leading by two car lengths on the last lap when Wally came from nowhere and beat him by about 10 inches at the flag. Now that's racing. God, it was wild."

Economaki, as you may have gathered, is a sprint car freak.

9. He isn't a writer, he says, although he writes the equivalent of a book every year.

"I am no writer. I do the column like Walter Winchell, three-dots style. I can crank out a good news story, but that's not writing, that's reporting.

"I think I have a nose for what's news, whether it's writing or putting news or a feature on television. News is something nobody knows about until you tell them about it. I'm pleased when we have a good issue of the paper, or I do a good telecast. The best ones involve some urgency. That's an element of news, too.

"I couldn't write a great magazine piece or a real book, I don't think." But we're working on him.

Economaki is a familiar celebrity at the Speedway each May. Here, he's interviewing an about-to-be-bumped Bill Simpson.

10. Chris Economaki is ambivalent about the future of racing in America and everywhere.

"Attendance is up, interest is rising, but the costs are incredible. And the sanctioning bodies never seem to get any wiser.

"There are smart people in USAC and NASCAR. There are smart promoters. There are intelligent team managers and constructors, but they're not always the ones listened to. The English, bless 'em, have that expression that tells it all: 'I'm all right, Jack,' meaning I've got mine and nuts to you.

"If racing continues in that vein, I'm very pessimistic.

"Sponsors are not an unlimited resource any more than gasoline is. You've got to give them something for their money, whether you are a driver, track or sanctioning group. USAC puts on a tremendous show at the Speedway, and the Speedway people even outdo them. The sponsors get a lot from their participation here, and the public at large is given a real show here and on TV and radio. But that's an exception. Often the public--and the sponsors--get a rooking.

"Racing is my life, and I want it to grow and prosper. I'm trying to do my part and I see others trying their best. But we need everyone pulling together, not just a dedicated few and the guys like me who report but who can't make it happen."

That last statement pretty well sums up Chris Economaki. Automobile racing is his life's work and he's as dedicated a worker as you'll find anywhere. His writing is considered gospel, and in this business we'd say that's a pretty enviable position to have obtained.

'MOM' KNOWS THEM ALL

When you walk past her you could think that she's probably someone's grandmother. They left her down in the first turn and told her to watch the race cars for awhile. The sun would be good for her.

Then Freddie Agabashian walks up and says, "Hi Mom, how are they doin' today?"

Pretty soon Lloyd Ruby comes by and chats for a few minutes. She's never alone for very long. And she is recognized by some very important Speedway personalities. Maybe she's a driver's grandmother.

No, but Margret Gray is more than just another face in the crowd to many who call the Indianapolis 500 Motor Speedway home throughout the month of May. For the past dozen years she has been a fixture in turn one.

"But only during practice days," she says. "I have a seat in the tower terrace for qualifying and race days."

Everyone seems to know her in various degrees. Some will go out of their way to say hello or ask about a mutual friend while others pass along a greeting.

"I've known them all," she says, "they are all like sons to me."

But 12 years in turn one haven't provided all her experience, far from it. Ask Margret when she first came to the Speedway and she will think a minute, smile and say, "I first came here in 1927. I was a fan then just as now. I always liked fast cars and this is the fastest place I knew of," she said.

But the races she saw weren't consecutive. Margret missed some years especially from 1945 to 1964.

"It really hurt to miss the race. I would sit home and almost cry but I had committments and I couldn't go," she explained.

In 1964 friends Chuck Arnold and Bud Tinglestad persuaded Margret to come back out to the Speedway. "From then on things have worked and I haven't missed a year," she smiled.

In the off season Margret is a part time cashier at the Indianapolis Zoo.

With stop watch and years of experience to guide her Margret Gray eyes the action from her favorite turn one vantage point ever ready to extend a greeting.

"The people there are so nice, they let me off in May so I can come out to the Speedway. They understand how much I like it here," she said.

Margret seems like a regular fan on the outside yet she appears to be more serious than most. "I enjoy seeing the drivers at work and I like to hear about their families. I like to think of them as part of my family especially the older drivers like Ruby, MacElreath, and Foyt," she explained. Margret seemed impressed by Janet Guthrie. When asked if she could consider Janet as part of her family, "Yes, I want to see her do well. I want everyone to do well. Janet will have to go with the times. If she makes it fine, if not I won't complain just because she is a woman," Margret emphasized.

Since she's been attending races since 1927 Margret has noticed things about the fans and the crowds in general. "I wonder these days if the people really care. I am happy to sit quietly and not bother anyone. How can the people be interested if they are always running around?" she asked.

Concerning A.J. Foyt, Margret replied, "I can't say A.J. will retire if he won his fourth 500. He has racing fever and as long as he has that he will continue to drive," she said.

"But," she added, "there will never be another one like him."

Margret refused to pick a winner for race day. "I don't make predictions because I want everyone to do well," she stated.

But as practice time ends and race day nears Margret explained how she begins to get sad. "When practice days are finished that means I can't get out here until next year, it's just too crowded for me," she said.

"On practice days the fans usually leave me alone but once in a while I will have to ask the boys to find another place to play. They usually do," she adds.

It was a special day for Margret, not just because she was in her favorite spot in turn one, but because more of her friends had stopped by. She showed off gifts that John Fugate, Freddie Agabashian, and some boys from Channel 13 had given her.

It wasn't the umbrella, pen and pencil set, notebooks, or the t-shirt, but it was what they said.

"The best thing they gave me was their wishes for me to remain here for many years to come," she smiled.

[173]

The First Lady
Janet Guthrie

By Bob Cutter

It didn't happen in 1976. But the betting is now in favor of its happening in 1977. A woman in the field of 33 cars at the Indianapolis Motor Speedway.

Several women said in 1976 they wanted to be there. Two tried very hard to get there. One made it, all the way through the rookie test, at speeds of better than 181 m.p.h. in a loaned car. But her own car just didn't have the stuff to qualify, even if she did.

And wisely she and her team decided not to even make the attempt and fail. While the men still raced at Indy, Janet Guthrie went to Charlotte, N.C., for the World 600, the first woman to race at a NASCAR superspeedway. She could have raced at Riverside, Calif., a few weeks later in another NASCAR start, but she wouldn't give up that precious USAC license to do so.

She will be back. For 1976, the slim, tall brunette from New York City had accomplished quite a bit: first woman entered at the Speedway for the 500, first woman to pass the Indy rookie test, first woman to start a

Our lady was subjected to some pretty heavy pressure from the press and the usual army of photographers found in the pits. She held up well.

Fisher

500-mile race (Pocono, a month later, where her gear box broke after 89 laps). She still wants to be the first woman driver to start the biggest 500 of them all.

In 1977, there may be tougher competition. Arlene Hiss, 28, stole one distinction from Guthrie. She was the first woman to start a USAC race, taking the grid at Phoenix, Ariz., in March, 1975. But her driving left a lot to be desired, and the uproar knocked Hiss out of Championship car contention and into USAC's stock-car ranks.

Hiss just didn't have the experience that Guthrie did. And certainly not the diplomatic, gracious touch that Guthrie displayed throughout her three-month-long ordeal to get to the Speedway and be treated like any other driver. Hiss waved her feminism like a red flag before a bull. Guthrie let her actions speak for her.

Hiss will try to be at the Speedway in 1977. And so will the so-called Tigress of Turin, Lella Lombardi of Italy, who spent a season in Grand Prix cars and who has Formula 5000 experience. Lella wants lots of money. If someone comes up with it, she will be at the Speedway in 1977, too.

Others? Perhaps. But from these three should come the first woman in the Indy 500. And the betting here is like that of many others, Guthrie will make it in 1977 if she has the car.

Her 1976 car, an older, rebuilt Vollstedt-Offy, just wasn't fast enough even to attempt to qualify. Builder Rolla Vollstedt readily admitted this himself: "We just don't have the money some others do. We can't put the best cars on the grid. We try to put the best-prepared cars there and hope."

In Janet Guthrie's mind, even though the chance to qualify was gone, the "super team" at the Speedway in 1976 had to be Vollstedt's Bryant Heating & Cooling squad. "There are nothing but class people at Indianapolis, but I'd have to say that Rolla, Dick Simon and the whole Vollstedt crew are super-class people. It has been the experience of my life, and I look forward to next year."

In 1976 A.J. Foyt loaned her his second Coyote-Foyt for some practice laps.

But A.J.'s car was not available to qualify or to race, and with the withdrawal of the No. 27 Vollstedt car, she had no ride after all in the 1976 Indy 500, after getting as high as 181 m.p.h. and change in this car.

Rolla Vollstedt, left, and the folks at Bryant found Janet easy to work with.

"Disappointed? I just can't say what a disappointment it is," she said, holding back tears, "but at the same time I'd have to say it has been the most thrilling experience of my life."

Janet Guthrie's life hasn't been exactly humdrum for most of her 38 years.

Born in Iowa City, Iowa, she was raised in Miami, home base of Eastern Air Lines in those days, for which her father was a pilot, and eventually, captain. Maybe that's why she started flying at age 13, soloed at 16, and had a commercial rating by age 19.

At home in her New York apartment, the worn log books start with a childish scrawl and the handwriting matures as the hours mount up to better than 400.

But the flying falls off by 1969. By then, Guthrie had a new passion called auto racing.

"Flying got sort of dropped when I discovered racing," she recalled. "Racing gives you something you can't find any more in flying. An opportunity for direct competition. A responsibility for the person alongside you, to go along with that desire to beat him."

"Women can do most things better than or at least as well as men," she said. "And I'm tired of male chauvinist ideas that women can't compete against men in any and all phases of racing. I certainly have the experience, and I'm not chicken.

"But I guess I'm not a feminist in the traditional sense. I believe in doing, not saying. In acting, not parading or protesting."

Janet Guthrie: She didn't expect special treatment, just wanted a fair chance.

"I say this even though I've faced prejudice. Not in racing, despite all those press reports about Bobby Unser and Billy Vukovich and such. But in flying. There is an intense opposition to women in flying, built up over the years for some inane reason.

"There's none of that in auto racing any more, at least that I can see. Oh, they still talk about USAC or NASCAR being all-male preserves, but it is amazing how quickly USAC is accepting the idea of a woman driver or two, and absorbing us into its mainstream."

Guthrie noted that driver opposition to a woman out there was vocalized by reactions to another woman's performance at a race, which the drivers didn't consider up to standards. "I can't blame them," she admitted. "I think I would have had many of the same reactions if I had to race against a slow driver, man or woman, who alternated between being a rolling obstruction and also a potential cause of an accident.

"When I showed up at Trenton, there was a genuine anxiety on the parts of some drivers who didn't want a repetition of something they didn't like. But when I got out there, and and they saw I knew what I was doing, the attitudes started to change."

It rained the first Trenton weekend, which postponed the race and gave Guthrie more track time and the drivers more time to get used to the fact that this was a different sex, to be sure, but not so different a driver.

Dick Simon, her teammate at Vollsteadt, remembered that at the Ontario test that put Guthrie into a Champ car for the first time, he raised

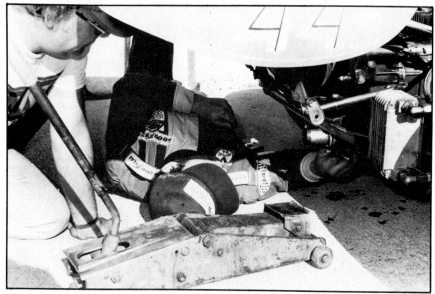

It's not uncommon to see a driver getting a hug from a crewman once the newcomer has passed the mandatory rookie test. Janet received high marks when judged.

Here's a fella who spent most of the month in this position: Dick Simon. Guthrie realized the the valuable assistance Simon was giving her and she recognized him publicly for it.

the boost a bit without telling Janet to see if she detected it. When she not only detected that change, but reported three or four other changes in the car and pitted because she was worried that something was happening with the engine, Simon reacted:

"I had proved to myself that the seat of her pants were just like those of the other real race drivers I knew. I said to myself, this here is a damn good race driver."

Johnny Rutherford noted the same thing quickly, and so did Foyt, one of Guthrie's earliest supporters. Others came around less quickly and vocally, but came around nonetheless.

When Janet's baggage was lost on the way to opening of practice at Indy, Vukovich loaned her a spare uniform and helmet of his. Rolla Voll-

stedt allowed as how Vuky wouldn't have to eat his hat after all—which he offered to do if Janet passed her rookie test at the Speedway—and Vuky said he was sorry. He was looking forward to eating a chocolate hat.

"The atmosphere changed at Trenton," Guthrie recalled about her fellow drivers, "and kept improving every week at Indianapolis. I've said Dick Simon has a lot of class. You can say that about just every real driver you'll meet here."

Acceptance has never really been a problem for Guthrie, even if it has been grudging, as in flying.

She graduated from the University of Michigan with a degree in physics and joined the aerospace industry, first as an engineer, then as a technical writer and editor. She applied for and

was accepted as a NASA scientist astronaut candidate.

She didn't make the space capsules because all non-PhD candidates were eliminated on the second round of tests. Only four women, including Janet, had made it that far.

And then there was motor racing, road racing to be more specific. The transition wasn't instant. Here was a pilot who had all those hours, who ferried open-cockpit, bi-winged crop dusters while in college, who had all that scientific background, and yet hadn't paid the slightest bit of attention to cars until a day in 1962 when she bought a used Jaguar XK120 coupe.

"I had to ask my 10-year-old brother how the clutch worked," she recalled with a hardy laugh, "But I learned rather quickly."

An SCCA touring school was quickly followed by a race school and a new car, an XK140, which she tore down completely and rebuilt for racing, including a three-month, part-time project of rebuilding the engine in the back of her station wagon.

"I started paying my dues rather early," Guthrie said. "In a way, you might say I didn't progress all that far in racing, despite all 120 races, all those races at Watkins Glen and Daytona and Sebring in the major endurance races, all of that.

"If you remember, just a year ago, I was still rebuilding engines, this time for a Toyota Celica, almost in the back of a station wagon. While other girls probably were watching the dawn come up over a romantic bay, I watched it come up over the hood of my car with a wrench in hand. Or I spent it rebuilding the tow truck's engine that gave out on the way back from a race course."

While she raced against the likes of Mark Donohue and Peter Revson and Mario Andretti, she also faced a lot of guys named Joe who often ran into her or spun out in front of her in a vain attempt to stay ahead of this upstart woman driver.

While she raced in those big races before thousands of spectators, she also was at Lime Rock, Conn., in the rain before a handful of people, or similar small races.

"The last five years, struggling to stay in racing has taken a lot out of me," she said in an interlude just before her dramatic Indianapolis project jelled. "A lot psychologically and monetarily. It's been a very hard struggle, curtailing my private life almost completely, giving up things I really enjoy, like the ballet and cooking and having friends in for dinner.

"I've never entertained any serious thought of chucking it in, though. The driving always has been rewarding. I admit the initial glamour wore off quickly for me, but I've always felt better when I'm racing than when I'm not."

Indy did not change Guthrie's outlook. "I wish I had this opportunity five years ago. I think I was not only younger, but a lot more eager in those days. But I guess I'm still eager, especially about something like Indianapolis, even though I never went there before this year and never even saw a race there except on TV."

She almost made the Speedway in 1975. Rolla Vollstedt first contacted Guthrie about trying the 500 in January, 1975, but the financing wasn't there. He told her in March, maybe next year. She didn't exactly believe it, she admitted, and she refused even to go and look at a Champ car. "I reasoned, why torture myself about something that might never happen," Janet said.

But last January, Rolla called again. In February, she met the Bryant Heating & Cooling people, her potential sponsors, for the first time in Indianapolis, and also got her first look at the Speedway in a street car driven by a Bryant PR man. One lap, at 60 m.p.h.

That same month came the crucial Ontario Motor Speedway test in California, and in March the project surfaced with an official announcement. Janet Guthrie was the first woman entered for the Indianapolis 500. Arlene Hiss beat her into a USAC race, but didn't even get a sniff at Indy. Maybe Hiss didn't have quite the same determination, the kind that sends you out for a car test with a broken bone in your foot that you hide from the team until after they like the test.

Hiss didn't have the background, nor the experience, perhaps, nor the gut feeling for racing that Guthrie has.

"There is nothing much in today's civilized existence," Janet said recently, "that demands that you use everything you've got. Auto racing sure does. Everything is better after a race. Everything looks better, tastes better, smells better, feels better, at least to me.

"It all comes down to what you

Janet Guthrie listens intently to advice from Johnny Rutherford before practice.

think you get out of something, balanced against what you think are the risks. Long ago I just decided racing was worth it."

She admitted her parents, particularly her father, now retired from the air and perhaps a man you'd think would understand Janet's position better than a landlocked dad, hated the idea of a racing daughter.

"They haven't tried to stop me, but they never really helped either, and I can't blame them for it. You have to do what you believe in. My father believes that, and he taught that to me."

Talking with her, you are convinced about anything she says. It goes with the person. The schoolgirl grin. The poised, reflective air. The careful responses, but the just as quick laughter. The flashing eyes. The gentle and graceful movements.

At the race track, she sounds like any other driver, but away from the track, she sounds like what she is, a college graduate with the polish of an honor graduate from Miss Harris's School for Girls in Florida.

It's a male shauvinist remark, but she took her situation at the Speedway in 1976, losing her chance to qualify after coming so close, like a man.

The full story behind the Foyt car loan has not been told until now. A.J. had been a Guthrie supporter from the beginning. "These guys forget how it was to get started," he remarked at Trenton when some driver criticisms still were being heard about Janet.

He made a point of stopping by to pass the time of day on the line several times, and to pass along encouraging words to Guthrie.

At the Speedway, when it was evident that the Vollstedt-Offy would have a tough time to even try and qualify, A.J. formed a plan. When

Janet's car was withdrawn, he was ready to offer her a practice session in his second Coyote-Foyt. All Vollstedt had to do was ask, with the good offices of Leo Mehl of the Goodyear Tire & Rubber Company.

The practice was arranged and an enthusiastic qualifying crowd saw Guthrie hit 181 m.p.h. plus, seemingly without effort. She herself later confided she felt she could have gotten as much as 4 m.p.h. more out of the car without trying that hard.

One person who asked the question was A.J. himself when she pitted. "I might let you try to qualify the car," he told Janet after she said how comfortable it was.

Several hours went by. A 5 P.M. decision time came and went without a decision. And the clockhands moved inevitably to 6 P.M. and the close of qualifying without Janet getting her chance.

Later A.J. revealed that his crew didn't want to have to service two cars. They wanted to concentrate on Foyt's own car to win his fourth Indy 500. He respected their wishes, perhaps regretfully in light of the rain-shortened race that was to follow.

But Guthrie's chance, just so near, went away. George Bignotti and others considered giving her a ride in their spare cars, but when Foyt moved in, they backed away. What's that saying about the road to a certain place being paved with good intentions?

Guthrie had no recriminations then, nor does she have them now. Foyt, Bignotti, all the men of USAC were, and are, class people to her. It takes one to know one.

Guthrie will be back, and she'll be welcome, at the 1977 Indianapolis 500. Just another driver, but also a kind of special person.

AMC V8
THE STOCK BLOCK

By Julie Klym

While Janet Guthrie was doing a pretty fair job of receiving the attention of the racing press at this year's 500, the fellas back in garage 67 were making history of their own.

They were running an American Motors Corporation stock block V-8. To the non-technically oriented fan, the idea of running an AMC passenger car engine might not be very impressive. But to the knowledgeable racer, the ones who can tell you chassis type, year and engine from a block away, an attempt at Indianapolis with the AMC engine was simply throwing good money after bad. It'd never work.

"How them guys with that Nash doin?" you could hear them say. And as usual, you could detect a tone of sarcasm that is directed toward those who show up with something new and bold.

For those of us who root for the underdog, the AMC became our hero. We had heard that it showed a little potential in practice runs at Ontario and we hoped it could get up to qualifying speeds for this year's 500. It was doubtful though. Less than ten months before May of '76 the AMC V-8 was just an idea. There were no real plans. Nothing was on the drawing board. Still, it turned out a winner.

The engine powered the No. 73 California-Oklahoma Eagle to a 183. 617 qualifying speed, eleventh fastest in the field. Practice speeds for the car were in the 185 range.

Though the car finished 27th in the 102 lap race, it was still running strong and would have finished higher except for a fuel miscalculation just before the rain fell.

The creation of the AMC racing engine began last July when Dick Jones, racing engineer for Champion Spark Plugs, designed the engine. The idea started turning around in his mind two years ago when the number of broken engines and the cost of racing were steadily rising.

"I thought it would be possible to reduce the cost with a stockblock engine, as well as improve dependability."

Jones explained that in the last five years there had been enough progress with valve technology so that a stockblock engine would be feasible.

"The valve gear is normally the problem of a stock block engine."

He added that the power potential for a stockblock is great enough to be competitive—even dominate—the Offy.

A recent ruling that allows 208 cubic inches of displacement for the stockblock versus 159 for overhead cammers gave the AMC a size break.

"I decided it was time to try to develop the stockblock," Jones said. He contacted American Motors for their block. "I felt the construction of their engine appeared to have sufficient strength for what I wanted to do."

Jones then contacted car owner Fred Carrillo about running the AMC engine in his Eagle for the 1976 season. "I felt it would be good for Fred because of his connecting rod

business (Carrillo Rods, San Juan Capistrano, California)." Carrillo was sold on the idea, and the development program began.

By the time parts for the engine arrived at the West Coast Champion facilities in Long Beach, it was early October. Engine builder Art Oerley, who had designed air craft engines for years and built Jim Hall's Chapparal engines, started work on the AMC stock-block Jones had designed. Engine builder Robert J. Cronin, 22, assisted Oerley.

"The set appearance date for Indianapolis put us under a great deal of pressure," Jones said. "Development was limited because of only one test vehicle and one prototype engine."

Chief mechanic Dave Klym was kept busy making special pieces to adapt the engine into a car designed for an Offy. "The AMC engine weighs 138 pounds more than an Offy," Klym said. "Because the engine is heavier, it had to be relocated in the chassis to maintain the designed balance of the car."

By the first part of 1976, the AMC engine and the chassis were together, and testing at Ontario Motor Speedway began. Adjustments and tuning to get the chassis and engine compatible were made. Dealing with so many unknown factors made the work slow and often frustrating.

Driver of the car, Jerry Grant, admitted that the project was disappointing at times. "Testing is often much more difficult than racing because of so many unknowns. However, I never had any doubts that we would reach

Fred Carrillo tells Jim Hurtubise about the advantages of the AMC stock block.

the point we did at Indianapolis."

Grant added, "In this type of development work, you need the ability to keep a positive attitude."

Overheating was one of the early problems. That was solved by a scoop that channeled a greater air flow through the radiator.

Another problem resulted from running two superchargers. The engine would perform on the dyno with two blowers, but the airflow on the track would unbalance the blowers. The solution was to use just one blower, and give up 200 h.p. in the process.

"But we'll regain it," Grant said. "By the end of the season, we should have an unfair advantage over the other engines."

Grant explained, "The engine development took away from chassis development. We were fortunate to gain as much (from the chassis) as we did at the Speedway."

Grant, as well as the rest of the team, is optimistic about the future of the program. "The engine is very dependable. It just runs and runs and runs. So far, the full potential of it hasn't been discovered. We just haven't had the time.

"I know of no other development program that has come as far as we have in such a short amount of time," Grant stressed.

And given more time, who can say what that AMC engine, with all of the talent behind it, can achieve.

[179]

THE DRAGON

Last winter when Grant King started building his two new Dragons for the '76 Indianapolis race, we asked one of his employees, Jerry Weeks, to follow the progress for us. Weeks is one of the finest metalsmiths in the racing business and is also a USAC Sprint and Midget car driver. He's not a bad photographer either.

Grant King has gained a reputation throughout USAC racing as being one of the hardest working independents in the business. His shop, located only a couple miles west of the Speedway, is one of the best equipped, for fabricating racing components, in the country. King prides himself with the fact his cars always make the Indianapolis starting field minus the assistance of expensive sponsorship.

Undressed, the Dragons (like all other Indy cars) reveal the aircraft type construction that goes into today's racers. Take a closer look now at how to build a Speedway car in your backyard.

No sleek lines here yet, just a basic rectangular shape that will require several hundred hours work to finish. Gordon Barrett, one of King's employees is shown fitting a side panel. He's an accomplished aluminum fabricator who takes pride in his work.

Sturdy roll bar construction is shown here along with some of the exacting aluminum fabrication necessary to build a Championship race car.

Now it's starting to look like a race car. That's an old Offy block bolted in place that is used throughout construction for measuring purposes.

Here's our photographer, Jerry Weeks, who's known for his race driving ability and is a fine metalsmith.

A few more rivets, the cowling is in place, and May draws nearer. Still a long way to go.

Driver John Martin, right, listens to Grant King explain a bracket he wants made. Martin helped the project through to the end.

"It's a race car!" Almost. Look closely and you'll see there's nothing holding the tires in place, but you can sit in it.

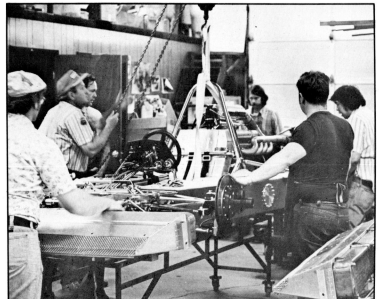

Everything's been painted and plated now. Time to install the engine and finish plumbing. Lots of help available.

Ready for the Speedway. Doris King has the easy job of installing the decals.

Owner Dick Beith Wants To Come Back

Ready for Round Two

by Ted West

Like hundreds of thousands of other kids around the country, Dick Beith knew the first time he ever heard about the Indianapolis 500 that someday, somehow he would have to go there. There was something irresistible about the place, something that draws people from every nook and cranny of the United States every year to sit and watch what is truly the Greatest Spectacle in Racing.

For Beith it took years, but he never lost sight of his goal. As time went on he realized that he wanted to do more than simply sit and watch though. One way or another, he wanted to become involved in the 500, to participate directly. Being a school teacher in Northern California hardly seemed to be leading him in the direction of the Speedway though. Beith is a venturesome man, however, and he saw in the early 1970s that the custom wheel business offered huge profits to anyone who knew what the kids wanted and was willing to spend the time to set up a profitable business serving those wants. Beith reckoned that he was the man, set up his business and by 1972 was a millionaire. He owned a beautiful home in the San Francisco Bay Area free and clear and had more money than he knew what to do with. When the right offer came along, he sold his company, the maker of E.T. Mags, in a deal that left him a huge block of shares in the company under the new owner. He watched the value of those shares go from $1.3 million straight up to $3.2 million. It was all just too good to be true.

But Dick Beith still had that cantankerous dream of going to Indianapolis. Now he had the means to make it come true. He bought an All-American Racers Eagle-Offy, called it the American Kids Racer, hired the under-rated Steve Krisiloff to drive it. and began preparing. In March of 1974 the team made its first appearance in the Ontario 500. A more impressive debut is hard to imagine. Krisiloff qualified the car in the middle of the second row and managed to

Dick Beith in front of the transporter for the former American Kids Racer Eagle.

lead the race before being black-flagged for an oil leak.

But an oil leak was the least of the problems that turned up for Beith at Ontario. Team difficulties began to crop up between Beith, Krisiloff and Krisiloff's father over how the team should be run. Before the weekend was over, Krisiloff had quit and Beith was left with a very fast, but very driverless, race car. By the opening of practice for the 1974 Indy 500 Beith had hired Bill Simpson to drive, but things didn't go as well as had been hoped for. Simpson qualified all right, but he was twentieth on the grid. He managed to finish thirteenth, but the car was no longer the front-runner that it had been. Simpson soldiered on that year to an eighth at Milwaukee, blew a piston while running far back in the field at Pocono, and then suffered another DNF at the second Milwaukee Champ Car race.

For 1975 the Eagle was still reckoned to be a very competitive car and Beith had high hopes of a major sponsorship deal with Levis jeans for the Indy 500. In the meanwhile, though, he had to demonstrate his car's competitiveness to his prospec-

tive sponsor. George Follmer was hired to drive the car in the Ontario 500, but disaster struck early. In one of the twin qualifying races which were to determine starting positions for the Ontario race, Follmer lost a U-joint at speed, hit the wall and wiped off the car's right side. Not only was it out of the 500, but Beith's chances of getting Levis to sponsor him at Indy were nearly gone. Desperately he tried to find an entrant at Ontario who had qualified and would paint Beith's American Kids Racer colors on his car so he could show Levis a bonafide entry. Since he couldn't tell the entrants he talked to that Levis sponsorship hung in the balance (he didn't want someone else to jump in and steal the Levis sponsorship away from him) nobody took his offers seriously. There was no American Kids Racer in the Ontario 500 and Levis was suddenly very cool towards Beith and the Indy 500.

Meanwhile everything else was going wrong for Beith. The cost of aluminum had doubled, temporarily ruining the custom wheel business, and Beith's shares in his old company plummeted. In an alarmingly short

[182]

period his stocks went from a net worth of $3.2 million down to only $135,000. He had spent over a quarter of a million dollars on racing already, depending all along on getting a major sponsor in order to keep going. The chances of that sponsorship had disappeared, but Beith had come this far and he was determined to carry on. He would be at Indy in 1975, sponsor or no.

The 1975 Indy 500 entry the American Kids Racer never seemed to have a chance. Beith started out with George Follmer again, but after one and a half weeks Follmer hadn't come anywhere near to running at a good qualifying speed despite having put over five hundred miles on the car trying. "I got tired of watching the car go by," Beith says of that week and a half. Finally Beith picked Rick Muther to take over the car, but that lasted only a day with no results. Then Beith tried Jan Opperman in his racer for three days. Jan gave it his all, but his lack of experience setting up Indy cars was too great. The car was dirt tracking—strictly a no-no at the Speedway—and Opperman did all he could to go quickly despite the incredible risks of running an Indy car hard that was set up wrong. It was no good and

in the last afternoon of qualifying Beith asked Lee Kunzman to give it a try. Kunzman was so amazed at the car's handling, that he couldn't believe Opperman had gone as fast as he did. Still there was just too much wrong to fix in time for qualifying and, knowing there was no chance, no attempt was made to qualify the car.

Elsewhere Beith's stocks had crashed, his checks were bouncing, his credit had given out, and the banks wouldn't even put a lien on his home because he wasn't officially employed anywhere. He stayed to watch the 500, but the next day he loaded the Eagle into his transporter and began a dispirited drive back west to California and bankruptcy. Every time he stopped the truck he knew that there was no money behind the credit card that was buying him $60 worth of gasoline per fill-up. As a final blow, the truck's clutch blew a thousand miles from home, and having no money for fixing it, he drove the entire last thousand miles with no clutch. When he finally got home he was a solid $15,000 in the red.

But racers are a tough bunch. Looking around at his assets, which were nil, he decided to go back into the custom wheel business. Things went

slowly at first, but Beith worked day and night, until six months later he had nearly all his debts paid and he was banking money again. He still had his house and his race car and, more important, he had vowed he would be at Indy again in 1976.

Sure enough, he came back this year. You had to look hard to find him, because he had leased his car, the same Eagle, to twenty-first starter Billy Scott. Ironically, for entirely unrelated reasons Scott's team had chosen to name the car "The Spirit of Public Enterprise Special". If there was ever a more appropriately named car, we haven't heard of it.

Indianapolis has taught Beith about racing the hard way, but he's back and will be back again and again. "When we were kids," he says, "we used to talk for hours about the Speedway. We'd talk with anyone who'd ever been there just to find out more about the place, how tall the trees were, how many people were in the grandstands, if the rain was wet." Beith knows more about Indy now, but the place still makes him smile. I've just begun to fight," he says. Once Indy gets into your blood, there just isn't any antidote.

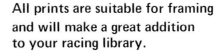

Turbine Returns!

TRACK DRYER

by Dave Parker

The jet engine returned to the Indianapolis Motor Speedway in 1976, but the vehicle it powered couldn't run as fast as the pace car.

Craig and his brother Terry pilot this strange looking vehicle at the Speedway unnamed but displaying the Arfons Drying Systems logo.

The vehicle resembles two giant vacuum cleaner attachments mounted on a frame with four wheels and a jet engine in the middle. Actually it is a sophisticated system with much potential that became a proven time saver, especially in the 1976 race day rain delay.

The project was completed in six sleepless weeks by the brothers whose father, Walt, and uncle, Art, were known for their land speed records in jet powered machines.

Craig Arfons explained that Clarence Cagle, Speedway superintendent, saw some preliminary drawings and gave his approval for construction.

"But we had only six weeks to meet the deadline Cagle gave us. It took up to 20 hours a day," explained the weary Arfons who now could sleep as long as the sun was out and the machine operative.

The vehicle is a combination cleaner and dryer, capable of removing liquids and solid material from the track surface.

It uses a 1959 4,000 horsepower Westinghouse J-34 jet engine for the cleaning and drying functions. It rests on a custom designed frame powered by a 4-cylinder engine straight from a Chevrolet Monza Coupe. The engine is linked to a Turbo-Hydramatic automatic transmission with a special Hurst shifter. The machine tips the scales at two tons.

The frame utilizes some stock parts: the power steering unit, rear end, and A-arms are straight from a Chevy ½ ton pickup truck.

The vehicle's suspension system enables it to tilt forward, backward, left, or right, through use of a special system derived from nose wheel landing gear taken off a jet fighter plane.

The system rests on four custom Cragar wheels, 13 inches wide and 15 inches in diameter. They are shod with prototype Goodyear all terrain vehicle tires.

The track dryer holds 148 gallons of jet fuel and 18 gallons of gasoline for the Monza engine. Fuel consumption worked out to about 14 mpg for the 4-cylinder and about two to three hours running time for the jet depending on shaft speed and output temperature.

The jet engine's starting power comes from a bank of bulldozer batteries. Once started, Arfons can vary the turbines's output temperature from 300 to 1200 degrees for maximum drying power.

Arfons explained that a 15 to 18 mph pace seemed about the best to dry a damp track while he must slow to about 5 mph to dry a wet track.

He said that the cleaner actually works better at a high speed usually at about 20 miles per hour.

Top speed for the machine? "She'll do about 50," Craig states.

The leading edge of the front in-

Parker

No locomotive cow catcher ever looked like this! From the front the Arfons track dryer is partially hidden by its large stainless steel intake scoop.

take scoop has a lip that contacts the track surface, picks up debris, and forces it into the intake suction created by the jet. This leading edge consists of a neoprene cord material similar to a conveyor belt about 3/8 of an inch thick.

Solid waste is caught and held by a triple layered screen that filters down to 50/1000 of an inch. The removable screen captures up to five pounds while particles smaller than 50/1000 of an inch are pulverized in the engine.

Liquid is diverted into the machine's 14 gallon holding tank and then injected onto the jet's flame, superheated, and vaporized. There is even a safety valve to bleed off liquid if pressure exceeds 35 psi.

The machine saw use throughout the month. It was used to clean up solid debris, oil dry material, and moisture, especially on race day.

Cagle said there were few bugs in the machine but in general he was pleased with its performance.

"But it sure burns jet fuel!" he added.

When asked about the turbine days at the Speedway, Craig smiles and then warns that turbine technology has not been standing still.

"There are engines today that could be competitive under current USAC rules if someone wanted to try it," he said.

Arfons stated that he has other projects besides the track dryer.

"I am working on a turbine powered bulldozer for one," Arfons said, "and some other things that I can't really talk about yet," he adds.

"I am motivated by innovation. I love to see a guy come in with something new and make it work. Then everyone copies him and he counters with something still better than before," Craig stated.

What about the future of the track dryer and changes that might be made?

"We want to change the 4-cylinder and add a V-6. Then we plan on adding some bodywork and clean up some of the details," Arfons said.

He added that other tracks have contacted him about using the dryer.

"Roger Penske has expressed interest in using it at his Michigan International Speedway," Craig announced.

Most who saw the dryer in action called it wierd looking and some even termed it ugly. But to Craig and Terry it was beautiful because it worked.

Track dryer at work. The Arfons' machine was called on numerous times when the weather threatened to slow down the program. It sure beats 40 men with brooms!

Steady Craig Arfons piloted the track dryer most of the month. A heavy steel roll bar protects him while to his right sits a 4,000 horsepower jet engine.

$calpers

They are the only sellers without a stand and their product is tickets. "Tickets, anybody here need tickets?"

The Peddler's License was designed for street vendors, but Scalpers use them too.

For the right price you can sit in any Grandstand you want to. The only catch is that you may have to hit your life savings.

By Dave Parker

They don't set up little wooden stands like most of the vendors do, but all major sporting events have them. They stand on the street corners and they don't have switchblades in their pockets.

Collectively, however, they've been labeled with a term most of us associate with Geronimo. The ticket scalper is as much a part of the 500 as chicken and A. J. Foyt.

The scalper is a mocked wage earner, who claims he actually gets the short end of his dealings. We visited a few of them this past May and here's what they said:

"People moan about our high prices but no one complains when food goes up or the prices of a motel room jumps from $15 to $50," said one.

The scalpers cluster around the 16th Street and Georgetown Road Intersection and work in packs or alone. Some will talk about their trade but most simply want to know if you are interested in tickets. If not, "Good bye!"

But Olin Willoughby consented and to witness his technique was something to behold.

Olin Willoughby and possible buyer discuss the possibilities. This scene is routine for the scalper when they meet ticket seekers. Would you call this sidewalk shopping episode an example of "the customer is always right?"

A looker will meander up and the question can come from either seller or buyer. "What do you have?" is responded with "What do you need?" or the scalper will ask first, "How many do you need?"

An older gentleman had been all over the corner looking for "the deal" He finally came up to Willoughby.

Willoughby: "How many tickets you need?"

Buyer: "I'm looking for some good seats."

Willoughby: "I got two Penthouse seats you can have for a good price."

Buyer: (the inevitable) "How much?"

Willoughby: "These seats are damn good, you can have the pair for $300."

Buyer: "Three hundred! What do they cost normally?"

Willoughby: "Fifty bucks, but try to get them for that."

Buyer: "That's too much!"

Willoughby: "I got two others you can have for two hundred and fifty."

Buyer: "No thanks, what about the Paddock?"

Willoughby: "I have two you can have for one hundred twenty."(Twenty dollar regular price.)

Buyer: "Thanks, but no thanks."

Willoughby: "Ok, but you won't do any better."

Willoughby turned out to be right. The same buyer was seen for the next hour trying. He seemed to get more frustrated but at least the prices didn't appear to shock him as much.

Willoughby explained how he determined the prices of each ticket.

"A lot of things make the price. You got so much invested right off. Usually we can't buy tickets first hand so we pay more than the face value to begin with. Then the longer you plan to stay in town the more expenses you must meet and that raises the price. You have to consider all these things plus how much you want to clear beyond expenses," he said.

Willoughby explained that he needed to make $500 this year but added that he has made up to $3,000 and had gone away losing money.

"Things aren't consistent and you have to be careful. The Speedway recognizes most of us and won't sell to us. We depend on other sources like people who can't use tickets or are forced to give them up for any price because they can't see the race," he added.

Willoughby fits the scalper mold. Most have southern accents and are

This youth was willing to spend one hundred dollars for two prime Grandstand E tickets. The seller didn't agree with his offer, however, and then tried to peddle him different seats.

from Atlanta. His paper peddler's license hangs from his belt. It reads Town of Speedway, Peddler's License. There are many to be seen and many to try for the right price.

Three other scalpers sit dealing down the street. They aren't friendly like Willoughby and are suspicious of camera and questions. Finally they realize there is no threat and begin to open up. A youngster comes up to them. He is looking for two Grandstand E tickets. The price, $125.

"Sheee-it," whines the scalper when the youth turns up in amazement at the quote. "Son, you won't do any better on this corner for these tickets." He looks and tries for his own deal.

"I got $100 and that's it. I want the tickets but this is all I have." he said.

"No way, son." is the reply.

"OK," replies the youth and he wanders off.

"We want buyers not shoppers."

The scalper leans over and begins to complain about kids who always want something for nothing.

"I hate coming to the Speedway. I can make more money at the Derby or football games," says one who won't give his name.

"The people at the Derby spend more than anyone. They think it is an insult to buy cheap tickets. They don't mind paying two or three hundred dollars for the right ticket even if the

whole scene lasts only a few hours." he urges.

"These people hassle and haggle for days' tryin to get the price down. The longer we have 'em the higher they are gonna get," he adds.

The same youngster returns to the scalper with two tickets in his hands.

"See, I could get what I wanted for $100," he boasts.

"Good son, but these are better." is the return.

Other scalpers settle in and form a group within a group. There seems to be some kind of credit system that allows scalpers to exchange tickets without exchanging money with them.

"Sure there is," says one. "We have credit between the sellers and we all try to help each other when we can. We are here to make money not deal with people who want to hassle us. We want buyers not shoppers," he states.

A heavy set scalper breaks into the conversation to tell of the best scalping opportunities.

"Besides the Derby, rock concerts are pretty good and the U.S. Open does well.

I ask about golf tournaments in general. "No, just the Open," is the reply. But he can't or won't tell me why.

The scalpers continue until race day when last ditch efforts to get any amount for the tickets creates a mad bargaining spree.

"I just wish it was football season again," said one.

"Boy, how you can make money off football games", he smiles.

500 SHRINE CLUB
MINI INDY CARS

by GEORGE MOORE
Courtesy of the Indianapolis STAR.

It is not every day you can make the claim "It's the only one like it in the world." But if you are a member of the Indianapolis 500 Shrine Club, you can.

The Indianapolis Motor Speedway has contributed to many offsprings during the 60-year history of running the annual speed classic—the "500" Festival, Detroit's participation in the Pace Car program, national sports television—and all have found their proper niche in the presentation of the race.

However, none is more unusual or long lasting than the Shrine Club which functions not only during May but during the 11 other months as an organization which has come up with a fine product mix of charitable works and automobile racing.

The members do the charitable work and, in the process, drive their models of 500-mile race cars in parades and at other functions.

"The Shrine started in Indianapolis in 1884," says 1975 club president James R. (Jim) Rodgers. "It's a reasonably good bet that the founders never thought that Shriners would be riding around in race cars.

"On a horse, maybe. But not in a race car."

In the parlance of the gambling trade, Rogers has what is known as a mortal lock on that one, for outside of Indianapolis, just like the man said, there are no Shriners riding around in race cars. That is an approach exclusive to the local Shrine Club.

"The idea of the club really goes back just a few years," Rodgers says. "It orginated back in 1964 during the action at the Speedway.

"Fellows like Walt Myers, who was the chief observer, Ed Jett, Charles Baugh, Hank Cook, all of them in racing, received favorable response from Shriners on the possibility of forming such a club.

"So after the first of the year, Jan. 18 to be exact, Charles H. Ellis who was the Potentate signed as his first official act the charter for the Indianapolis 500 Shrine Club."

With the signing of the charter, certain qualifications were laid down which gave the club a degree of exclusiveness. Members not only had to be a Shriner in good standing in a recognized Temple, but they also had to have served in some capacity at the Speedway during the racing season.

The club definitely was for racers only, as the first president was Cook, who still is an active United States Auto Club official, and its vice-president was Clay Ballinger, former dirt track driver and riding mechanic who also is an active USACer.

Over the years the club's membership roster has carried names of many famous drivers, mechanics and car owners. Four—Henry Banks, Al Miller, Bobby Grim and Jimmy Wilburn—competed in the 500.

The track itself also has contributed members. Speedway vice-president Clarence Cagle was the club's '66 head and safety director Joe Quinn joined the organization.

There is a certain similarity between the Shrine Club and the beginning of automobile racing. At first, there were no cars. The start was a case of being just a club.

The first car on the scene owed its appearance to Indianapolis businessman Dick Hunt, who had one built as a scaled down model of a 500 machine, and then other members got into the swing of things and either began constructing their own or having them fabricated by professional race car builders.

There is a scattering of front engine jobs, but the majority are rear engine, smaller versions of the championship equipment which races at the Speedway. A few actually were road racing chassis which ran in smaller engined sports car club events.

The Shrine Club wanted the racers to look like scaled down 500 jobs, so it owns the body molds used to fabricate the outer shell. A member can,

The Shriners call on Barney Wimmer to keep their cars running especially during parades. Wimmer is a former 500 mechanic who lends a hand when a Shriner needs one.

of course, create his own body configuration should he wish to emulate some particular national championship car design.

Of the 32 cars in the club, about 80 per cent of them use a VW for power. Others are powered by Corvairs or BMWs, and there is one four-cylinder Chevrolet water-cooled engine. The aircooled powerplants, however, seems to work a little better in parades at low speeds.

The automobile is a wonderous thing, but at times it can be cantankerous, and much of the "detankering" of the Shrine parade cars falls on the shoulders or veteran 500 chief mechanic Barney Wimmer. Wimmer, who was the club's parade marshal in '74, functions as a much helpful member to fellow Shriners who need mechanical assistance, sometimes right on the spot.

"An unexpected breakdown can be frustrating and embarassing thing to a man trying to put on a show in a parade," Wimmer said "But sometimes it takes some funny twists.

"We were in Toronto once when the manifold and carburetor on a car came loose. I had Jim (Rodgers) run back to the truck for the tool box, and before he got back some Toronto motorcycle gang had jumped in with their own tools and were working like mad.

"And they were good. They got everything hooked up and it ran beautifully."

The 500 Shrine Club is a traveling club which likes to show off its equipment. The cars as a whole are worth close to a quarter of a million dollars, and are put to excellent use by being loaned for display at various charity functions.

The clubs' contributions go to the Shrine's Crippled Children and Burns Hospital. Rogers says that the Shrine maintains 22 of these all over the United States.

In addition to traveling to Shrine parades at places like Miami, Atlanta, Toronto, Canada and this year at Kansas City in July, the club puts in appearances at functions which are not Shrine oriented.

Some of the cars are shipped by van while others are towed individually. "We travel 7,000 to 8,000 miles a year making about 30 parades," Rogers said.

It was at one of these that Wimmer, whose racing experience goes back before a lot of the young hot shoes of today were even riding in a perambu-

lator, showed them what a Shriner with a wheel in his hand looked like.

The setting was the Winchester Speedway where a parade was held through the streets of Winchester prior to going out to the high banked, high speed half mile track. Wimmer began running the paved track right up on the rim where the leaders who have that "I can't do anything wrong" philosophy ride and had the kids watching from the pits, mouth agape.

"Say, old man," said one of the impressed young chauffeurs, "you're pretty brave riding up there. How long you been driving one of those things?"

"He wouldn't have believed me if I told him," Wimmer said.

May is naturally a peak time for a club member. Not only is there a job to be done at the Speedway, but there are local appearances in the "500" Festival Parade plus circling the oval

on the first day of qualifications. And there is the more serious function of providing a day at the track for 33 handicapped children selected by the PAL Clubs.

Many years ago there was a motion picture made about automobile racing. The film starred James Cagney and was titled The Crowd Roars.

The Shriners turning the track in rows of three that first morning of time trials have no aspirations to be movie actors, but they know from actual experience the feeling Cagney portrayed on the screen when that mass of humanity packing the grounds comes to its feet in acclaim for the men parading before them. And it has caused more than one driver upon climbing out of his replica car after the 2½-mile journey to exclaim, "That makes it all worthwhile."

No, this isn't the parade lap at the Indianapolis 500 but it is a full field of Shriner cars. The mini-Indy replicas are an important part of the annual 500 ceremonies.

The Shriners are featured in programs across the nation. Here they participate in a 1972 parade in Lansing, Michigan to honor Oldsmobile Division's seventy-fifth anniversary.

OLDTIMERS CLUB

by Jack Fox

Despite the absence of several familiar faces, the 1976 gathering of the Indianapolis 500 Oldtimers Club was even more successful than it has been in past years. Once again the Huddleston Brothers made a spacious mobile home available as a club room and was parked in its usual spot right behind the Press Building with an excellent view of the southwest turn and adjacent partially-defanged "Snake Pit."

The always-gracious Mary Owen acted as hostess and put in long hours making sandwiches, serving drinks (soft!), registering members and keep-

Herman Winkler, Oldtimers President, poses with a 1923 Hispano Suiza.

Lee Oldfield has been a driver, head of the AAA technical committee and built the first Speedway rear engined car.

ing the books on who would attend the barbecue. This big event held under a tent behind the Tower, was hosted by the Hooks Drugs people (Bud Hook and Norman Reeves are Club members as are the Huddlestons). Assisting Mrs. Owen were two of the traditional first arrivals, Elmer Lombard and Freddie Mangold who come up from Florida each year. Big John

This mobile home serves as headquarters for the Oldtimers during their May get-togethers.

Mary Owen, The Oldtimers "Den Mother" and Ed Hitze pause outside the Oldtimers "Den."

Ira Hall, Pop Dreyer, Joe Leneki and other Oldtimers enjoy another story about the past.

Emil Andres, Tony Gulotta and Harry McQuinn are familiar faces at Oldtimers gatherings.

Berry was a daily visitor as was Lee Oldfield, 87 year old former driver, owner, and Chairman of the AAA Technical Committee. It will be remembered that Oldfield (no relation to the fabled Barney) entered the first rear-engined car way back in 1937. Another most welcome visiting member was Ernie Olson who was Jimmy Murphy's riding mechanic when the little Irishman won the 1921 French Grand Prix and who chief-mechaniced cars for many years.

The most asked question was "Is Charles Lytle coming this year?" Unfortunately the Sharon, Pa. historian was under the weather and missed his first race since 1935 but everyone's thoughts were certainly with him as they were for Frank Kurtis, Jimmy Wilburn and Fritz Duesenberg who were recovering from critical illnesses. A few days after the race, Jo Quinn, long time Safety Director, passed away at Methodist Hospital after a three-year illness. He had earlier been given a

Ira Hall is 84-years-old but that is only middle age by Oldtimers standards.

special award by the Club at the barbecue which was accepted by his son.

With Tom Carnegie presiding at the Barbecue, two drivers were inducted into the Hall of Fame...Cliff Bergere and Joe Dawson. Bergere, now 79 years old, was there to receive his honor and still retains his ramrod-straight military posture, crew cut and ever-present pipe. He would be the perfect stand-in for a British colonel, and it may be remembered that he played a cameo role of a Speedway guard in the 1949 movie "To Please A Lady."

Joe Dawson, who passed away in 1948, won the 1912 race at the wheel of a National as Ralph DePalma pushed his crippled Mercedes down the front stretch. Later he became an AAA representative in the Philadelphia area and served as an official at numerous races.

Other awards from the Oldtimers went to John Serbin of Monroe, Al Del Pico, of Sunnen, and Chris Economaki, publisher of National Speed Sport News and a commentator for ABC's Wide World of Sports. Another award went to Joe Cloutier, Tony Hulman's right hand man who was back after missing last May due to a serious heart attack.

Fred Young presented Peter DePaolo with the yearly Automotive Organizational Team award and the Bill Klein Award, in memory of the Club's late president, was given to Karl Kizer who has done so much work making the new Speedway Hall of Fame Museum a reality. Kizer, who is rarely seen in the trailer during May, is one of the key men in the success of the Club, doing most of his work behind the scenes.

Three Feminine members of the Speedway staff were given honorary memberships in recognition of 20 years service to the Speedway: Jan Binford, secretary to Jo Quinn; Lucille Raehn, assistant director of ticket sales; and Glad Cagle who is secretary to her husband, Clarence.

All of the nostalgia of a month of reminiscences culminated on the morning of the race when Fred Agabashian drove a lap around the track in George Robson's winning Thorne Special. Many of the grand old guys had departed after the Barbecue which saw over 200 members and a very few guests partake of the lavish meal. But those who remained, some still serving in official capacities, were thrilled to hear the deep-throated roar of the big blue six-banger. They don't sound like that any more.

How to Improve Race Car Performance

Brand new book, RACE CAR ENGINEERING & MECHANICS, jam-packed with priceless information no matter what you drive: sports cars . . . dragsters . . . NASCAR stock cars . . . formula iron . . . high performance sedans . . . USAC championship cars . . . it even will help you bring out the tiger in your street machine. Written in plain English, it's yours . . .

FREE

Above: Dry sump pump and toothed drive belt on a sedan engine. Note that water pump belt has no idler and rides in deep-groove pulleys. Below: Shaded area shows relative air pressure on different sections of race car at 100 mph.

. . . with money-saving Trial Membership in the Autos Unlimited Book Club and your agreement to buy just four other Club Selections during the next two years — all at DEEP CLUB DISCOUNTS that save you 15% to 70% off regular store prices.

THERE YOU STAND, staring at the car you race. It might be a Z . . . a Vette . . . something you did up from a basic VW . . . a Formula job. The questions are always the same: How are you gonna make this jewel of yours *lighter . . . faster . . .* more *stable* "at speed" . . . more *responsive* . . . run *cooler* . . . be more *maneuverable* . . . and *SAFER?*

Friend, we've got a new book for you that you're not going to believe! RACE CAR ENGINEERING & MECHANICS is by Paul Van Valkenburgh, who is world-famous for his work with Donohue and the Penske Team . . . as Tech Editor of *Sports Car Graphic* and for his contributions to the highly confidential "Chevrolet Racing Team". Van Valkenburgh has taken the subject of advanced race car technology and boiled it all down to simple every-

> "... many of the things I write here were previously known only by a very few professional racers." — Paul Van Valkenburgh
>
> "... the only book that really covers the subject in depth, in a modern way, with current information." — Don Cox, Chief Engineer, Penske Racing
>
> "... must reading for any aspiring race car mechanic, designer, engineer or driver." — John Dinkel, Engineering Editor, Road and Track

day English so YOU can doll up your car's performance *without* needing an engineering degree! Here are some samples:

Do you know the 4 factors that point like an arrow to the *best gear ratio* for *your* car? Page 192 tells you. On page 282 you find out how to find your car's exact center of gravity. Then turn back to 187 for Van Valkenburgh's 14 recommendations for endurance car *wiring* — advice that will save many precious pit-stop seconds, and maybe, the race itself.

Now flip to page 190 for the 2-step procedure that will keep header flange bolts absolutely tight under severe racing conditions. Go to page 161 where you get the 13 ways your car sends you *signals* while you're actually racing, so you can control it right at the "fine edge of traction". On page 240, there's a dynamite trick that enables you to *read up to eight cockpit instruments at once* — all in about 6/10ths of a second!

Thinking of putting in a Watts Linkage — or a deDion axle? Better read pages 51-54 before you sign the order. Thinking about acid-dipping for weight reduction? You need page 215.

Starting on page 120 you'll get some of the best information you've ever read on spoilers, wings, ducts and guide vanes. How to choose them. How and where to mount. How to set the angles. What to *avoid.*

But this section is not just about juggling around the hardware. You learn how to *drive* spoilers and wings . . . how other cars on the track affect the air flow around *your* car. AND — you learn the high art of drafting and slingshoting the way the pros do it!

There isn't a topic that hasn't been covered in easy-reading text and loads of clear photos, sketches, diagrams, charts and formulas. Whole sections teach you about racing wheels and tires. Brakes. Suspensions. Springs, shocks and roll bars. Stability. Gearing and differentials. Frames and bodies. Testing methods. Working out the fuel, oil, water systems. The ignition system. The exhaust system. How to engineer and construct your car for maximum pit-stop efficiency . . . and a whole lot more!

BIG DISCOUNTS . . . FREE SUBSCRIPTION MANY OTHER BENEFITS OF MEMBERSHIP

We don't care if you're a quiet-type guy looking to get a tad more zip out of your wheels on the way to the office . . . or you're a young buck with the smell of Indy in your nostrils. We have something BIG for you here: membership in the *Autos Unlimited Book Club.*

The first thing that happens when you join — you get the $15.00 *Race Car Engineering & Mechanics* — FREE. You also get — FREE — a subscription to *Autos Unlimited,* the Club's tremendously informative publication which is issued fifteen times a year. *Autos Unlimited* not only describes the Club's latest Selection and a load

of alternates, it's jammed with useful information for everyone interested in cars . . . and it also alerts you to *special sales* and other events "for members only". Everything you order from the Club is delivered at *deep discounts* ranging from 15% to 70% off regular store prices.

You'll be offered close to 200 books and products from which you need select only 4 in the next two years . . . including books on tuning, modifying or customizing your car . . . on the great cars, both the classics and today's high performance iron . . . the great race car builders. Others on dragging, rallying, track competition . . . technical guides for both foreign and domestic vehicles . . . books for modellers and collectors . . . *every* subject of interest to the auto enthusiast. And, since Club offerings are not always books, but also will cover items like accessories, special tools and instruments, etc. — your deep discount privileges are *worth even more!*

Hey, man. This is a green-flag opportunity! Fill out and mail the Trial Membership Application — to *Autos Unlimited Book Club,* Box 2008, Latham, New York 12111.

The Duesenberg

by George Moore
The Indianapolis Star

IMAGES DIE hard as far as America's romance with the automobile is concerned. And in some instances if you are dealing with a name like Duesenberg, they never die at all.

Probably there are no 10 letters in the history of the automotive industry or automobile racing which have more magic than those which spell Duesenberg. In fact, the magic is as alive and thriving today as it was when the last Indianapolis-built Model J rolled out of the plant on West Washington Street back in 1937.

The record books are well scribed with the names of the Duesenberg brothers, Fred and August, and like the mythical bird Phoenix, rising from the ashes to new triumphs, the Duesenberg brothers, 1976 version, are planning to add their own names to automotive lore.

Duesenberg brothers 1976?

Yes. Their names are Kenneth and Harlan Duesenberg, and they are the grandsons of a third Duesenberg. Henry, who was the brother of Fred and Augie. He stayed home in Iowa while his brothers went eastward to follow the lure of the early day period of automotive racing. But not his son, Wesley C., or his grandchildren.

THOSE PEOPLE who are fatalists, who believe everything is predestined and has a purpose, will understand what is happening now. The Duesenberg brothers are re-establishing the Duesenberg Corporation to Manufacture the Duesenberg automobile and have begun construction of the prototype in Chicago, Ill.

The artist's rendering shown was taken from the clay mockup which Ken did in his Duesenberg Designs, Inc., studio in Scottsdale, Ariz.

"It's something we should have done a long time ago," Harlan said. "We talked about it, but never put it into actual operation until now."

The Model J was a big automobile, and the new Duesey is continuing this concept. At a time when Detroit will be going the other way starting with the 1977 models this fall, the big job should stand out something like a lighthouse beacon in the middle of a dark night.

Today, in a period of bureaucratic governmental regulation, a small producer cannot manufacture an entire automobile. The limited production maker must work around an existing base, and that is precisely what the Duesenbergs are going to do.

THE ENGINE, drive train, chassis and inner body shell structure will be the 133-inch wheelbase Cadillac Brougham, the model which probably will be Cadillac Division's limousine in '77. But from that point on there will be no relationship to the Cadillac automobile

The sheet metal is entirely changed, as is the interior. And the electrical system will be modified. The famous Duesenberg grille — which is costing $2,000 to build — and the bow tie bumper is being contemporized to give a modern look to the J's appearance.

The construction work is being done in the Chicago shops of Robert W. Peterson, the Peterson of Lehmann-Peterson who made long wheelbase limousines out of Lincoln Continentals for a number of years and who built the presidential limousine during the administration of President Lyndon Johnson.

Ken, a graduate from the School of The Art Institute of Chicago, was manager of Whirlpool Corporation's industrial design center at Benton Harbor, Mich., before leaving and establishing his own design studio in Scottsdale. He was with Whirlpool 19 years, during which he worked with the company's international division designing products for use in France, Spain, Australia and Canada.

Harlan was the "racer" of the two, being a stock car driver right after World War II. One of the tracks he ran on was the old West 16th Street Speedway which was located across the street from the Indianapolis Motor Speedway.

He transferred to a more mundane set of wheels equipped with air conditioning, stereo, etc., to become a Chicago businessman in the insurance and printing industries..

Can the Duesenberg brothers 1976 make the car an active part of the automotive scene again? It will be a very interesting and very difficult undertaking. But like some philosopher once said, "Nothing is impossible."

1916

by Jack Fox

The 1976 "500" might have been the shortest Speedway event on record but the next shortest was the 1916 which was 300 miles in length...on purpose!

In the early days of Speedway racing, there were few privately-owned cars and Messers Fisher, Allison, Newby and Wheeler had to depend almost entirely on the company-financed teams to fill up their entry lists. It was hoped that a shorter race would insure a larger finishing field since it was obvious that there would be fewer starters. Why were there so few private owners? Race cars in that era were pretty exotic creations and there were few good mechanics who could work on them not already working for the mushrooming automotive industry had absorbed most of the mechanical technologists and not too

many other people knew metallurgy well enough to build or convert stock cars into competitive racing creations. This would not come until after the War (the Kaiser War, that is) when Louis Chevrolet and Cornelius Van Ranst began manufacturing speed equipment for Model T Fords and hundreds of "backyard mechanics" got into racing on dusty half-mile tracks.

A few homemade race cars did, find their way to the "brickyard" driven and built by eager, young men oblivious to the almost unsurmountable advantage held by the large company teams, but they were rarely successful. There were also AAA regulations which prevented the entry of more than a given number (usually three) cars of a certain make. This did even more to discourage the private owner.

Unfortunately for the Fisher group, the European War had depleted their

entry list for the 1916 race as the foreign teams which had won the 1913 and '14 events were not available as their personnel and some of their cars had returned to Europe because of the War. A few of their cars had been left and two Peugeots which were purchased by the Fisher group in case of just such a problem. So without foreign participation, the Speedway would still be able to field a group of highly competitive cars. Fisher's Prest-O-Lite Company had also taken over the ownership of two white Maxwells and placed them under the operation of Eddie Rickenbacker. Eddie, a fine mechanic and highly successful driver, would eventually buy the Speedway from Fisher and Allison a decade later.

The Peugeot Co. did enter one car in its own name driven by Italian-born, English-reared Dario Resta and Sun-

[194]

bean entered a car for Josef Christiaens.

Johnny Aitken was put in charge of the two Speedway Peugeots and it was decided that three additional replicas could be built by the Premier company. Aitken was also put in charge of this project and both the Speedway and Prest-O-Lite Teams repaired to a corner of the Allison Co. which became headquarters for these racing activities.

Aitken, the "swinger" of the prewar racing set, was the man who helped organize social events, entertain visiting firemen and on occasion act as Carl Fisher's "court jester." He was also a darn good race driver and won the 100-mile Harvest Classic held at the Speedway in September of 1916. It was his last victory as he fell victim to the Spanish flu epedemic and died in 1918.

Ralph DePalma was the most significant name among the missing entrants and his temporary departure resulted in a policy which the Speedway continues to this day; one which might have well saved the "500" from drivers overblown with their own importance. DePalma had not entered his Mercedes when the usual blanks had been sent

out. He was reported to be testing an aircraft engine at Sheepshead Bay, N.Y. with his close friend, the famed automotive engineer, Col. J. G. Vincent. It was "mentioned" to Carl Fisher that the previous year's winner wanted appearance money to enter the race...somewhere in the neighborhood of $5,000.

The explosive Fisher for once held his temper and totally ignored the demands. The deadline for receipt of entry blanks passed and there was no word from DePalma. The situation looked black for the Speedway with less than 20 entries on May First. It was announced that the deadline would be extended by one week due to the shortage. The delay proved fruitful as three Crawfords from Hagerstown, Md. were entered by Billy Chandler for the Crawford Motor co. and Grover Cleveland Bergdoll entered cars for himself and Eugene "Ike" Stecher, the Bergdoll family's chauffeur.

Bergdoll, and his brother Erwin, were wealthy Philadelphians but quite eccentric in their personal lives. Neither driver would attend the driver's meetings-always being represented by a proxy-and even to this day the

powerplants of their cars remain a mystery despite years of investigation by race historian, Charles Lytle. Even the existing photos of the Bergdolls show them with masked faces. When America entered the War against Germany, the Bergdolls and Ike Stecher escaped to Germany via Mexico and their case became front page news. For years after the cessation of hostilities the criminal charges hanging over them were aired by the courts in Congress and in the press. After two decades of legal maneuvers, the Bergdolls were allowed to return to Philadelphia where they lived out their lives as recluses.

Colorful Barney Oldfield, who had been feuding with DePalma-"The Barber" as Barney called him-personally brought his entry to Carl Fisher. Like the other drivers, Barney had heard that DePalma was demanding deal money or as the Grand Prix road racing circuit now calls it "Starting Money." Barney laid the entry blank on Fisher's desk. The cigar-chewing leadfoot told the promoter that he would gladly enter the race and compete for the ample $30,000 purse but IF the Speedway gave De-

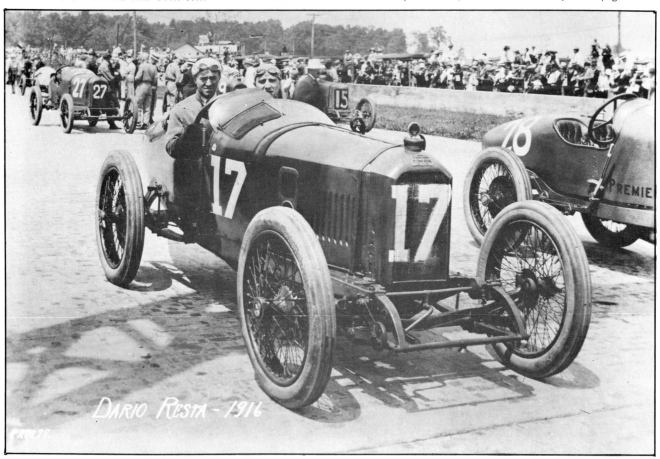

IMS

Dario Resta won the 1916 Indianapolis "300" in the blue and white factory entered Peugeot. From his fourth place starting position the Italian born, British bred racer won easily by pulling away in the early laps never to be seriously challenged.

IMS photos

Howdy Wilcox led the Indianapolis Speedway Co. Team in his green and white Premier.
He qualified sixth and topped his team with a seventh place finish.

Palma any additional money then he wanted an equal amount. Fisher gladly assured Oldfield that NO One would get anything he didn't race for and the men shook hands. This policy remains in force to this day. After the final entries had been accepted, DePalma asked permission to enter his Mercedes with, not him, but Frank P. Book as the driver. Book, who supposedly had driven in a few amateur races was the Detroit millionaire sportsman.

While the conjecture was running rife that if Book actually started the race DePalma might become the "relief" driver after only a few laps, it was announced that Book would not be able to drive the Mercedes due to family objections.

The Books' objections were nothing compared to some of the previously entered drivers who stated flatly that if DePalma was allowed to drive they would withdraw. They had nothing to fear since Fisher had not the slightest intention of allowing him to compete unless the entire field signed waivers for him to do so. These were not

forthcoming although DePalma did have a certain amount of support from the fans and one or two directors.

The shortened race solved several serious problems which faced the directors besides that of a car shortage. Both Chicago and Minneapolis-St. Paul had already held 500-mile races, the latter particularly unsuccessful, and thus cheapened the mystique of a 500-event heretofore reserved for Indianapolis. A certain group of vocal Speedway fans had been complaining to the management that the race was too long and that the competition would be closer if the distance were reduced. Frank Wheeler, who had already lost a bundle on the Twin Cities race, was particularly in favor of the shorter distance.

In view of the problems besetting the Speedway in 1916, 300 miles was a wise decision although the original distance was restored in 1919 and never reduced. . .on purpose! When the 300 mile race was set the directors had figured that DePalma would be an entrant and they had also counted heavily on Harry Harkness' team of three Delages. Unfortunately two of

these were wrecked in mid-May at Sheepshead Bay-Carl Limberg being fatally injured-and Louis Chevrolet's cracked a cylinder head and was withdrawn after qualifying. Two Duesenbergs failed to show up and the elusive Bergdolls withdrew their entries. Two of the three Harkness cars finally arrived but one broke a crankshaft after qualifying. Only 21 cars started the the race. The smallest field ever.

Dario Resta made a runaway of the race and after the first few laps it was virtually no contest.

The three green Speedway Premiers didn't offer much competition. Tom Rooney clobbered the wall on his 48th circuit and broke his hip: Gil Anderson broke an oil line on his 75th lap and Howdy Wilcox was the only one of the three still running at the finish and he trailed in 7th place. Only 11 cars were still running, which indicated that a 500-mile race would have had a slim finish indeed and might have been a real disaster.

While the official attendance wasn't given-a tradition which still exists-the crowd was estimated at 85,000; not quite up to expectations but with the Speedway's cars winning a part of the $30,000 purse the organizers made out rather well financially and bought the farm adjacent to the backstretch where the golf course now stands.

True to his promise, Carl Fisher left Ralph DePalma out in the cold and this must have proved a lesson to the Italian-born champion. When the entries for the Fall Harvest Classic were received, DePalma's Mercedes was among the first. Shortly before the race it threw a rod with no time to get the engine back in racing form. To show his sincerity-or contrition-he offered to drive any available car just to lend his name and support to the race. Fisher gave him one of the Speedway-owned cars and they remained friends for years.

Oldfield finished fifth in the "300" in his blue Delage, his best Indianapolis finish. . .and his last. The colorful barnstormer whose name was synomous with auto racing retired during the War and later was often quoted by the Hearst newspapers during their periodic anti-racing campaigns. Barney habitually referred to the Speedway as a "Murder Factory."

DePalma, whose actions in 1916 might well have wrecked the "500" died a beloved elder statesman of auto racing and Oldfield, whose gesture helped save the race, died a drunken outcast from the sport which he almost singlehandedly popularized.

Barney Oldfield drove his blue Delage to fifth place in his final Speedway appearance. In later years he turned against the track and even called it a "Murder Factory."

500 Yearbook Features Index

Official Photographers

by Jack Fox

"We Picture The Race For You" was the slogan accompanying Charlie Bell's Tower Studios ad in the official Indianapolis "500" program back in the late 1930's. Officially-recognized Speedway photographers have been doing just that since Messers Fisher, Allison, Newby and Wheeler first opened their wooden gates on 16th Street some 67 years ago.

While the Speedway always had the final say in who would take their official photographs their "in plant" production of these photos has been, more or less, a recent endeavor. It is a small miracle that a large percentage of the thousands of negatives taken through the years remain in reasonably good states of repair since there have been some pretty hairy situations arise which might have seen them consigned to a trash dump, traded for a bottle of wine or become victims of age, flood, fire, or pestilence. There have also been a few amusing incidents connected with the shooting of Speedway pictures.

Until 1958 the Official Photographer was a concessionaire granted reasonable exclusive access to shoot pictures in the pits and garage areas and the equally exclusive

right to sell his results at the track, in downtown stores, hotel lobbies and across the counter at his studio. Photos in the media were also obtained from this official source more often than not.

There were few amateur photographers in the early days although the finest set of photos of the 1911 race were supposedly taken by one Henry Ford who was a VIP in the original Pagoda. They are sharp, well composed and every bit as good as the 1976 product of modern technology.

The gentleman who had the exclusive rights to photograph the race in the several years before and after World War I was Harry Coburn, a meticulous man who really took his assignment seriously. He shot both stills and movies of the race and took his exclusive contract as just that! While there weren't too many amateur shutterbugs in 1914 there were of course some. Coburn didn't want an alien camera on the grounds and with the Speedway's compliance he ordered all guards to confiscate any camera they could find-paying them a small sum for everyone they turned in. Mr. Coburn had either underestimated the number of box Brownies in the hands of the spectators or the diligence of the guards as he was deluged with a huge pile of cheap cameras for which he was expected to pay a bounty. The order was not repeated the following year.

The photographers in the old days had it much rougher than they do today...especially those who were assigned to get action shots. These iron men were expected to carry bulky 8 x 10 view cameras, complete with tripod, around the inside of the track (or outside depending on where a wrecked car might quit bouncing) to get shots of the debris after a battered driver and mechanic had been removed from the scene. The actual racing was shot with a big 5 x 7 Graflex which did a pretty fair job of slowing down, if not stopping, the action. Both cameras were designed to engender hernias and it's doubtful if Mr. Coburn or his immediate predecessors had too much competition for the unique privilege of recording the "500" on film.

When Coburn put away his glass plates in favor of a more mundane job with the Indiana State Library, F.M. Kirkpatrick was named Official Photographer and he did an excellent job. He compiled a fine set of 8 x 10 negatives of every (well ALMOST every) car and driver, the starts, the finishes and finishers, officials, informal shots, visiting politicians (fortunately only a tiny fraction of those hordes who deluge the track and garage area today), and engines and mechanical features.

For over a decade Kirkpatrick went about his job with precision and missed only a handful of car and driver shots so dear to Speedway historians. This wasn't always easy as there were a few drivers who shunned cameras like the bubonic plague and fled at the click of a shutter. One of the most notorious camera-haters was W.W. "Cockeyed" Brown who drove a loud and greatly modified Hudson in 1919 during the Coburn era. The only existing racing photo of him that I know was one poorly blurred action shot of Brown speeding down the front stretch, that found its way into a newspaper prior to the 1919 race.

Mark Billman was another driver who didn't like to be photographed, especially before a race. He was able to evade Kirkpatrick after completing his qualification run but as he lined up for the actual race he couldn't get away. After the photographer explained that it was his job to get every starter Billman relented and allowed the man to shoot both a side view and a cockpit shot of himself and his riding mechanic, Elmer Lombard. Two hours later Billman was dead and Lombard critically injured.

In the late 1930's Kirkpatrick sold out his negative collection and official photographership to Charlie Bell, a fine lensman but a man who had a decided affinity for the grape. The fact that there were fewer photos taken during Bell's era may have been a result of his weakness or for the logical reason that there were fewer cars entered in the years just before World War II.

Bell had an assistant named Rose who did most of the actual work at the track. Through no fault of his own he missed some great shots of the burning of Gasoline Alley on the morning of 1941 race.

Let's backtrack a few days in May, 1941. Charles Lytle, famed Speedway historian and photographer was walking through Gasoline Alley snapping away with his Leica when a distinguished, elderly gentleman stopped him. Not too many people carried cameras in those days and the Leica had caught the gentleman's eye.

"Would you consent to taking my picture on my bicycle," asked the man and the affable Lytle readily

Great clouds of dust were an added problem for 1911 photographers.

agreed. It turned out that the man was one of the members of the Speedway Fire Department and held an important position. When Lytle refused to accept payment for his photo the man asked if he would like track credentials for race day.

In those pre-Hulman years credentials were much harder to come by (or not as regularly requested) and even Lytle did not have a pass which would get him on the track before the start of the race. When offered the rare cardboard badge Charles readily accepted.

Lytle was acquainted with Mr. Rose (remember Mr. Rose?) and asked if he could ride to the track in the photo truck on race morning. The Official Photographer was located downtown in those days and Rose and Lytle proceeded out 10th Street and turned up Main Street in Speedway where they were stopped by a traffic jam. Lytle asked a guard at the Prest-O-Lite plant if they could proceed through the grounds to avoid the stalemate and soon they were at the front gate of the track. Lytle flashed his credentials and the truck was waved in.

Once inside the gate Rose confessed that he didn't have any photographers' credentials as Charlie Bell was under the influence on the previous evening and had failed to give him any. Lytle was asked to stay with the truck

Wall standing may have been OK in 1911 but is a no-no these days.

[199]

Two rooftop photographers record Tommy Milton's 1921 win.

Photographers take choice rooftop locations prior to the 1930 race.

while Rose cornered Major Carpenter (the pre-Hulman Jo Quinn) for the necessary pieces of cardboard which would enable him to do his job. In a few minutes he returned with a funny smile on his face.

"I explained to Major Carpenter that Bell had been imbibing and had forgotten to give me my credentials" Rose related to Lytle, "and he agreed that it was a not unusual situation with the Chief Photographer. He handed me the necessary badges and then asked where the truck was parked outside the gate." I told him it was already inside the gate and he blew up. Dammit! You're the first person to get through these gates without a ticket,' and with that he snatched the badge back and threw me out of the office." How, and if, Mr. Rose ever got in to photograph the garage fire and race is unknown. The Speedway possesses a number of photos of the burned ruins but they were apparently taken the following afternoon. Lytle, with the proper badge, blythly said goodbye to Rose and went about snapping photos from the very best locations just as you and I would have done.

Charlie Bell retained official negatives during the war but it is believed that some of them were lost or quite possibly traded for a supply of liquid refreshment. Thankfully, only a few of the posed shots disappeared and other sources have been able to produce most of the missing views for copying by the Speedway.

After the War Bill Mickler took over the concession from Bell and about 1950 O'Dell and Shields bought out Mickler who went into the restaurant business. The quality

This official photo session of the mid-fifties looks like 1976.

of the photography under O'Dell-Shields left something to be desired but it improved rapidly once the Speedway began shooting their own photos in 1958 after buying the original set of negatives.

Photographer Bud Jones ran the Speedway's photo operation from 1968 through '71. His lab was located under the Tower Terrace grandstand and had to be considered less than ideal.

Charlene Ellis has been photo shop manager since Jones left and she too did a yeoman job from the cramped photo facility that still sees use throughout the month of May. Charlene's work has brought her in and out of the pits for years and she has performed her functions without ballyhoo. She never could understand all the fuss about women being allowed in the pits because it was always just one of the places she had to visit in order to function. Ladies in automobile racing could learn a few things about manners from Miss Ellis.

The opening of the new Hall of Fame has changed the face of the photo lab like the proverbial Jekyll and Hyde. The new photo lab must be considered one of the finest that money can buy. It's easy to elicit an, "I can't believe it" comment from Charlene and her assistant Cathy Craib, when referring to their new working area. And although a huge investment has been made in the photo lab, prices to race fans for 8" x 10" prints remain at a reasonable $2 for a black and white and $6 for color.

During May the Speedway's photographic staff is increased from its usual three to 20 or 25. Cameras ranging in size from 35mm to 8 x 10 are used for various purposes; action, candid shots, posed photos, color and portraits. The color photos are done with a 4x5 and Speed Graphics and smaller cameras account for the more informal and action shots.

Two cameras used by Kirkpatrick, an 8x10 view and a smaller Graflex have found their way into the Hall of Fame Museum since they have been quite important-particularly to racing historians-in visually recording the "500".

Just how many rolls of film are used in a given May may never be known but I'll bet the number would be staggering. Whether it be from Instamatics or expensive telephoto jobs (who seem to need a small man just to carry the protruding lens) the click of shutters is heard all over the grounds. It remains that if you really want a beautiful posed shot of a car, driver and crew you can't do better than get one from the Official Speedway Photographer.

Hints On Taking Good Racing Photos

Despite the constant battle to shoot through or over fences or from a distance while fighting the crowd, it is still possible for the average race goer to produce good, interesting photos.

Having the right equipment helps greatly. Most professionals use Nikon cameras, lenses and accessories. The F-2 body is very popular and usually is used in conjunction with the MD-2 motor and MB-1 cordless battery pack. The amateur, however, can do quite well with either the FT2 or EL.

At least three lenses are needed: a wide-angle (24mm or 28mm is best), a medium telephoto (105mm or 135mm) and a long telephoto (200mm to 300mm range).

When it is possible to get close to the cars without having to shoot through a fence, the wide angle lense is good for shooting over-all views of the cars although the photographer needs to be aware of the distortion such a lense will create from many angles. A three-quarter front view from a standing position will give optimum results. Shooting from close to the car at a low angle will enlarge the wheels or nose for instance and create interesting new perspectives of the car.

The medium length telephoto will give good pictures when used to shoot cars in the pits from along the pit fence if care is taken to shoot when no one is standing between the camera and the car. The same lense will give good results shooting through chain link fences if it is held against the fence and aimed through a hole.

The same lense is best for getting good portrait type shots of drivers and other personalities.

At most tracks the long lense is needed to record the race action and produce enough magnification to show the details of the cars involved.

Link

The photo above shows Bear wheel service personnel in their shop. People are well arranged and lighting is good. Photo below has subjects posed like firing squad victims. Background is inappropriate and lighting is harsh and makes subjects squint.

Good candid shot shows famous faces with crews enjoying a light moment without distracting foreground or background.

This good idea misses for several reasons. Track traffic should be race cars; Pat Vidan should be holding flag and camera should be raised slightly to put dark background behind hair and remove tower from his skull.

Whitlow

This shot would be much better if taken an instant later while Hank Higuchi is actually tying Jim Hurtubise' bandana on.

Whitlow

300 mm telephoto lense from high in stands gives enough scope to show car is alone but provides enough detail to identify car.

Hall of Fame

(Continued from page 117)

Finally, the racing fans of the world have a facility that is equal to the automobiles it represents.

The new Hall of Fame has modern exhibits in addition to vintage ones. This unique drag racing vehicle is powered by a rotary engine.

Curator Karl Kizer looks over "Old Calhoun" the roadster that Parnelli Jones drove to victory.

Restoration men Bill Spoerle, left, and Barney Wimmer shown with Kizer during final assembly of another roadster.

The Eddie Rickenbacker Duesenberg shown above was located in a barn after many year's searching. Although nearly gutted, enough of the car existed to make restoration possible.

Headlamps always have been important to an automobile's styling. These examples have more class than today's new square lights.

Ever wonder where bucket seats got started? These seats from a pair of brass era speedsters would cost you a small fortune today.

These three cars represent from left, the Novi, one of Al Dean's roadsters, and Bill Vukovich's 1953 winning Fuel Injection Special.

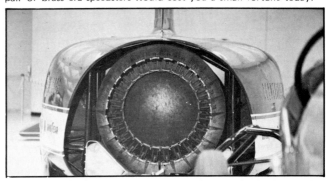

Here's the business end of Craig Breedlove's land speed record Spirit of America jet car he drove on the Bonneville salt flats.

down to a display board to keep it. I'm hoping we can expand our literature collection in the new museum."

Bloemker is another Speedway principle who's office has been moved to the new facility. His publicity department is located behind the car display area. Across the hall there are more executive offices, including one for Grounds Superintendent Clarence Cagle, the man who is responsible for nearly every physical change and upkeep of the entire Speedway facility. Virtually nothing happens to the grounds without Clarence's supervision. He's as much a fixture at the track as the yard of bricks that make up the start finish line. Sometimes he talks of retirement, but this quarter couldn't imagine the place without him, at least on a part-time schedule.

Upstairs there are meeting rooms and the all-important photography lab headed up by pert Charlene Ellis, the gal who is in charge of fulfilling the thousands of photo requests the Speedway annually receives. For the first several years Charlene was employed by the track her facilities were located under the grandstands north of the Tower Terrace: a lab that was fondly referred to as the Black Hole of Calcutta by her dedicated crew. (See companion feature story on the Speedway's photographers). Charlene and assistant Cathy Craib are also awed at the completeness of their new workshop.

There is a basement in the new facility too, not open to the public, that currently houses more vehicles that are either awaiting restoration or will be displayed on a rotating basis.

The last, and probably one of the most interesting additions constructed along with the new museum is the Louis Chevrolet Memorial, a display located to the left of the entrance.

One Fred Wellman (1889-1973) conceived the idea after visiting Chevrolet's grave and finding it to be marked only by a gray headstone. Wellman believed that Chevrolet's accomplishments in the automotive world deserved a more

fitting final tribute and set out to construct a lasting memorial. He formed the Chevrolet Memorial Committee and in 1965 began soliciting 200 cash contributions of $200 each in order to raise the $40,000 he and sculptor Adolph Wolter saw necessary to complete the project. Wellman also enlisted the services of William B. Ansted, Jr. to act as chairman of the committee along with A.W. Herrington as honorary chairman and Charles Keogh as treasurer.

Sculptor Woltor was an eminent choice as he had earned respect through his works that have included: the American Legion Office Building in Washington; the World War II Memorial at Detroit; the Powerama Exhibit at the Allison Division of General Motors.

Wellman himself visited the stone quarries in New England and chose the white Imperial Danby Marble and fine-grained granite. By 1970 the memorial, termed Greek Exedra, was finished and stored on the Speedway grounds while plans for the new museum were still under way.

Wellman, Ansted, Herrington and Keogh all died prior to the erection of the memorial but their successors, Karl Kizer, Charles Brockman, and Al Bloemker carried out the original plan. Tony Hulman assumed the necessary expenses to erect the monument and Clarence Cagle supervised the actual work.

We think that the only thing missing from the new facility is a proper dedication to Tony Hulman and his dedicated staff, one of the most important being Joe Cloutier, the man in the background who directs finances. In the bygone days of auto racing's dust and glory, we've heard more than one documented story about the racing promoter who absconded with the prize money. The new Hall of Fame is standing evidence that those behind the Indianapolis Motor Speedway have put their gate receipts to good use.

by Carl Hungness

Schuppan

Cont'd.

road-race circuit, rather than an oval track," said Schuppan, whose ride in the pace car at Trenton in April had been "the first oval race I'd ever seen in my life."

"There's really no difference," continued Vern, "except for the banked turns. Of course, the cornering speeds are so much greater you begin wondering why the thing isn't flying off the corners.

"The turbocharger did take some getting used to, naturally, since I'd never driven a turbocharged car before. It was fine, but you still feel that thing pushing you in the back as you go along."

Schuppan took time to explain what went wrong on his first qualifying attempt. "After our last practice we found the rear-wing position had changed, so we had to guess at the setting when we went out for the earlier run," he noted. "When I got up to speed, the car was unstable and difficult to drive at the right speed, so we came back in and got the wing set right."

The day was, of course, a huge success for someone from so far away that you might think the Indianapolis 500 gets about as much notice in his hometown as a minor-league hockey match. "No, actually many people in Australia are very much aware of Indy and, whenever I'd go back, they would ask me when I was going to be racing there," Vern reported, correcting that impression.

The news from Indy '76 probably was followed most closely by a Whyalla Chrysler dealer who once tried to stop his son from getting involved in automobile racing. "My father will be pretty pleased I imagine," said Vern.

"He has gone from being very angry with me and not writing me any letters to becoming my number one fan. He may even turn up in the U.S. later this year to see me race Formula 5000."

That was a far cry from the day Vern Schuppan left the shipbuilding town of 30,000 in South Australia to make his name as a motor racer. After a few years of training in go-karts, Vern moved to England to learn the ropes of international road racing.

He raced Formula Fords in England, his first race coming in 1969 at Oulton Park. He stayed with the FFs until 1971, when he moved into the Formula Atlantic series in England and won the series championship.

In 1972, Schuppan was at the top level of formula racing, driving the Grand Prix circuit for BRM. He did the same the following year, but also branched out into the endurance races of the World Championship of Makes series.

In 1974, he did those two circuits—switching to the Ensign team in Formula one—and expanded his endeavors to the U.S. by competing in the Formula 5000 series there. It was there that Schuppan was first noticed by the man who would eventually make his life-long dream of driving at Indy come true.

At the F5000 event at Riverside, Calif., that season, Schuppan qualified a privately entered machine for the outside spot of the front row. On the inside was the sleek and powerful turbocharged Indy-car built and owned by Dan Gurney and driven by 500 champ Bobby Unser.

Gurney noticed the performance of the soft-spoken Australian and, for 1975, he signed Schuppan as his lead driver on the F5000 tour. Schuppan rewarded Gurney with a second-place finish in the F5000 race run through the streets of Long Beach, Calif.

Vern also ran F5000 in England that season, finishing second at Silverstone and again at the Oulton Park. He also took a third in the 24 Hours of LeMans at the wheel of a Gulf Mirage.

Over the winter, he drove to the Australian Tasman championship, topped off with a victory at Oran Park.

Which brings us up to Indy 500 time. Starting 17th, Schuppan was in the best position of all the first-time Indy drivers to win Rookie of the Year honors. Ultimately he did just that, but not without some unfortunate setbacks first.

Schuppan had to make an extra pit stop early in the race when a blistered tire went undetected on his regular stopover for service. That set him well back in the field, but eventually he worked his way back up to 18th by the time the rains called a halt to the '76 race.

"Basically, I tried to keep out of trouble and not overextend myself or my car," he related later. "I have to admit I thoroughly enjoy this type of auto racing. I'd like to continue in it."

But for the additional pit stop, he might have enjoyed it even more, since the young Australian seemed to settle into the Indy groove as naturally as any veteran. "Yes, once we got it in the groove, everything was fine," he said, smiling. "I could run 180s and 181s with no problem. About 10 or 15 laps before the red flag, I passed Mosley and Parsons running in the high groove."

So, the personable Schuppan ended up with 18th place and his name on the Stark-Wetzel Trophy. Not bad for someone no one imagined would be anywhere near the Indianapolis Speedway on May 30. They won't make that mistake again next year.

or modifications, Bobby Unser's Cobre Eagle was even more radical, and the Sinmast Wildcats of George Bignotti and Al Unser's American Racing Wheels Parnelli-Cosworth were basically new for 1976.

Probably the most classic example of modifying an "old" car for the rule was Bobby Unser's Cobre Eagle. Without discarding the basic Eagle Model 6 chassis, the Cobre team had virtually redesigned it aerodynamically. The radiators, which were originally located just behind the front suspension, had been relocated just ahead of the rear wheels facing sideways, as is done in the Penske and March Formula 1 cars. Out of the airstream and with no ducting leading to them, it would seem the air had no reason to find its way to the radiators, but that isn't the case at all. The huge rear tires of an open-wheeler push so much air along ahead of them that a large part of it spills around the sides of the wheel. With the radiators placed back there in the flanks of the car, plenty of air feeds through them, albeit the radiators must be larger (and therefore, heavier) in order to generate enough cooling. However if you're going to carry a lot of extra weight, just behind the cockpit is a good place to have it in terms of weight distribution. More importantly, the great deal of aerodynamic drag caused by conventionally-mounted frontward-facing radiators is eliminated almost entirely. The air flows across the nose of the car much more efficiently, while the engine is being cooled just as effectively as if it had regular forward-facing radiators. This is yet another aerodynamic advance promoted by the extremely high speeds of Championship Car racing.

Even more aerodynamically acute than the Cobre Eagle was the all-new Hopkins-Offy for Roger McCluskey. Designed by Roman Slobodynskyj, who designed the precedent-shattering 1972 Eagle Model 6 (still the most popular car in the field four years later—there were sixteen Model 6's in the 500 this year), the Hopkins was in all respects the most advanced car at the track. It too had hip-mounted radiators, again fitted sideways in the chassis and depending on rear-wheel air for cooling. The Hopkins, though, had air-dams on the side of the tub as well in order to direct air to the rads. Slobodinskyj chose to adopt the hub-centerline front suspension first introduced by Bob Riley for A.J. Foyt's

Mahoney

This year the Gilmore car sported a new nose and turned the fastest practice lap.

Wick

The new George Bignotti built Wildcat II featured a Coyote-like nose piece. Here the car is about to be unloaded from the trailer for its maiden run during March tire tests.

Coyote several years ago, but Slobodynskyj's version employed very different suspension geometry than Riley's. Despite constant engine trouble, the Hopkins was fast almost immediately during practice, thanks in large part to its being aerodynamically the cleanest car at Indy so far. Even the turbocharger intake, normally stuck out in the airstream on most Indy cars, had been neatly fitted into the engine cover to reduce drag on the Hopkins. The car received the Indiana Society of Automotive Engineers Award and deserved it.

Another dramatically new car was the Parnelli 6B-Cosworth DFX for Al Unser. Superficially it looked very much like last year's Parnelli-Cosworth, but the car was actually very much changed. The chassis was much stiffer, incorporating three skins in a triangulated shape, both to promote better airflow to the hip-mounted radiators, and to provide greater crash protection for the driver. The wheelbase was longer for 1976, the transmission was a Weismann instead of a Hewland, and the suspension for the 6B was all

by shock/coil units instead of 1975's torsion bars. The rain-shortened race went badly for the Parnelli team because they had purposely held back, planning to run hardest in the second hundred laps, so unfortunately the race told little about just how fast the Parnelli really was.

While neither Team McLaren nor Dan Gurney's All American Racers brought all-new cars this year, both entrants had made a major change in their chassis. Without changing overall length, which is limited by the USAC rules, both had lengthened their wheelbase and shortened their nose pieces to allow further rearward placement of the rear wing. In both cars the change proved beneficial, particularly for Johnny Rutherford's McLaren, which brought Johnny his second Indy 500 victory in three years. Both Gurney and Team McLaren have new cars on the drawing board, McLaren's using their own version of the Parnelli turbocharged Cosworth DFX V8. After five years, though, you begin to wonder if a new McLaren is ever going to be necessary. The basic M16 format,

The Bignotti Wildcats had an excellent race day finishing third and fourth. The Foyt resemblence is obvious but Gordon Johncock and Wally Dallenbach relied on the four cylinder Drake-Goosen-Sparks engines. The cars had engine cowlings but they were not used in the race.

first introduced in 1971, is still as competitive as any Indy car to date and at the rate that things are going, the M16 may go on being competitive forever.

Another older car that just seems to get more and more competitive every year is A.J. Foyt's Coyote. Basically unchanged in the last-three

years, it still set the fastest lap of practice at the Speedway with a speed of 190.880 mph, and it also turned quickest lap in the race, at 186.027 mph. There is nothing like starting out with a basically good design and refining it piece by piece, which is what the Gilmore-Foyt people have done. In fact, their car has been so impressive

that it has influenced several other teams to imitate it. This year two teams did so in a big way-Grant King's Genesee-BottomHalf team and no less than Foyt's arch-rival, George Bignotti himself.

King's Dragon was an almost exact copy of the Coyote, from nose to hub carriers to overall aerodynamics. Unfortunately, though, the car was based on a misunderstanding of why the Coyote is so blindingly fast. Foyt's car emphasizes blistering straightaway speed, at the expense of cornering speed. It is an inevitable trade-off, because good cornering speed requires a lot of aerodynamic downforce, and aerodynamic downforce inevitably means a lot of drag. What makes Foyt's trade-off sensible, though, is the incredible horsepower generated by his Foyt V8. With the lower 75-inch boost rule, Foyt has an even greater horsepower advantage over the Offy this year than before. However Grant King's Coyote copy was using an Offy, which meant that it not only had to sacrifice cornering downforce because of its overall low-drag shape, but it also sacrificed straightaway speed due to its weaker engine. Without that storming turbo-Foyt engine, the rest of the Coyote formula isn't terribly useful. Both John Martin and Sheldon Kinser successfully qualified the King

The Hopkins Offy used this unique turbocharger mounting. This airbox fits through the engine cover to feed the unit but reduces drag without lowering efficiency.

cars, but they were at a serious disadvantage and had to run in the middle of the pack.

George Bignotti's imitating the Coyote was more successful. It shouldn't really be called an imitation, but more properly a "modification." The Sinmast Wildcats which first appeared in 1975 were designed by ex-Foyt designer Bob Biley, so similarities were understandable. For 1976, though, Bignotti and Riley decided to relocate the old side radiators in a broad, low "sports car" nose nearly identical to Foyt's. They too were looking for greater straightaway speed and were willing to sacrifice some cornering speed to get it. It had become clear that, while the Riley-style hub-center-line front suspension used in the Coyote, the Wildcats and the Hopkins

was no match for the conventional McLaren front suspension through the turns, straightaway speeds could be made much higher by optimizing aerodynamic efficiency. Like Foyt, Bignotti had decided to let the McLarens have the turns-you can't pass there anyway in most circumstances-Bignotti would take the straightaway speed instead. Of course that would require that the Wildcats have enough horsepower (as King's didn't) to take advantage of those straights. Since the Wildcats were using Bignotti's DGS engine, a redesign of the basic Offy, Wildcat drivers Johncock and Dallenbach seemed at first to have more than enough power for the race, and in fact in the early running they were able to run right along with Rutherford and Foyt. However, as time wore on

Rutherford and Foyt gradually pulled away, Johnny establishing his biggest advantage in the turns, and Foyt being strongest on the straights. Until someone devises an engine as powerful as A.J.'s, the only way to beat him will be in the turns, and it seems only McLaren realizes that. Perhaps the turbo-Cosworth is the engine that will match Foyt, but when the rains came on lap 102 and stopped the race, the only Cosworth, Al Unser's, had not yet begun to run hard enough to tell the story. We'll have to wait till next year to see if anyone can match A.J.'s incredible V8 and Rutherford's even more incredible corner-demon, the McLaren M16. But next year Rutherford may have both a dynamite Cosworth and a new McLaren corner-burner. That should be a combination to see.

Bobby Unser tries to hold off a charging Mario Andretti. Here you can see Unser's rear mounted radiators and how they clean up the car's frontal area. Unser finished in tenth place while the faster Andretti in a McLaren moved to get eighth spot.

After a tire change early in the race Johnny Rutherford's McLaren was the best handling car shown here as Gordon Johncock attempts to pass. Note the differences in the rear wings as Rutherford's was set lower and farther to the rear.

John Martin in No. 98 had the slippery Foyt inspired King Dragon but didn't have the horsepower to make the combination work. Mario Andretti passed Martin easily while Martin fought to finish in twenty first place, six laps behind winner Johnny Rutherford.

Driver Biographies

This Year, A Few Even Told Us About Their First Race

MARIO ANDRETTI

Mario Andretti had decided to pass up the Indianapolis 500 in 1976 because it conflicted with the Monaco Grand Prix and this was the year Mario was going to go all out to win the world championship. Then Roger Penske offered him a ride in one of his McLarens.

Andretti missed the first weekend of qualifying to run another Formula One race but still picked up some extra cash for his qualifying efforts as he registered the quickest qualifying time of the month when he ran 10 miles in 3:10.07 for a speed of 189.404, bettering pole sitter Johnny Rutherford's speed by nearly a half mile an hour.

Mario started 19th but wasted no time moving through the field to reach seventh by the 10 lap mark. He consistently ran in the top 10 throughout the rest of the race and had the three cars in front of him lined up in his sights when the race was stopped. Just as he had been in 1969 when he won, Mario was driving a red car he hadn't expected to be driving. If it hadn't rained. . .

His eighth place finish was his best in recent years and indications are that the little Italian immigrant may soon be back to the form which helped him rule USAC from 1965 to 1970 during which time he won three national Championships and a host of wins in addition to his 500 victory.

GARY BETTENHAUSEN

One of the second generation drivers at the Speedway, Gary Bettenhausen has been dogged by some of the same tough luck which kept his father Tony from ever winning at the Brickyard.

Gary's best year at the track was 1972 when he qualified fourth and led much of the race before engine failure slowed and finally stopped him late in the race when he was beginning to look like a sure winner. That honor went to his teammate Mark Donohue.

He ran his first four races under Thermo-King Sponsorship before joining the Penske team. That marriage resulted in wins at Trenton in 1972 and Texas in 1973 but otherwise was disappointing to both parties. A Syracuse Dirt Championship race in 1974 ended for Gary in a nasty accident which nearly destroyed his left arm.

Although his arm was slow healing, Bettenhausen was back at the Speedway in 1975, again with Thermo-King but a shredded tire put him into the wall and out of the race after 158 laps. This year he was the last car to drop out of the race when his turbocharger failed on lap 52.

TOM BIGELOW

Tom Bigelow made his third 500 this year after moving from the Rolla Volstedt team to the A. J. Watson-Leader Card combination. He barely sneaked into the field, qualifying 32nd but happy to be starting there instead of 33rd where he began the 1975 race.

Once again he worked his way steadily through the field to finish 14th. In three races he has started 23, 33, 32 and finished 12, 18, 14. If he ever gets his qualifying act together he might blow everybody else off the track.

He began racing Midgets in 1957, moved into IMCA Sprinters then joined USAC fulltime in 1968. In 1969 he won the Astrodome Grand Prix Midget race and his first Sprint feature. He won his first Dirt Champ race at Du-Quoin in 1972 and was runnerup in the Sprint and Dirt divisions in 1974. After a slow start in 1975, he won the last three Dirt Championship races but fell 60 points short of catching Jimmy Caruthers for the title.

Photos by deBrier, Flynn, IMS, Link, and Wick

LARRY CANNON

"It was in an old jalopy at the Eastern Illinois Fairgrounds at Danville, Illinois; I think it was 1958.

"The thing I remember most is, I'm going down the backstretch lined up in about the fourth row, which is the same as I'm in here at the speedway. But I was in the middle of the fourth row, and it was the first race I ever drove in.

"I looked over to my left--I was driving along with my elbow out the window, like you do in traffic--and this car is about six inches from me. I thought, 'Boy, he's a little close, I'd better give him some room.' So I leaned to the right just a little bit and I bumped the car on my right.

"All of a sudden, I looked and there's cars in three or four rows in front of me, a car on my left, a car on my right, and in the mirror I look and there's a couple of cars behind me. That makes you kind of tense up a little bit more.

"That's my recollection of the first race I ever drove. I did not win my first race, like a lot of guys are lucky enough to do."

Once he got the lining up part down, Larry Cannon was on his way. He moved from stock cars to super-modifieds and won 130 features at tracks near his Oakwood, Illinois, home.

He came to the USAC sprint and midget ranks in 1969, winning a race in each division that season. He has since won five more sprint car features.

The first start for the 39-year-old politician, barber, and racer at Indianapolis came in 1974 when he squeezed into the field near the end of qualifying time. He was a victim of mechanical trouble in the race and placed 24th.

For 1976, he put the American Financial Eagle into 10th starting spot and finished 17th.

DUANE CARTER JR.

Second generation driver Duane "Pancho" Carter could well be the first of that select group to reach Victory Lane at the Speedway. This year, his third at the Speedway, he drove last year's winning car for Dan Gurney, America's top race car builder and head of one of the strongest racing teams.

He was his usual consistent self this year starting sixth and finishing fifth. The fact that some observers were a bit disappointed with that showing shows how highly touted he is. The four drivers ahead of him have won 10 500's between them.

When not running the Championship cars, Pancho keeps busy running and winning Sprint and Midget races. He is the only driver to have won both of those divisions.

Gurney is said to have a completely new Eagle in the works for the 1977 race. With Pancho behind the wheel it could very well fly right into Victory Lane.

Art Pollard's misfortune may have been the start of something good for Wally Dallenbach but it couldn't have seemed so at the time.

Dallenbach had labored in relative obscurity on the USAC trail until 1972 when Andy Granatelli chose him to drive the STP Lola in the 500 after Pollard had crashed the car and broken his leg in the process.

Although Dallenbach was running at the finish, his car had caught fire on three of his four pit stops. That ride eventually led to a ride with the Pat Partick team which had later picked up the STP sponsorship.

Now under the Sinmast banner, Dallenbach regularly runs in the top notch cars of George Bignotti and has a 500 win (at Ontario) under his belt.

Although he had only a few days to set up his brand new Wildcat this year, Wally qualified safely and led three laps while running near the front of the field all day and thinks he could have done better than his fourth place finish if the race had continued.

When not racing the former New Jerseyite spends his time working with a rescue team he formed after moving to his Basalt, Colorado home.

WALLY DALLENBACH

The broken suspension on his car would have finished the race for many other drivers before the rain did but A. J. Foyt was running second and working hard for an unprecedented fourth Indianapolis win when Indiana's fickle May weather stopped the 1976 race. "I hope to Hell it ain't a race," he told a questioner as he eyed the sky and his newly repaired car.

But it was over and he had lost again. He had another one of his fits which have marked his career then started planning to win the next race and undoubtedly the next Indianapolis race.

In his nearly quarter century of racing A. J. never has learned how to lose--he's been too busy winning. About the only races he hasn't won several times are those he hasn't entered. He has won six USAC 500 mile races and six National championships. In his spare time he has picked up a dirt champ title and a USAC Stock Car title.

During the past winter he won the International Race of Champions championship although not winning any of the four races in the series.

He has proven his versatility with wins in the Daytona 500 and the 24 hours of LeMans. He still runs occasional Sprint and Midget races and wins his share but he still has not achieved his ultimate goal--winning a fourth Indianapolis 500. You can bet he won't quit trying until he does.

A.J. FOYT

"It started when I was 16, at a midget race at Joe Shaheen's quarter-mile dirt track in Springfield, Illinois. I went over there on Saturday and just jumped into it, went out and made a couple of hot laps in it, came in, and qualified it.

"I think it was fast enough to make the race, I can't even remember what it was. We started the race in the back and, the first time, I just went out there and drove it around for awhile to see if I could get to like it. If I did like it, I thought I could get going faster with each lap.

"It was just kind of a research deal on the first one."

Spike Gehlhausen went on to race more midgets with SLARA the remainder of the 1971 season and on into 1972. He raced CORA midgets through the 1973 season before mov-

ing into the USAC ranks in 1974.

He ran his first USAC dirt championship event at Springfield in 1975 and placed seventh. His pavement champ-car debut was at Milwaukee the same year and he finished 10th. His performances on the champ trail earned him the title of Rookie of the Year in that division.

A 21-year-old bachelor from Jasper, Ind., he qualified the Spirit of Indiana McLaren owned by his father for the '76 Indy 500, but had to pull out on the pace lap when the car's oil pressure dropped drastically.

SPIKE GEHLHAUSEN

JERRY GRANT

Fishermen talk about the "one that got away" but Jerry Grant had

his hooks in racing's biggest catch in 1972.

He was leading the Indianapolis 500 with just a few miles to go when a tire went flat and he had to limp into the pits and out of the clouds. To make matters worse, he was penalized for going to the wrong one and ended up 12th instead of second.

Losing that whopper hurt, but the gregarious Grant still keeps coming back and casting his line.

Maybe, just maybe, he'll get another bite.

BOB HARKEY

"I was in the 11th grade in high school in Charlotte, North Carolina, and two buddies and myself built a hot-rod. We took a '29 Model A roadster and we put a '34 Ford V-8 engine in it.

"Now there were posters all along the telephone posts at that time saying, "Auto Races." It didn't specify like they do today--Sprint, Midget, Stock Car. It just said Auto Races.

"So we took the hot rod to Gastonia, North Carolina, Robinwood Speedway, which is a quarter-mile high-banked clay track. We got to the speedway and it was actually a sportsman amateur race mainly. There were a lot of '37, '39 Ford coupes with limited sportsman engines.

"So, a modified showed up with three carburetors, burning alcohol, a midget showed up, with no top on it, of course, and burning alcohol, and I showed up in a roadster with no top on it. We were all illegal to run with the amateurs.

"At this particular time, I guess

Chuck Berry or someone had a record out called "A Kid In A Hopped-Up Model A," and the announcer asked the crowd if they wanted to see the kid in a hopped-up Model A race and they said yes, so I ran a 15-lap race with the midget and the modified in my hot rod.

"I won the race and made 15 dollars. It was two years before I won the next one."

From that beginning came the racing career of Bob Harkey, one of the longest among active Indy driver. The 45-year-old racer, who has often doubled as an airplane stunt pilot and now resides in Indianapolis, ran midgets and roadsters through the late '40 and most of the '50s. He was NASCAR midget champion in 1957.

He drove his first Indy 500 in 1964, bringing the Wally Weir roadster home eighth. Despite an ensuing period of near-misses at Indy, he logged many miles in champ cars, dirt cars, midgets, and stocks. He returned to the Indy lineup in 1971, missed in 1972, and has made the show every year since.

He placed eighth in 1974 and was 10th in '75, relieved by Salt Walther. He made the '76 race in one of Grant King's entries and was running 20th when the race was called to a halt.

DAVID HOBBS

David Hobbs first came to the Speedway in 1971 from the unlikely sounding place in England called Upper Boddington to drive for Roger Penske. His first race ended near the finish line when he was clobbered by the wildly careening car of Rick Muther on lap 107.

After a year's absence he returned in 1973 and again ran 107 laps before rain ended the proceedings. The next year he finally got to run all day and completed 196 laps before being flagged.

His finishing record of 20th, 11th, and fifth must have led to a certain amount of anticipation when he landed the second Dayton-Walther ride this year. However he could qualify only 31st and a water leak put him in the pits at the start of the race and he finally had to give up after only 10 laps.

He began racing in 1959 in a sports car and moved through the sports and formula car ranks until reaching the international racing scene in 1968. His main claim to fame is in the F-5000 Series where he won the most races, scored the most points and recorded the most top qualifying laps of any driver. He won the F-5000 Continental Championship in 1971 and is still one of the top drivers in that series.

GORDON JOHNCOCK

Gordon Johncock was ready to run 500 miles on May 30, 1976 and win. He started in the middle of the front row and ran the way he wanted to all day but the rain short circuited his plans.

Gordie has been one of the top threats to win any Championship race during the past few seasons and he has won several but he has had some bad luck along the way. In 1966 he was involved in the first lap crash and lost time in the pits undergoing repairs but returned to run the distance

faster than winner Graham Hill.

He won in 1973 but the win was tainted by the tragic events and bad weather that year and the 5-7 charger is determined to win a full length 500.

SHELDON KINSER

"The first race I ran was at Bloomington Raceway, a quarter-mile high-banked dirt track south of Bloomington, Indiana. We built an old rat racer, which was back when they ran the six-cylinders.

"We didn't finish the first one, but we took it home and repaired it, then came back and were lucky enough to win the second one. I must have won at least 40 or 50 races down at Bloomington over a period of time after that."

Sheldon Kinser went on to be a top competitor in the tough super-modified circuit that runs at southern Indiana tracks like Bloomington, Paragon, and Haubstadt. He came to the USAC sprint car circuit full-time in in 1974, driving Grant King's familiar number 56 sprinter.

He won his first USAC sprint race at Terre Haute in August of 1974. His other sprint victories came at Illiana in 1975 and the '76 season opener at Eldora. He also won the 100-mile dirt championship race at Syracuse on July 4, 1975.

He became King's Indy-car driver in 1975, driving the Spirit of Indiana entry to a 12th at Indianapolis and 15th at Pocono. The strapping 33-year-old from Bloomington placed 19th in the 1976 Indy 500 with King's THEBOTTOMHALF Dragon.

STEVE KRISILOFF

Just about everybody remembers Steve Krisiloff's first May at Indianapolis.

He showed up in 1970 with an old chassis, a tired engine and alone. He did all his own mechanical work and chased his own parts.

He got bumped from the starting lineup and thumped by a mugger outside the track, but his desire, knowledge and ability impressed everyone and the next year he came to 16th and Georgetown with Andy Granatelli.

And he hasn't watched the Speedway classic since.

AL LOQUASTO

"The first race I ever competed in was a hillclimb in the Pennsylvania Hillclimb Association in Mt. Pocono, Pennsylvania. That was 1958 and I drove a '57 Corvette which was owned originally by Roger Penske.

"First time in the car, first outing, we finished first overall and first in class. We were really tremendously happy with it and the car owner was just tickled pink.

"Funny story about it was, the first time out in practice, we spun out and cracked the right front fender and I figured, 'Boy, that's the end, the guy's going to take the car away from me.' But he came back the next day and said, 'No problem, Al, we'll fix it and get you out there so you can race tomorrow.'

"And, like I said, we did very well. So, that was the starting of my career."

Al Loquasto kept on winning in the hillclimbs and was national overall champion for five straight years beginning in 1962. He also branched out into sports car and sprint car racing at various Eastern circuits during that time.

He came to USAC in 1968 and first passed his rookie test at Indianapolis in 1970. Though he ran many championship races in the succeeding years, his Indy experiences were an exercise in futility, or so it seemed.

He actually qualified for the '75 race, the first driver to do so, but a seemingly safe speed turned unsafe on the last day of time trials and he was bumped. The 35-year-old racer from Easton, Pennsylvania, finally made it in '76, putting the Clint Brawner-prepped Frostie Root Beer McLaren into the race and finishing 25th.

JOHN MARTIN

"The first race was at Mid-America, which is in Wentzville, Missouri. I kind of grew up on that track, being as it was at home.

"I won every race there that year in SCCA. It was like a bootleg road course, you might say. It was like running down South, running booze or something. It was down through the woods, and trees and all that stuff were your sideline, more or less.

"My first race there was in a Corvette. In those days, a 327 Corvette was classified as A Production and I had those nasty Cobras to contend with, but my first year I think I got 13 out of 15 races. So, naturally, I was Midwest champion."

That was 1965 and, operating out of Houston, Missouri, John Martin raced USAC stock cars and Trans-Am cars over the next three seasons. He went Formula A racing in 1970, placing 11th in the series standings.

He first made the Indy 500 field in 1972 and, for four years, was noted for bringing his famed Unsponsored Specials to the champ car trail. Acting as his own car owner, mechanic, and driver, he still managed to become a genuine contender on the Indy circuit, finishing eighth in the 500 in 1973 and 11th the next year. He also has finished fifth in the California 500 on two occasions.

In 1976, the 37-year-old resident of Long Beach, California, finally gave up being a one-man gang and became the lead driver in the Grant King stable. He put the Genesee Dragon in 15th starting position at Indy and placed 21st in the finishing order.

ROGER McCLUSKEY

Roger McCluskey has been racing

at the Speedway almost as long as anyone else (14 times) but could challenge Lloyd Ruby for the hard luck title. In all those races the most laps he has ever run are 188 in 1971 when he was flagged while running ninth. His best finish was in 1973 when he was running third when rain stopped the race. He was still running in 1975 when rain again stopped the race with Roger in fifth spot.

This year many observers thought the Tucson, driver had his best chance ever to win but he faded quickly from his 13th starting position and crashed heavily into the third turn wall on lap eight.

During his long career McCluskey has had his good fortune winning 23 Sprint races, 22 Stock contests, four Championship races, He won the National championship in 1973, the Sprint title in 1963 and 1966 and the Stock crown in 1969 and 1970. The biggest win of his career was the California 500 in 1972.

After a couple of frustrating months and a few spins, Larry McCoy qualified as a race driver in 1975.

That was the year he made his first Indianapolis 500 and finally got some respect.

And he made it two in a row this past May, although mechanical trouble KO'd him once again.

But he's getting experience--and that's what it takes.

LARRY McCOY

It seems hard to believe Mike Mosley has been in nine 500's but the records show he first ran in 1968

and finished the race to take eighth. But from then on his Speedway fortunes have been less than good.

In 1971 he and Bobby Unser tangled with each other and both the outside and inside walls and five cars parked in the fourth turn. Mosley was trapped in his completely smashed and burning car for several minutes and spent most of the rest of the season recovering. He returned to the Speedway the next year only to hit the same wall in nearly the same place again. He avoided broken bones the second time but the new burns nearly called a halt to his career.

A sixth place start in 1974 and fifth the next year finally got the charger good ink in the papers but engine failures ended both races prematurely.

He won at Phoenix in 1974 and at Milwaukee in August of 1975. He retired shortly after but missed the action and decided to return to the tracks at the start of the 1976 season.

MIKE MOSLEY

"Driving midgets was so easy compared to racing cycles I couldn't believe it at first."

So says Jan Opperman about his early racing days.

Opp was banging off the fences on two wheels before trying his hand at midgets.

He's not exactly sure what year or what track, but he does vividly recall the facts of his initial effort.

"I won my heat and the race," says the desperado of the dirt,"

From there, Opp went to the super modifieds where he became the most feared outlaw in sprint racing.

He's since settled down with USAC, but continues his winning ways in the sprinters and midgets.

Opp's made the show at Indy twice, is starting to run all the champ races with his new deal and will probably have to be reckoned with at the Brickyard after he gets a few more laps under his helmet.

JAN OPPERMAN

JOHNNY PARSONS

Ever since he got Ayr-Way to sponsor him, Johnny Parsons has been shopping for his first championship trail victory.

And it should happen any day now.

J.P. has blossomed into a constant contender in the Indy cars and with a little luck, he might have already won one this summer at Michigan.

He "just" made the show in 1974, but the past two Mays, Parsons has been running strong fifths when mechanical ills set in.

And since '75, he's been passing people he's not supposed to in the midgets and sprints.

But he knows where the money and the satisfaction is. His dad found it first and Johnny won't settle for second.

BILL PUTERBAUGH

Bill Puterbaugh made Speedway history while setting a record which still stands in 1968 but never got to start the 500 until 1975. Lee Elkins finally put a car under him that would run and Bill took his 83 seriously and qualified at 183.833 to start 15th.

He ran well all day, finished seventh and was named Rookie of the Year. He was running steadily along again this year when the rain ended his second race with him running 22nd.

Oh, yes. His record is for the latest qualifying run ever. He took the checkered flag at 7:40 p.m., in the dar. He was bumped the next morning.

Abe Rayborn had no idea what was in store for the young man he was strapping in his midget back on that humid Texas afternoon in 1946.

It was a sultry Sunday and Abe was hot-lapping his racer when a cycle riding buddy came over to talk. The kid's right arm and leg were encased in plaster (compliments of a two-wheeled race the week before) but Abe asked his friend if he wanted to try out his little bundle of horsepower.

The kid accepted and that was the start of a saga named Lloyd Ruby.

And you'd think a guy that had been racing for 30 years would have trouble recalling his first fling in the sport of speed.

Not Rube.

"I had a couple of half-casts on but I could move pretty well so I decided to give it a try," reflected Rube. "Before the afternoon was over I was runnin' as fast as a lot of the guys that had driven for him.

"So the next week I began driving steady for him and it wasn't long after that we began racin' four nights a week."

Since then, Rube has been through the seven-nights-a-week barnstorming, the tiny dirt bowls, the roadsters, the rear-engined racers, the good times and the many disappointments that have stalked him.

He's led a bunch of laps at Indianapolis, but never the one that counted.

But Rube, as always, isn't getting excited. After all, he's only 48.

LLOYD RUBY

Johnny Rutherford's victory in the rain-shortened 1976 500 was accepted by the Texan as kind of poetic justice. He admitted A. J. Foyt might have beaten him if the race had resumed but recalled last year when rain stopped the race with Bobby Unser in front. Rutherford felt he could have won that one. "I would have liked to have gone the whole distance and won but the rain stopped us last year and this year we were in front so we won it."

His second win in the 500 was also his second win in two races this season and continued the good show-

ing the one time hard luck driver has been making in recent years.

Until winning the 1974 event Rutherford had finished only two of 10 races with ninth place his top achievement. He missed the 1966 race while recovering from two broken arms suffered in a Sprint car accident which nearly ended a career which had been looking very good in that division.

"Lone Star J.R." as he is now known on the Citizen's Band frequencies, first gained special notice at the Speedway in 1970 when he came from nowhere to just miss knocking Al Unser off pole position. He joined the McLaren racing team in 1973 and set the qualifying record of 198.413 which still stands.

His charge from 25th starting position in 1974 will not soon be forgotten by racing fans.

John and his wife Betty, a former track nurse, are one of the most popular "teams" ever to have been to Victory Lane.

JOHNNY RUTHERFORD

"My first race was in September 1969 at Oulton Park in England. I moved to England in 1969 and started out in Formula Ford. I think there were 32 starters in the race and I finished 12th, as I remember.

"Nothing at all unusual happened, really. I had come from karts three or four years prior to that and I remember feeling that the Formula Ford was nothing like a go-kart to drive. The handling was lousy. A kart handles fairly well, and the power-weight ratio of a good go-kart is much greater than that of a Formula Ford.

"So, my first experience with a racing car was to feel it--that type of racing car, anyway--was a bad handling car and just had no power.

Vern Schuppan, whose original home was in Whyalla, South Australia, later moved into a variety of formula racing cars in international competition. He drove formula one for BRM in 1972 and 1973 and split his time between an Ensign F1 car and a Teddy Yip F5000 entry during the 1974 season.

For 1975, he became the F5000 driver for Dan Gurney's factory Eagle, placing second at Long Beach. He also placed third in the 24 Hours of LeMans in '75 and began the '76 season by winning the Australian Tasman championship and placing third in the Pocono F5000.

At Indy for the first time, the 33-year-old road racer finished 18th in the second of Gurney's Eagles to become 1976 Rookie of the Year.

VERN SCHUPPAN

"My first race was 1964 at Fontana dragstrip and I was driving a top fuel dragster. I only made a half-pass on my first run; it was 141.

"I was driving my dad's top fuel car, and it really was exciting. It was somethin' else. The weird part was that we started right in top fuel, and then we went in top gas for awhile. I think my next run was 170, then 180, and then it was a few weeks later we ran 200."

After becoming the first 16-year-old to do 200, Billy Scott spent the next five seasons becoming one of America's top drag racers. He was inducted into

that sport's Hall of Fame in 1968.

He started driving stock cars and sprints in California then, competing in major NASCAR sportsman and CRA sprint races. He came to USAC in 1974 and placed 14th at Phoenix in his USAC champ car debut.

The 27-year-old bachelor from San Bernardino, California, placed 29th in the 1975 California 500 but failed to make the lineup at Indy that year. In '76, though, he was the best rookie qualifier there, putting the Spirit of Public Enterprise Eagle in the field at 183.383 mph. He finished 23rd.

BILLY SCOTT

"It was in Salt Lake City, in 1963, I guess it was. I watched some races at the local fairgrounds there, and then one day I asked a fellow if he would sell his car.

"He sold it to me for $350 and I went out the next weekend and took my first race in a supermodified on a quarter-mile race track in Salt Lake City. I rolled the car immediately, after qualifying. About the third lap of the main event, I rolled it over and totaled the car.

"We started over with another one the following weekend. That taught me a little bit of courtesy to the car. In other words, I felt I could leave my foot in it, and the car obviously wasn't able to do so. I learned that very rapidly."

Born in Seattle, Washington, Dick Simon was already a ski jumping and parachuting champion before turning to auto racing. After winning a supermodified championship in Utah in 1965, he turned to sports car racing in 1968.

He ran Formula A in 1969 and won the Continental Divide event, winding up eighth in the point standings for the SCCA series. Indy racing came along in 1970, and he placed 14th that year at the 500. He then finished third in the California 500.

He has been a starter in every Indy 500 since, as well as most of the other events along the championship trail. The 42-year-old former insurance company executive, who has a home in Sandy, Utah, put Rolla Vollstedt's Bryant Heating and Cooling entry in the '76 race but a blown engine put him out ofter only one lap.

DICK SIMON

"The first race I ever ran was in a 1938 Chevrolet coupe, just a jalopy, at a three-eighths-mile pavement track in Spokane, Washington.

"I can remember it was going to be our first win. It was about a 20-lap race and we were rounding the corner on the last lap and tried to pass a slower car. Well, he moved over and put us right into the wall, so it took away our first win in our first race.

"It was sort of disappointing to me at that time. We finished about 50 feet short and halfway over the fence."

After that almost-auspicious start in 1969, Tom Sneva drove a supermodified to the CAMRA championship the next year. He came to Indianapolis for the first time in 1973, a virtual unknown in those parts, and failed to make a qualifying run.

Later in the season, however, he made himself known to Midwest race fans by winning six USAC sprint car features in a controversial rear-engine sprinter. The following May, he was the quickest rookie qualifier at Indy in Grant King's Kingfish and ran as high as fourth before dropping out to be classified 20th.

For 1975, he joined the Roger Penske team and put the Norton McLaren in fourth spot in the Indy 500 lineup. He was running well after 125 laps when he crashed spectacularly in the second turn. He escaped serious injury, however, and returned to drive at Pocono. He then won the Michigan 150 for his first championship trail victory.

The 27-year-old former schoolteacher from Spokane qualified Penske's Norton McLaren for the outside of the front row in '76 and was running sixth when the rains came.

TOM SNEVA

GEORGE SNIDER

Nobody pays much attention to George Snider.

And he doesn't do too much to attract it.

But if you've ever watched him run on the dirt you probably couldn't take your eye off him.

Ziggy, as he's known in the racing world, doesn't stir up much dust unless he's in a race car.

He's made Indianapolis for 11 straight years, won the dirt championship and been a continuous front runner in the sprints.

Quick and quiet.

AL UNSER

Al Unser was just getting ready to run hard when rain ended the 1976 500. Had the skies not opened the race may have had another three time winner instead of a two time champ.

The youngest of the Racing Unsers had finally gotten the new Cosworth engine and Parnelli chassis sorted out and was ready to redominate the Championship trail.

Although still in his 30s Unser has become one of the greatest drivers in the history of the Speedway. He started his first 500 in 1965 driving for A. J. Foyt.

A motorcycle wreck kept him out of the 1969 500 but he came back to take the pole, lead 190 laps and win the 1970 race. He repeated the next year and settled for second place in 1972. Along the way he won nearly every other Championship race and picked up a national title.

He won the dirt championship in 1973 then went into a mild slump until this year.

He is also a regular on the Formula 5000 trail where he has shown he can turn right quite well also.

BOBBY UNSER

Bobby Unser had an unfamiliar look about him when he arrived in Indianapolis for the 60th running of the 500. He was still driving a Dan Gurney Eagle but it was a highly modified version and carried the colors of the Fletcher Racing team.

The defending champion had left the Gurney team last year because he wanted to spend more time racing the USAC Championship trail than the team was planning. He still had most of last year's crew with him and Bob Fletcher put plenty of money into the race effort but things just never quite clicked. Two of the latest Offenhauser engines failed and Bobby finally had to qualify on the second day using an older engine.

He managed to improve on his 12th starting position to finish 10th but was not able to run as quickly as he has in recent years.

The older of the Racing Unsers first ran at the speedway in 1963, crashing his roadster in the second turn of his second lap. He piled into the McDonald-Sachs wreckage the next year before finally getting in some racing in 1965 in one of Andy Granatelli's Novi's. He ran very consistently until a small inexpensive part failed.

He drove his first Eagle in 1967 and hasn't been in a different chassis since. He finished ninth that year and first and third the next two. The wing got his bird flying again in 1972 but fast qualifier and DNF were the story until 1976 in most races although he held together long enough to pick up four championship wins in 1972.

BILL VUKOVICH

Billy Vukovich sums up his first race in his typical tell-it-like-it-is style:

"Man I stunk," laughs Vuky.

"I had a flat-head Ford I bought for $600 and everybody else had Chevrolets. The race was at Airport Speedway in Fresno, where my dad became famous, and I took off work early to make it in time for practice.

"I was scared and I started my heat on the pole, went straight to last and finished seventh out of eight cars.

"I just did make the semi and I started last in a 15-car field and chugged around and finished 11th. I was slow and bad."

But that was in 1963 and today the 32-year old Vukovich is good and fast.

He graduated from the California modifieds to midgets and it didn't take him long to go to the head of that class. He came to USAC with sharp tongue and cocky attitude, but he also packed a lot of ability.

He was as good a midget shoe as there ever was and he made Indianapolis at the tender age of 24 and he's been a front-runner there ever since 1971.

He hasn't been THE front runner yet, but he's working on it.

SALT WALTHER

"I raced the boats from the time I was 12 years old on, but the first time in a car was a sprint car for Casey Newberry. It was called the Broadway Radiator Special, which I think Sammy Sessions had driven.

"I was only 20 and you had to be 21 to even run them, so USAC threw me out. But they didn't throw me out until the next race I went to and they found out how old I was. As best I can remember, that was about 1967; I don't even remember where it was.

"I do remember that I didn't make the feature, but I made the consy and was running pretty respectable. We had a water leak, or an oil leak, where I didn't get to finish. It was quite a thrill, though, and I was tickled to death to even make the consy.

"That was the beginning--good, bad, or whatever."

David "Salt" Walther continued to divide his racing time between the hydroplanes and the sprint cars until he moved into Indy-type cars in 1971. He qualified for his first Indy 500 in 1972, but suffered magneto failure on the first lap. His first-lap luck continued the next year, as he was involved in a fiery crash on the front-stretch.

He ran 17th in 1974, then placed 33rd for the third time in 1975. He relieved teammate Bob Harkey, however, and finished 10th in the second of his father's Dayton-Walther McLarens. He also placed eighth in the California 500 that year.

In 1976, the muscular 28-year-old bachelor out of Dayton, Ohio, was running a strong ninth after starting 22nd when rain cut short the Indy 500.

Performance Records

Year	Car	Qual.	S	F	Laps	Speed or Reason Out

MARIO ANDRETTI, Nazareth, Pennsylvania

Indianapolis 500 Record (Passed Driver's Test 1965)

Year	Car	Qual.	S	F	Laps	Speed or Reason Out
1965	Dean Van Lines	158.849	4	3	200	149.121
1966	Dean Van Lines	165.899	1	18	27	Engine
1967	Dean Van Lines	168.982	1	30	58	Lost wheel
1968	Overseas Natl. Airways	167.691	4	33	2	Piston
1968*	Overseas Natl. Airways			28	10	Piston
*(Rel. L. Dickson)						
1969	STP Oil Treatment	169.851	2	1	200	156.867
1970	STP Oil Treatment	168.209	8	6	199	Flagged
1971	STP Oil Treatment	172.612	9	30	11	Accident
1972	Viceroy	187.167	5	8	194	Out of fuel
1973	Viceroy	195.059	6	30	4	Piston
1974	Viceroy	186.027	5	31	2	Piston
1975	Viceroy	186.480	21	28	49	Accident
1976	CAM2 Motor Oil	189.404	19	8	101	Running

GARY BETTENHAUSEN, Monrovia, Indiana

Indianapolis 500 Record (Passed Driver's Test 1968)

Year	Car	Qual.	S	F	Laps	Speed or Reason Out
1968	Thermo-King	163.562	22	24	43	Oil cooler
1969	Thermo-King	167.777	9	26	35	Piston
1970	Thermo-King	166.451	20	26	55	Valve
1971	Thermo-King	171.233	13	10	178	Flagged
1972	Sunoco McLaren	188.877	4	14	182	Ignition
1973	Sunoco DX	195.599	5	5	130	Running
1974	Score	184.492	11	32	2	Valve
1975	Thermo King	182.611	19	15	158	Accident
1976	Thermo-King	181.791	8	28	52	Turbocharger

TOM BIGELOW, Whitewater, Wisconsin

Indianapolis 500 Record (Passed Driver's Test 1973)

Year	Car	Qual.	S	F	Laps	Speed or Reason Out
1974	Bryant Heat-Cool	180.144	23	12	166	Flagged
1975	Bryant Heating	181.864	33	18	151	Piston
1976	Leader Card	181.965	32	14	98	Running

LARRY CANNON, Danville, Illinois

Indianapolis 500 Record (Passed Driver's Test 1974)

Year	Car	Qual.	S	F	Laps	Speed or Reason Out
1974	American Financial	173.963	33	24	49	Differential
1976	American Financial	181.388	10	17	97	Running

DUANE (Pancho) CARTER JR., Brownsburg, Ind

Indianapolis 500 Record (Passed Driver's Test 1974)

Year	Car	Qual.	S	F	Laps	Speed or Reason Out
1974	Cobre Firestone	180.605	21	7	191	Flagged
1975	Cobre Tire	183.449	18	4	169	Running
1976	Jorgensen Steel	184.824	6	5	101	Running

WALLY DALLENBACH, Basalt, Colorado

Indianapolis 500 Record (Passed Driver's Test 1967)

Year	Car	Qual.	S	F	Laps	Speed or Reason Out
1967	Valvoline	163.540	15	29	73	Accident
1968	Valvoline	165.548	12	17	146	Engine
1969	Sprite	166.497	19	21	82	Clutch
1970	Sprite	165.601	24	17	143	Magneto
1971	Sprite	171.160	23	24	69	Valve
1972	STP Oil Treatment	181.626*	33	15	182	Flagged
1973	Olsonite Eagle	190.194	20	24	48	Conn. rod
1974	STP Oil Treatment	189.683	2	30	3	Piston
1975	Sinmast	190.648	21	9	162	Piston
1976	Sinmast/Goodyear	184.445	7	4	101	Running

A. J. FOYT, Houston, Texas

Indianapolis 500 Record (Passed Driver's Test 1958)

Year	Car	Qual.	S	F	Laps	Speed or Reason Out
1958	Dean Van Lines	143.130	12	16	148	Spun out
1959	Dean Van Lines	142.648	17	10	200	133.297
1960	Bowes Seal Fast	143.466	16	25	90	Clutch
1961	Bowes Seal Fast	145.907	7	1	200	139.130
1962	Bowes Seal Fast	149.074	5	23	69	Accident
1962*	Sarkes Tarzian		17	20		Starter failure
*Rel. E. George 127-146						
1963	Sheraton-Thompson	150.615	8	3	200	142.210
1964	Sheraton-Thompson	154.672	5	1	200	147.350
1965	Sheraton-Thompson	161.233	1	15	115	Gearbox
1966	Sheraton-Thompson	161.355	18	26	0	Accident
1967	Sheraton-Thompson	166.289	4	1	200	151.207
1968	Sheraton-Thompson	166.821	8	20	86	Engine
1969	Sheraton-Thompson	170.568	1	8	181	Flagged
1970	Sheraton-Thomp ITT	170.004	3	10	195	Transmission
1971	ITT-Thompson	174.317	6	3	200	156.069
1972	ITT-Thompson	188.996	17	25	60	Engine
1973	Gilmore Racing	188.927	23	25	37	Conn. rod
1974	Gilmore Racing	191.632	1	15	142	Gearbox
1975	Gilmore Racing	193.976	1	3	174	Running
1976	Gilmore Racing	185.261	5	2	102	Running

JERRY GRANT, Irvine, California

Indianapolis 500 Record (Passed Driver's Test 1964)

Year	Car	Qual.	S	F	Laps	Speed or Reason Out
1965	Bardahl MG Liq. Sus.	154.606	17	27	30	Magneto
1966	Bardahl Pacesetter	160.335	10	10	167	Flagged
1967	All-American Racers	163.808	30	20	162	Piston
1968	Bardahl Eagle	164.782	15	23	50	Trans. lubr. leak
1970	Nelson Iron Works	165.983	29	7	198	Flagged
1972	Mystery Eagle	189.294	15	12	188	Flagged
1973	Olsonite Eagle	190.235	18	19	77	Conn. rod bolt
1974	Cobre Firestone	181.781	17	10	175	Flagged
1975	Spirit of Orange Co.	184.286	14	20	137	Piston
1976	California/Oklahoma	183.617	20	27	91	Running

BOB HARKEY, Indianapolis, Indiana

Indianapolis 500 Record (Passed Driver's Test 1963)

Year	Car	Qual.	S	F	Laps	Speed or Reason Out
1964	Wally Weir's Mobilgas	151.573	27	8	197	Flagged
1971	Joe Hunt Magneto	169.197	32	22	77	Rear end
1973	Bryant Heating-Cooling	189.733	31	29	12	Engine
1974	Peru Circus	176.687	31	8	189	Flagged
1975	Dayton-Walther	183.786	23	10	162	Running
1976	Dave McIntire Centers	181.141	28	20	97	Running

DAVID HOBBS, Upperboddington, England

Indianapolis 500 Record (Passed Driver's Test 1971)

Year	Car	Qual.	S	F	Laps	Speed or Reason Out
1971	Penske High Perf. Prod.	169.571	16	20	107	Accident
1973	Carling Black Label	189.454	22	11	107	Flagged
1974	Carling Black Label	184.833	9	5	196	Running
1976	Dayton-Walther	183.580	31	29	10	Water leak

GORDON JOHNCOCK, Phoenix, Arizona

Indianapolis 500 Record (Passed Driver's Test 1965)

Year	Car	Qual.	S	F	Laps	Speed or Reason Out
1965	Weinberger Homes	155.012	14	5	200	146.417
1966	Weinberger Homes	161.059	6	4	200	143.084
1967	Gilmore Broadcasting	166.559	3	12	188	Spun out
1968	Gilmore Broadcasting	166.775	9	27	37	Gearbox
1969	Gilmore Broadcasting	168.626	5	19	137	Piston
1970	Gilmore Broadcasting	167.015	17	28	45	Engine
1971	Norris Industries	171.388	12	29	11	Accident
1972	Gulf McLaren	188.511	26	20	113	Valve
1973	STP Double Oil Filter	192.555	11	1	133	159.036
1974	STP Double Oil Filter	186.750	4	4	198	Flagged
1975	Sinmast	191.652	2	31	11	Ignition
1976	Sinmast/Goodyear	188.531	2	3	102	Running

SHELDON KINSER, Bloomington, Indiana

Indianapolis 500 Record (Passed Driver's Test 1975)

Year	Car	Qual.	S	F	Laps	Speed or Reason Out
1975	Spirit of Indiana	182.389	26	12	161	Flagged
1976	THE BOTTOM HALF	181.114	29	19	97	Running

STEVE KRISILOFF, Parsippany, New Jersey

Indianapolis 500 Record (Passed Driver's Test 1970)

Year	Car	Qual.	S	F	Laps	Speed or Reason Out
1971	STP Gas Treatment	169.835	27	31	10	Accident
1972	Ayr-Way/Lloyd's	181.433	10	21	102	Turbocharger
1973	Elliott-Norton Spirit	194.932	7	6	129	Flagged
1974	STP Gas Treatment	182.519	15	22	72	Clutch
1975	Lodestar	182.408	29	11	162	Running
1976	1st National City T.C.	182.131	23	24	95	Running

JOHN MARTIN, Long Beach, California

Indianapolis 500 Record (Passed Driver's Test 1971)

Year	Car	Qual.	S	F	Laps	Speed or Reason Out
1972	Unsponsored	179.614	14	16	161	Fuel leak
1973	Unsponsored	194.384	24	8	124	Flagged
1974	Sea Snack Shrimp	180.406	22	11	169	Flagged
1975	Unsponsored	183.655	16	27	61	Oil rad. cooler
1976	Genesee Beer	182.417	15	21	96	Running

ROGER McCLUSKEY, Tucson, Arizona

Indianapolis 500 Record (Passed Driver's Test 1961)

Year	Car	Qual.	S	F	Laps	Speed or Reason Out
1961	Racing Associates	145.068	29	27	51	Accident
1962	Bell Lines Trucking	147.759	9	16	168	Spun out
1963	Konstant Hot	148.680	14	15	198	Spun out
1965	All-American Racers	155.186	23	30	18	Clutch
1966	G. C. Murphy	159.271	21	13	129	Oil loss
1967	G. C. Murphy	165.563	22	19	165	Engine
1968	G. C. Murphy	166.976	7	29	16	Oil cooler
1969	G. C. Murphy	168.350	6	14	157	Exhaust header
1970	QuickKick	169.213	4	25	62	Crank case
1970*	Sprite		16		52	Accident
*Rel. M. Kenyon						
1971	Sprite	171.241	22	9	188	Flagged
1972	American Marine	182.685	20	24	92	Valve
1973	Lindsey Hopkins Buick	191.928	14	3	131	Flagged
1974	English Leather	181.005	27	16	141	Rear end
1975	Silver Floss	183.964	22	5	167	Running
1976	Hopkins	186.500	13	30	8	Accident

Performance Records

LARRY McCOY, Bristol, Pennsylvania

Indianapolis 500 Record (Passed Driver's Test 1973)

Year	Car	Qual.	S	F	Speed or Laps	Reason Out
1975	Shurfine Foods	182.760	28	30	24	Piston
1976	Shurfine Foods	181.388	26	26	91	Running

MIKE MOSLEY, Fallbrook, California

Indianapolis 500 Record (Passed Driver's Test 1967)

Year	Car	Qual.	S	F	Speed or Laps	Reason Out
1968	Zecol-Lubaid	162.499	27	8	197	Flagged
1969	Zecol-Lubaid	166.113	22	13	162	Piston
1970	G. C. Murphy	166.651	12	21	96	Cracked block
1971	G. C. Murphy	169.579	19	13	159	Accident
1972	Vivitar	189.145	16	26	56	Accident
1973	Lodestar	198.753	21	10	120	Conn. rod bolt
1974	Lodestar	185.319	6	29	6	Engine
1975	Sugaripe Prune	187.833	5	26	94	Piston
1976	Sugaripe Prune	187.588	11	15	98	Running

JAN OPPERMAN, Noxon, Montana

Indianapolis 500 Record (Passed Driver's Test 1974)

Year	Car	Qual.	S	F	Speed or Laps	Reason Out
1974	Viceroy	176.186	32	21	72	Spun out
1976	Routh Meat Packing	181.717	33	16	97	Running

JOHNNY PARSONS, Indianapolis, Indiana

Indianapolis 500 Record (Passed Driver's Test 1973)

Year	Car	Qual.	S	F	Speed or Laps	Reason Out
1974	Vatis	180.252	29	26	18	Turbocharger
1975	Ayr-Way WNAP	184.521	19	19	140	Trans. shaft
1976	Ayr-Way/WIRE	182.843	14	12	98	Running

BILL PUTERBAUGH, Indianapolis, Indiana

Indianapolis 500 Record (Passed Driver's Test 1968)

Year	Car	Qual.	S	F	Speed or Laps	Reason Out
1975	McNamara	183.833	15	7	165	Flagged
1976	McNamara	182.002	18	22	96	Running

LLOYD RUBY, Wichita Falls, Texas

Indianapolis 500 Record (Passed Driver's Test 1960)

Year	Car	Qual.	S	F	Laps	Speed or Reason Out
1960	Agajanian	144.208	12	7	200	135.983
1961	Autolite	146.909	25	8	200	134.860
1962	Thompson Industries	146.520	24	8	200	138.182
1963	John Zink Trackburner	149.123	19	19	126	Accident
1964	Bill Forbes Racing	153.932	7	3	200	144.320
1965	DuPont Golden "7"	157.246	9	11	184	Engine
1966	Bardahl Eagle	162.455	5	11	166	Cam gear
1967	American Red Ball	165.229	7	33	3	Valve
1967*	Wagner Lockheed		26		82	Spun out
	*Rel. G. Snider					
1968	Gene White Company	167.613	5	5	200	148.529
1969	Wynn's Spitfire	166.428	20	20	105	Fuel connector
1970	Daniels Cable Vision	168.895	25	27	54	Ring-pinion
1971	Utah Stars	173.821	7	11	174	Gearbox
1972	Wynn's	181.415	11	6	196	Flagged
1973	Commander Homes	191.622	15	27	21	Piston
1974	Unlimited Racing	181.699	18	9	187	Out of fuel
1975	Allied Polymer	186.984	6	32	7	Piston
1976	Fairco Drug	186.480	30	11	100	Running

JOHNNY RUTHERFORD, Ft. Worth, Texas

Indianapolis 500 Record (Passed Driver's Test 1963)

Year	Car	Qual.	S	F	Laps	Speed or Reason Out
1963	U.S. Equipment Co	148.063	26	29	43	Transmission
1964	Bardahl	151.400	15	27	2	Accident
1965	Racing Associates	156.291	11	31	15	Rear end
1967	Weinberger Homes	162.859	19	25	103	Accident
1968	City of Seattle	163.830	21	18	125	Fuel tank
1969	Patrick Petroleum	166.628	17	29	24	Oil leak
1970	Patrick Petroleum	170.213	2	18	135	Brkn. header
1971	Patrick Petroleum	171.151	24	18	128	Flagged
1972	Patrick Petroleum	183.234	8	27	55	Conn. rod
1973	Gulf McLaren	198.413	1	9	124	Flagged
1974	McLaren	190.446	25	1	200	158.589
1975	Gatorade	185.998	7	2	174	Running
1976	Hy-Gain	188.957	1	1	102	148.725

DICK SIMON, Salt Lake City, Utah

Indianapolis 500 Record (Passed Driver's Test 1970)

Year	Car	Qual.	S	F	Speed or Laps	Reason Out
1970	Bryant Heating-Cooling	165.548	31	14	168	Flagged
1971	TraveLodge		33*	14	151	Flagged
	*Qualified by J. Mahler					
1972	TraveLodge	180.424	23	13	186	Flagged
1973	TraveLodge	191.276	27	14	100	Piston
1974	TraveLodge	184.502	10	33	1	Valve
1975	Bruce Cogle Ford	181.892	30	21	133	Running
1976	Bryant Heating-Cooling	182.343	16	32	1	Rod

TOM SNEVA, Spokane, Washington

Indianapolis 500 Record (Passed Driver's Test 1973)

Year	Car	Qual.	S	F	Speed or Laps	Reason Out
1974	Raymond Companies	185.147	8	20	94	Ring, pinion
1975	Norton Spirit	190.094	4	22	125	Accident
1976	Norton Spirit	186.355	3	6	101	Running

GEORGE SNIDER, Bakersfield, California

Indianapolis 500 Record (Passed Driver's Test 1965)

Year	Car	Qual.	S	F	Speed or Laps	Reason Out
1965	Gerhardt	154.825	16	21	64	Rear end
1966	Sheraton-Thompson	162.521	3	19	22	Accident
1967	Wagner-Lockheed	164.256	10	26	99	Spun out
1968	Vel's Parnelli Jones	162.264	29	31	9	Valve
1969	Sheraton-Thompson	166.914	15	16	152	Flagged
1970	Sheraton-Thomp ITT	167.660	10	20	105	Suspension
1971	G. C. Murphy	171.600	21	33	6	Stalled
1972	ITT-Thompson	181.855	21	11	190	Flagged
1973	Gilmore Racing	190.355	30	12	101	Gearbox
1974	Gilmore Racing	183.993	13	28	7	Valve
1975	Lodestar	182.918	24	8	165	Running
1976	Hubler Chevrolet	181.141	27	13	98	Running

AL UNSER, Albuquerque, New Mexico

Indianapolis 500 Record (Passed Driver's Test 1965)

Year	Car	Qual.	S	F	Laps	Speed or Reason Out
1965	Sheraton-Thompson	154.440	32	9	196	Flagged
1966	STP Oil Treatment	162.272	23	12	161	Accident
1967	Retzloff Chemical	164.594	9	2	198	Flagged
1968	Retzloff Chemical	167.069	6	26	40	Accident
1970	Johnny Lightning 500	170.221	1	1	200	155.749
1971	Johnny Lightning 500	174.622	5	1	200	157.735
1972	Viceroy	183.617	19	2	200	160.192
1973	Viceroy	194.879	8	20	75	Piston
1974	Viceroy	183.889	26	18	131	Valve
1975	Viceroy	185.452	11	16	157	Conn. rod
1976	American Racing Wheels	186.258	4	7	101	Running

BOBBY UNSER, Albuquerque, New Mexico

Indianapolis 500 Record (Passed Driver's Test 1963)

Year	Car	Qual.	S	F	Laps	Speed or Reason Out
1963	Hotel Tropicana	149.421	16	33	2	Accident
1964	Studebaker STP	154.865	22	32	1	Accident
1965	STP Gas Treatment	157.467	8	19	69	Oil line
1966	Vita Fresh Orange Juice	159.109	28	8	171	Flagged
1967	Rislone	164.752	8	9	193	Flagged
1968	Rislone	169.507	3	1	200	152.882
1969	Bardahl	169.683	3	3	200	154.090
1970	Wagner Lockheed	168.508	7	11	192	Flagged
1971	Olsonite Eagle	175.816	3	12	164	Accident
1972	Olsonite Eagle	195.940	1	30	31	Distributor
1973	Olsonite Eagle	198.183	2	13	100	Conn. rod bolt
1974	Olsonite Eagle	185.176	7	2	200	Running
1975	Jorgensen Steel	191.073	3	1	174	149.213
1976	Cobre Tire	187.520	12	10	100	Running

BILL VUKOVICH, Fresno, California

Indianapolis 500 Record (Passed Driver's Test 1968)

Year	Car	Qual.	S	F	Laps	Speed or Reason Out
1968	Wagner Lockheed	163.510	23	7	198	Flagged
1969	Wagner Lockheed	164.843	26	32	1	Brkn. rod
1970	Sugaripe Prune	165.753	30	23	78	Clutch
1971	Sugaripe Prune	171.674	11	5	200	154.563
1972	Sugaripe Prune	184.814	18	28	54	Rear end
1973	Sugaripe Prune	191.103	16	2	133	Flagged
1974	Sugaripe Prune	182.500	16	3	199	Flagged
1975	Cobre Tire	185.845	8	6	166	Running
1976	Alex Foods	181.433	9	31	2	Rod

DAVID (SALT) WALTHER, Dayton, Ohio

Indianapolis 500 Record (Passed Driver's Test 1972)

Year	Car	Qual.	S	F	Speed or Laps	Reason Out
1972	Dayton Steel Wheel	180.542	27	33	0	Magneto
1973	Dayton-Walther	190.739	17	33	0	Accident
1974	Dayton-Walther	183.927	14	17	141	Piston
1975	Dayton-Walther	185.701	9	33	2	Turbocharger
1976	Dayton-Walther	182.797	22	9	100	Running

ENTRIES IN SIXTIETH ANNUAL INTERNATIONAL SWEEPSTAKES

MAY 30, 1976

Distance—500 Miles

Statistics Courtesy of Indianapolis Motor Speedway Program

Eligibility: supercharged four-cycle overhead camshaft engines will be limited to a maximum piston displacement of 161.703 cubic inches (2,650 cc); non-supercharged four-cycle overhead camshaft engines will be limited to a maximum piston displacement of 274.590 cubic inches (4,500 cc); stock production block design, single non-overhead camshaft, removable head, supercharged engines will be limited to a maximum piston displacement of 209.3 cubic inches (3,430 cc); stock production block design, single non-overhead camshaft, removable head, non-supercharged engines will be limited to a maximum piston displacement of 355.136 cubic inches (5,820 cc); special rocker arm, single non-overhead camshaft, removable head, non-supercharged engines will be limited to a maximum piston displacement of 320.355 cubic inches (5,250 cc).

All cars Turbocharged except No. 52.

The Bore, Stroke and Piston Displacement figures are taken from entry forms prior to inspection by USAC Technical Committee. Consequently, this information is NOT OFFICIAL.

Car No.	Driver	Car Name	Entrant	No. Cyl.	Bore	Stroke	Piston Disp.
1		Gilmore Racing Team	A. J. Foyt Enterprise	8	3.760	1.800	161
2	Johnny Rutherford	Hy-Gain McLaren/Goodyear	Team McLaren Limited	4	4.281	2.750	159
3	Bobby Unser	Cobre Tire	Robert L. Fletcher	4	4.281	2.750	159
5	Bill Vukovich	Alex Foods Special	Alex Morales	4	4.370	2.650	159
6	Mario Andretti	CAM2 Motor Oil Special	Penske Racing, Inc.	4	4.281	2.750	159
7	Roger McCluskey		Lindsey Hopkins	4	4.281	2.750	159
9	Duane Carter, Jr.	Jorgensen Eagle	E. M. Jorgensen Co.	4	4.370	2.650	159
11	Mike Hiss		Lindsey Hopkins	4	4.281	2.750	159
12	Mike Mosley	Sugaripe Prune Special	Jerry O'Connell	4	4.281	2.750	159
14	A. J. Foyt, Jr.	Gilmore Racing Team	A. J. Foyt Enterprise	8	3.760	1.800	161
16		McLaren/Goodyear	Team McLaren Limited	4	4.281	2.750	159
17	Dick Simon	Bryant Heating and Cooling	Vollstedt Enterprises Inc.	4	4.281	2.750	159
19	Spike Gehlhausen	Spirit of Indiana	Carl Gehlhausen	4	4.281	2.750	159
20	Gordon Johncock	Sinmast-Goodyear Wildcat	Patrick Racing Team, Inc.	4	4.281	2.750	159
21	Al Unser	American Racing Wheels Special	Vel's Parnelli Jones Racing	8	3.375	2.250	161
23	George Snider	Hubler Chevrolet Co. Special	Leader Cards, Inc.	4	4.281	2.750	159
24	Tom Bigelow	Leader Card Racer	Leader Cards, Inc.	4	4.281	2.750	159
25		American Racing Wheels Special	Vel's Parnelli Jones Racing	8	3.375	2.250	161
27	Janet Guthrie	Bryant Heating and Cooling	Vollstedt Enterprises, Inc.	4	4.281	2.750	159
28	Billy Scott	Spirit of "Public Enterprise"	Warner W. Hogdon	4	4.375	2.650	159
29		Scio Cabinet Special	Leader Cards, Inc.	4	4.281	2.750	159
32	Mike Mosley	Sugaripe Prune Special	Jerry O'Connell	4	4.281	2.750	159
33	David Hobbs	Dayton-Walther Special	Walmotor, Inc.	4	4.437	2.600	159
35		Cobre Tire	Robert L. Fletcher	4	4.281	2.750	159
36			Spirit of America Racers, Inc.	4	4.281	2.750	159
38	Bill Simpson	Simpson Safety Eagle	E. J. "Bill" Simpson	4	4.281	2.750	159
40	Wally Dallenbach	Sinmast-Goodyear Wildcat	Patrick Racing Team, Inc.	4	4.281	2.750	159
41		ICP-2	ICP-2	4	4.281	2.750	159
42		Don Mergard's Racing	Donald H. Mergard	4	4.281	2.750	159

Car No.	Driver	Car Name	Entrant	No. Cyl.	Bore	Stroke	Piston Disp.
44	----------------------	Lan Eagle ------------------	Dick Simon, Ltd. -----------	8	3.760	1.800	161
45	Gary Bettenhausen ------	Thermo King Eagle -----------	Gerhardt Racers, Inc. --------	4	4.281	2.750	159
46	Eddie Miller -----------	Thermo King Eagle -----------	Gerhardt Racers, Inc. --------	4	4.281	2.750	159
48	Duane Carter, Jr. -------	Jorgensen Eagle ------------	E. M. Jorgensen Co. ---------	4	4.370	2.650	159
51	----------------------	----------------------------	Michael Devin -------------	4	4.281	2.750	159
52	----------------------	----------------------------	Kenny Moran --------------	8	4.000	3.520	355
53	----------------------	California-Oklahoma Special ----	Fred W. Carrillo -----------	8	3.750	2.360	208
54	Woody Fisher ----------	Schlitz Special -------------	Opal Voight ---------------	4	4.301	2.750	159
55	----------------------	Cobre Tire ----------------	Robert L. Fletcher ----------	4	4.281	2.750	159
56	Jim Hurtubise ----------	----------------------------	Kenny Moran --------------	4	4.050	3.125	161#
58	Eldon Rasmussen -------	Indy Instrument'n-Anacomp Spl.	Rasmussen Racing Products ---	8	3.760	1.800	161
60	----------------------	Sinmast-Goodyear Wildcat -----	Patrick Racing Team, Inc. -----	4	4.281	2.750	159
61	Mel Kenyon -----------	----------------------------	Lindsey Hopkins ------------	8	3.760	1.800	161
62	Mel Kenyon -----------	----------------------------	Lindsey Hopkins ------------	8	3.760	1.800	161
63	Larry McCoy ----------	Shurfine Foods Special --------	Spirit of America Racers, Inc. --	4	4.281	2.750	159
64	----------------------	City of Syracuse/Crane Mos. Chev.	Patrick Santello ------------	8	3.760	1.800	159
65	Larry Dickson ---------	City of Syracuse/S & M Electric--	Patrick Santello ------------	4	4.281	2.750	159
66	----------------------	Penske GM Power -----------	Penske Racing, Inc. ---------	8	3.375	2.250	159
67	Ed Crombie -----------	----------------------------	Ed Crombie ---------------	8	3.760	1.800	161
68	Tom Sneva -----------	Norton Spirit --------------	Penske Racing, Inc. ---------	4	4.281	2.750	159
69	Larry Cannon ---------	----------------------------	Hoffman Auto Racing --------	4	4.281	2.750	159
73	Jerry Grant -----------	California-Oklahoma Special ----	Fred W. Carrillo -----------	8	3.750	2.360	208
75	Gary Allbritain --------	Routh Meat Packing Special ----	Richard Routh -------------	4	4.281	2.750	159
76	Jimmy McElreath -------	Webster Offy --------------	M. Webster ---------------	4	4.020	3.125	160
77	Salt Walther ----------	Dayton-Walther Special --------	Walmotor, Inc. ------------	4	4.281	2.750	159
78	Bobby Olivero ---------	Alex Foods Special -----------	Alex Morales --------------	4	4.370	2.650	159
80	----------------------	Racing Associates Special -------	Herb Porter ---------------	4	4.281	2.750	159
82	----------------------	Greer Special --------------	J. H. Greer ---------------	8	3.760	1.800	161
83	Bill Puterbaugh --------	----------------------------	McNamara Motor Express, Inc. _	4	4.375	2.600	159
84	----------------------	Gilmore Racing Team ---------	J. H. Greer ---------------	8	3.760	1.800	161
85	Al Loquasto, Jr. -------	Frostie Root Beer ------------	Al Loquasto, Sr. -----------	4	4.281	2.750	159
86	Al Loquasto, Jr. -------	Frostie Root Beer ------------	Al Loquasto, Sr. -----------	4	4.281	2.750	159
87	----------------------	Jim Robbins Company Special ---	Jim Robbins Co. ------------	8	3.760	1.800	161
89	----------------------	Racing Associates Special -------	Herb Porter ---------------	4	4.281	2.750	159
91	Spike Gehlhausen -------	----------------------------	Margie Gehlhausen ----------	4	4.281	2.750	159
92	Johnny Parsons ---------	Ayr-Way/WIRE Special --------	Vatis Enterprises, Inc. --------	4	4.281	2.750	159
93	Johnny Parsons ---------	Ayr-Way/WIRE Special --------	Vatis Enterprises, Inc. --------	4	4.281	2.750	159
94	----------------------	----------------------------	Vatis Enterprises, Inc. --------	4	4.281	2.750	159
96	----------------------	----------------------------	Agajanian-King ------------	4	4.281	2.750	159
97	Sheldon Kinser ---------	THEBOTTOMHALF Dragon ---	Agajanian-King ------------	4	4.281	2.750	159
98	John Martin -----------	Genesee Dragon -------------	Agajanian-King-Hammond -----	4	4.281	2.750	159
99	Rick Muther -----------	Joe Hunt Magneto Special ------	Joe Hunt -----------------	4	4.281	2.750	159

Peeled Eye continued

each other, bang wheels and slide around one another like there was no tomorrow. Then they'd come in the pits after the race, pop open a beer and laugh about the mistake the other guy made. Jimmy Caruthers had never sat in a Sprint car before running at Manzanita, but he didn't let anyone there know it.

Then they transferred him over East with only a couple of races to go and McClung said, "Caruthers, it's a good thing you're gettin' transferred. I'd hate to embarrass you. You'd have to finish second, you know."

Over East, Jimmy talked his way into a Midget ride with long-time owner Ken Brenn and once again conned the commanding officer into a little time off for racing. Brenn and Caruthers won some races.

Once he was out of the service he was interested in getting to the Speedway soon as possible. But after his mediocre record in '69, he was ready to stay home and run with the local Sprint car organization in 1970. Doug told him that he could go back to the Midwest by himself if he wanted, Doug couldn't make it.

"I kinda wanted to prove to the old man that I could cut it by myself," Jim had said. "But it'd sure be easier if he were around."

I remembered seeing Doug and Jimmy in '69 and meeting them just briefly. They sort of scared me. I was sure they were rich characters who were probably a little snooty. But they were very friendly. They just wanted some ink I thought. After all, I was the editor and founder of the USAC NEWS newspaper, the journalistic hit of the 1969 racing season. All the USAC members loved it. It replaced their little old newsletter, and now the racers could actually get their name in headlines and their photo in print. Everybody talked to the editor of the paper. Especially if they wanted some publicity.

But now it was 1970 and USAC had killed the idea of having a newspaper and given me the bum's rush in the process. All of a sudden I was on the outside looking in when Jimmy Caruthers came up to my one room office one day and said, "Wow. This place stinks. You oughta get outa here. You want to go to Springfield with me?"

I didn't even hardly know the guy. What was he doing in my office? He was right, anyhow. The place did stink. It was located just across the street from the USAC office on 16th Street in Speedway, above the Rosner drugstore. I thought that I should stay close to the action because I was sure that USAC had made a mistake by firing me and killing my newspaper. In the meantime, I believed, I'd help guys find sponsors for race cars, sell some free-lance stories too. Wrong. I was broke and miserable. Felt sorry for myself and was bitter at USAC. Jimmy Caruthers opened the door and it was like someone deodorized the joint.

"What? Me? Springfield? Yeah, sure. Um, how come you want me to go?"

"Cause I heard you were gonna be a famous Midget race car driver and you can't do it by sittin here. Let's go."

My old friend Jim Chini, probably the best racing photographer this country has ever seen, had told Caruthers I'd make a good stooge for him at the races. Besides, Chini had said, maybe Hungness will get a Midget ride, kill himself, and then he'll be happy. Chini always did have a sense of humor.

About half-way to Springfield Jim said, "Give me those three bottles on the floor. Driving's getting boring. We gotta liven things up a little."

"What are you going to do with them?"

"You just happen to be riding with the Champeeeeen Bottle Chucker of Southern California. Watch the next road sign."

Sure enough, when the next speed limit sign appeared in the distance Jim rolled down the window, took a bottle out and heaved it over the top of the truck some yards before passing it and, Crash! The bottle burst against the sign. Next sign, same thing. Third bottle, third crash.

"I never miss," he smiled.

All the way to Springfield Jimmy told me about his life, ambitions, and just how he was gonna do it. I felt a little ashamed of myself. He wasn't a rich kid at all. He was just another guy on his way to a damn competitive race. And if anything, he had an anchor with him because my general state was a mood of depression.

"So you want to drive a Midget?" Caruthers said. "Now you just listen to me and we'll get you a ride."

Jim explained that I should find the best car at the race track that didn't have a driver, ask the guy for the ride. It was simple.

"But you don't ask like everybody else," he said. "Just walk up and say, 'Who's drivin' this box anyhow?' and I'll bet you money you get the ride."

After we arrived at Springfield and unloaded Jim's Midget, I scoured the pits for a driverless car. A nice one. There was this gleaming black beauty. Even the wheels were polished like no other car at the track. It looked too pretty to get dirty. I found out that the owner's name was "Dink" Cornell. Dink? Dink was kind of a dumpy looking little guy who had two young helpers both dressed with pretty red shirts. They looked like racers. Professional. I looked a little bit like a skinny accountant who had just fouled up the corporate books. Not too confident.

"Hi"

"Hi"

Dink didn't look twice. He was talking to one of the kids.

"Hey, who's drivin this box anyhow?"

Boy that got their attention. All three of them walked around the other side of the Midget and Dink said, "No one. Just who in the hell are you?"

"Carl Hungness. I can drive it for you."

"Paul who?"

"Hung. . .ness."

"Never heard of you. Besides, it don't look like a box does it? You run much?" Dink asked.

"Who me? Sure. Um. . . .lots. Yeah, just came up here with Caruthers. Need a ride."

I didn't know what to say next. He actually asked me if I'd run much. I had run two Midget races in my entire life and nearly killed myself in the second one.

"Hey Carlie, want a Coke?" the voice asked.

It was Caruthers. Thank God someone broke the conversation.

Dink sort of glanced over at Caruthers, then me, then said something to the kids.

"Okay, you can warm it up. Get your stuff on."

I ran back to Caruthers' pit and got my helmet. Jimmy had been watching the little skit all the while and said, "See, what'd I tell you? Now just keep that thing between the fences. It's a pretty safe bet that you ain't gonna win the race."

The ride lasted through warm-ups. Springfield is a very fast, tricky little bowl that some of the best Midget racers in the country don't like. In racer's lingo, you better have your act together before you try and run Springfield. It was no place for a rank rookie.

And it was almost no place for Jimmy Caruthers either. He was leading the feature event when, coming out of the fourth turn, he spun. But rather than allow the car to stop near the guard rail he flat-footed it and tried to keep on going. Springfield is barely wide enough for two cars to run side by side: it isn't wide enough to park a Midget in the turn sideways and have anyone else get around you. Consequently, Jimmy's move caused one helluva chain reaction behind him. Mel Cornett rode over his wheel and nearly slammed his head into a fence post. Gary Irvin crashed along with two or three others. Jim's car was bent a little too.

"Boy, that was a dumb move," Midget Supervisor

[222]

Bob Stroud told him.

"Yeah," Jim said sheepishly. "Everybody okay?"

"Yup," Stroud said.

"Good. But didja see that? I almost made it," Caruthers laughed.

The next day, bright and early, we fixed the car. I wanted to keep working on it but Jim said we were going water skiing. The car was good enough.

So water skiing we went with Ralph Taylor, a racing fanatic whose doors are always open. Then Caruthers went out and won the feature event at Lake Hill, Mo. that night.

And so the summer went. Jerry McClung had obtained a Midget and came to the Midwest. He shared a garage with Jimmy and they were a happy-go-lucky pair. They bought trail bikes and used to race each other at every opportunity. There was hardly a time we came back from a racing jaunt that there wasn't something memorable to talk about. All the while he kept chuckin' bottles. . . .mostly in front of McClung.

Caruthers and I arrived in South Bend early one day and rather than sit around the entire afternoon Jim suggested we rent an airplane. We found the old Studebaker proving grounds, a two and one-half mile oval laid out very similar to the Indianapolis Motor Speedway. Of course Jim had to "get a better look at the place," and soon we were skimming the treetops. I was supposed to be timing our laps around the track because we didn't know how big it was when we spotted it from the air. After a little calculation and more than one suggestion that we climb back up where normal people fly, Caruthers simply said, "Take it easy. I told you I needed some laps around a two and a half mile joint. Here, you fly it for a while."

Then we buzzed the quarter mile at South Bend and had all the' waiting racers pointing in the air. After we landed, car owner Howard Linne asked Jimmy if he'd fly that way if his old man were around.

As usual, Jim would put both hands in his pockets, close his eyes for a couple of seconds, tilt his head back just a little, think for another second and say, "What the old man don't know won't hurt him," and walk away.

From the grandstands Jim always looked a little snobbish. Before he answered your question, or began his walk down the pits his posture was always the same. He never looked down. He didn't have to.

He possessed a fine quality of not outwardly displaying his personal problems too. His attitude throughout the summer didn't change despite the pressures of swapping the point lead back and forth. He and Strickland remained close friends during the campaign. At one point Jim said to me, "What's wrong? You forget how to write? How come you don't get us some ink? This is a pretty exciting season you know. Besides, a little publicity won't hurt me or Strickland."

So I had Jim tape a full size brick to his right foot and posed a picture with he, Strickland and McClung all looking at it. It wasn't exactly a Madison Avenue public relations job, but we did get the picture printed in every race paper in the country.

Jim went on to win the championship, running the last few races with his dad's help on the West Coast. I'm sure Doug was proud and younger brother Danny was just a tad jealous.

The next year Jim, Danny and Doug all came back to Indiana and Danny blasted his way into USAC stardom as he won 12 Midget features on his way to the 1971 division title. Jim ran fewer races than he had the year previous but still wound up second in the point standings. And Doug worked his tail off trying to keep up with both of them.

A couple races after Danny clinched the title he was the victim of a stuck throttle which ultimately caused his death. Doug had to accept Danny's posthumous award and did so with an eloquent speech that made everyone swallow kind of hard. Inside he might have been cursing auto racing for a time.

The next May, Jimmy Caruthers was in the starting lineup at the Indianapolis Motor Speedway. He had earned his way. And he said he'd never quit racing the Midgets either. Too much fun. Besides, he had to give the old man a hard time once in a while.

And old Doug kept right on thrashing. He's a ruddy sort of looking character, missing parts of a couple of fingers, lots of deep lines in his well-weathered face. He sucks on a toothpick sometimes and when he listens to you he chews the inside of his left cheek a little. He grumbles a lot when he works on his race cars too. When something on the car breaks, or doesn't fit right because of a manufacturing defect, old Slugger, as he's been called over the years, has been known to insert his tools back in their box from 40 paces. He'll throw a wrench in the tool box, stomp around for a couple of seconds, and then accepts his fate. He does, however, have a sense of humor about him that he passed on to his sons along with a penchant for practical joking. See if you can have some fun with the situation, make your own fun.

We recall a Midget race at Manzanita once where there was a jam-up in the third turn involving Vukovich, Bettenhausen, Caruthers and numerous others. The race was stopped. Jimmy had done a quick flip and landed no worse for wear back on his wheels. Supervisor Stroud informed Caruthers that he was out for the night, couldn't run, rules say if you get upside down, no matter what, you have to withdraw from competition.

"I didn't get upside down, Bob," Jimmy told him. "It was Vukovich."

Doug whispered to Vuke, "Tell 'em you were the one who flipped. You can't run anyhow."

"Yeah Stroud," Vuky said. "Maybe you're getting old. Everybody could see that it was me who flipped. See there, my car's all bent up. Jimmy's ain't."

And we all went back to the pits laughing about the caper that had been pulled on poor old Stroud. Caruthers ran second. Slugger and Jimmy talked about that one for a long time. Vuky had responded like one of the family. Doug had always treated him like a son too.

Then there was the re-enactment of the banquet scene. Doug Caruthers had to accept another posthumous award, this time for Jimmy who had won the USAC Dirt Championship title in 1975. The speech was, "Just. . . .just thanks to everyone," and was followed by a long standing ovation that was not only for a great little race car driver, but for the guy accepting the award, Slugger Caruthers. This one was almost too much to swallow. Jim had contracted cancer the year previous, went through some hectic treatment and recuperated to register his best racing season. He had more stamina than ever before. He used to come in from a race panting for breath, but after the cobalt treatments he performed like a well-trained athlete. He talked about the difference and even joked about his bout with cancer by telling fellow drivers, "Never try to out-brave a cancer patient."

But the cancer came back and Jim died soon after the '75 season had ended.

"It just doesn't seem fair," Doug said. "We thought he had it beaten once."

It wasn't fair, but neither was the stuck throttle that caused Danny's death. It wasn't as though Danny had made his own mistake that cost him his life.

Doug Caruthers went home and buried his first born. I didn't know if I'd ever see him again. Maybe he'd just close the door. But that's never been his style. They don't call him Slug for nothing. Besides, he has a lot more sons out there in the world of auto racing and the place would never be the same if he weren't around grumbling about an ignition wire that fell off and cost him the race. So in '76 Doug came back strong as ever. And even though the pits have lost a little of the romance that the Caruthers kids brought to them, Slugger is still around making sure that the Midget racers earn their wins. After all, in order to win a USAC Midget race you still have to beat a Caruthers. And that's a damn hard thing to do.